Selected Correspondence of Bernard Shaw

Bernard Shaw and Gabriel Pascal

Selected Correspondence of Bernard Shaw

Bernard Shaw
and
Gabriel Pascal

Edited by Bernard F. Dukore

UNIVERSITY OF TORONTO PRESS

Toronto Buffalo London

Published by University of Toronto Press Incorporated

Toronto Buffalo London
Printed in Canada
ISBN 0-8020-3002-5

Printed on acid-free paper

Canadian Cataloguing in Publication Data

Shaw, Bernard, 1856–1950
   Selected correspondence of Bernard Shaw

   [v. 1] – Bernard Shaw, Theatrics / edited by Dan H.
Lawrence – [v. 2] – Bernard Shaw and H.G. Wells /
edited by J. Percy Smith – [v. 3] – Bernard Shaw and
Gabriel Pascal / edited by Bernard F. Dukore.
   Includes bibliographical references and index.
   ISBN 0-8020-3000-9 (v. 1)   ISBN 0-8020-3001-7 (v. 2)
   ISBN 0-8020-3002-5 (v. 3)

   1. Shaw, Bernard, 1856–1950 – Correspondence.
   I. Smith, J. Percy. II. Title.

PR5366.A4 1995   826'.912   C95-930151-8

University of Toronto Press acknowledges the financial assistance to its
publishing program of the Canada Council and the Ontario Arts Council.

The Press also acknowledges a generous subvention from Mr John Wardrop.
We also thank the Academy of the Shaw Festival for its support.

Contents

General Editor's Note

This volume is the third in the series entitled *Selected Correspondence of Bernard Shaw*, the first two volumes having appeared in 1995. A great many of the thousands of letters written by Shaw have been published in various forms; how many have never appeared it is impossible to say. In any case, what is astonishing about them is not their sheer abundance. That a professional author with wide interests should be a prolific writer of letters is not remarkable. That one should write in unfailingly athletic prose, invariably directing at his correspondent a fund of detailed knowledge and a combination of forthrightness, penetrative argument, teasing wit, and good humour – in short, continuously projecting the persona of the author – is extraordinary indeed. These qualities appear whether Shaw is writing to friends or adversaries, public personages or private citizens, in the world of theatre, of letters, or of political affairs.

Yet in any genuine correspondence there is another voice, joining with Shaw's in a dialogue that might be brief or long-continued, a voice often capable of responding to Shaw in terms as forthright and downright as his own – if seldom as witty. The intention in this series is to make available, using for the most part letters hitherto unpublished, some of the dialogues in which Shaw engaged with particular friends and colleagues in various fields: fellow workers in literature or socialism or the theatre, translators of his plays, the film producer Gabriel Pascal, the illustrator John Farleigh, and so on. One or two volumes, exceptional to this description, will for obvious practical reasons comprise letters written only by Shaw to a large number of individuals, focusing on particular aspects of his career, such as the theatre and publishing. Volume One in the series – *Theatrics* – provides an example of the latter sort; Volume Two – *Bernard Shaw and H.G.Wells* – of the former and more usual collection.

This volume continues the more standard pattern. Its editor is Bernard F. Dukore, University Distinguished Professor of Theatre Arts and Humanities at Virginia Polytechnic Institute and State University. A noted Shavian scholar, he has assembled and edited the letters that were exchanged by Gabriel Pascal and Shaw as the film producer pertinaciously, and at last successfully, badgered the elderly playwright into a collaboration in filming – and in eccentric friendship – that lasted virtually until Shaw's death. The volume not only reveals the changes in relationship between the two men, but tells us something of the development of British film-making in the period in question, under the stress of the Second World War: a presentation both of personalities and of history.

Introduction

Among Bernard Shaw's many interests and recreational activities was what nowadays is called skinny-dipping. While this expression is less formal and dignified than the term usually used, nude swimming, it may be more appropriate to another unorthodox individual, Gabriel Pascal, the movie-maker whose correspondence with Shaw forms the contents of this volume.

One morning at dawn in the summer of 1925, as S.N. Behrman records Pascal's account, or – less mysteriously and less precisely – on a beautiful summer morning in the mid-1920s, as Valerie Pascal, Gabriel's widow, records it, while Pascal was at Cap d'Antibes on the French Riviera, he rose at dawn for a skinny-dip. As he splashed happily in the waters of the Mediterranean, the swarthy Pascal met another nude-swimming enthusiast, the white-bearded, fair-skinned Shaw. After introducing themselves to each other, Pascal told Shaw his profession, displayed his knowledge of Shaw's plays, and regaled Shaw with his dreams of filming them. When he swam away, Shaw called out that if Pascal were to go broke one day, as Shaw believed he undoubtedly would, he should visit him and at that time Shaw might let him make a movie of a play of his.[1]

Like many of Pascal's stories, this one seems too good to be true. Shaw does not confirm it, and he was not on the Riviera in 1925 – or in 1924, 1926, or 1927 either. About Pascal's stories, however, the title of one of Shaw's plays is apt: you never can tell. Shaw was on the Riviera with his wife Charlotte – at Cap d'Antibes, in fact – from 20 July to 2 September 1928. Possibly, only the year in Pascal's tale is too good to be true, since, as this introduction will narrate, a penniless Pascal visited Shaw and obtained Shaw's permission to film a movie of one of his plays in 1935. Perhaps the tidiness of a single decade appealed to Pascal for the sake of the story, or perhaps he merely forgot the year – assuming, of course, that the story is otherwise accurate. At times, truth itself seems too good to be non-fictitious. A decade after Shaw gave Pascal permission, as this introduction will also recount, came the opening night of their last film collaboration, this time ten years later to the very day. Was the selection of the date coincidental or deliberate? While, as before, you never can tell, you can suspect either.

Before returning to the meeting of Shaw and Pascal, and to the exploration of their cinematic collaborations, let us examine the activities, chiefly in motion pictures, of each man.

Unlike many Victorians, Shaw embraced labour-saving and technological innovations. To him, they were not the wave of the future, they were the wave of the present. By 1880, he was practising shorthand; in 1890, he bought a typewriter on credit and learned to type. The chief character of his 1883 novel *An Unsocial Socialist* defended photography as an art, an opinion shared by Shaw, who reviewed photographic exhibitions in 1887 and 1888. In 1898, he bought a camera. Ten years later, he learned to drive and bought an automobile.

Almost from its start, cinema appealed to Shaw and his writing attracted movie-makers. In the 1880s, he attended social and economic lectures by Wordsworth Donisthorpe, who filmed Trafalgar Square on a camera he made in 1889. Although there is no evidence that Shaw was familiar with Donisthorpe's film, the convergence of Shaw's fascination with photography and the drama, as well as the overlapping artistic and political circles of which he was a member, not only make it likely that he was aware of developments in cinema, they make it unlikely that he would be unaware of them.

On 22 March 1895, during a lecture at the Society for the Encouragement of National Industry, in Paris, the Lumière brothers, Louis and Auguste, demonstrated the cinematograph, which projected motion pictures on a screen. In November and December, in Berlin and Paris, motion pictures were projected on screens for a paying public. By then, Shaw had written six plays and directed one of them. In March 1896, in London, Robert W. Paul became the first person to exhibit a British-made film (*Rough Sea at Dover*) to the public, and later that year he showed a film of the 1896 Derby on the very night of the race. In 1897, movies were introduced into music-hall programs. One year later, Shaw published both *Plays: Pleasant and Unpleasant* and his first photograph. In October 1908, he declared the unity of all art, pictorial as well as literary. By then, he was familiar with silent movies and with experiments synchronizing recorded sound with film; and he recognized the economic implications of cinema to dramatists. In December, he received his first proposal to write an original screenplay; soon, he received numerous offers for adapting his plays to the new medium.

On 7 October 1915, the *Kinematograph and Lantern Weekly*, a trade journal, advertised a three-reel motion picture titled *The Devil's Disciple*, made by Reliance Productions, an American firm. Shaw, who was furious, wrote to the Society of Authors denouncing the film as 'contraband: a flat piracy,' claiming 'the title is unique,' urging the Society to threaten distributors 'with unheard-of damages' and exhibitors with legal action, and indicating that he was 'actually in negotiation with a firm for the film of this play.'[2] Although his claim was accurate, titles are not subject to copyright. Since Reliance advertised its *Devil's Disciple* as one of the '"thrill" films' in which it specialized, and since its star, Ralph Lewis (d. 1937, age 65), an American screen actor whose more than one hundred silent movies were chiefly action types, the title of this *Devil's Disciple*, of which I could learn no more, may have duplicated Shaw's only by chance. Did Shaw overreact? More likely, his negotiations for a silent screen version of *The Devil's Disciple* were serious and he did not want potential audiences, upon seeing the title, to think they had already seen the movie. His statement, years later, that he had begun to write his own scenario of this play, with 'a practically complete history of the causes leading up to the American Revolution ... together with vivid scenes from the Boston tea party, a close-up of Indians, and so forth' was apparently accurate.[3]

Hollywood frequently offered him extravagant inducements to film his plays, including a million dollars for movie rights to all of them and £1000 in advance of either 15 per cent of the gross or a third of the profits. He refused, partly because of high taxation in both England and the United States, partly because he believed that audiences who saw a film version of a play stayed away when the play was revived on stage, but mainly because movies were silent. To Shaw, the quality of a silent movie version of a play was in inverse proportion to the quality of the play's dialogue. His view of subtitles as fatuous underlies Shotover's injunction in *Heartbreak House,* written in the silent era, that Mangan should talk like a human being, not a movie.

When *The Jazz Singer* opened in 1927, 'talkies' began to replace 'movies,' to use the argot of the period. With the advent of sound, which could accommodate Shavian drama, Shaw changed his mind. What stood in the way were movie-makers, whose view of films was unchanged. As the studio owner says in MGM's *Singin' in the Rain* (1952), set during the transition of motion pictures from silence to sound, when he decides to make talkies despite the objection that no one at the studio knows anything about sound films, 'What do you have to know? It's a picture. You do what you always did. You just add talking to it.' To such movie-makers, dialogue consisted of spoken subtitles or of unrecorded words actors used to utter while performing in silent films. To Shaw, talkies were not merely films with spoken subtitles and dramas were not simply illustrated stories. He was convinced that the chief uses movie-makers had for his plays were to rearrange his scenes, add frequent changes of locale, pare his dialogue to a minimum, and exploit his name. By contrast, he considered cinema to be drama: it had to tell a story, develop characters, and employ dialogue to convey ideas, rather than display actors opening and closing doors or ascending and descending stairs, with cuts to picturesque exteriors. To him, film was a dramatic medium, and devices like close-ups and dissolves were technical features that should be at the service of dramatic qualities.

To claim that Shaw refused to permit a word of his plays to be cut or changed for the screen is untrue. What is true is that he refused to permit cuts or changes by studio hands who understood photography and editing but not drama, although they thought they did. If movie studios undertook to film plays, he insisted, they should either assume that dramatists knew their job and let the writers make necessary adaptations, or else they should leave the plays alone.

He had no illusions about art and commerce. Well before the First World War, he foresaw that films would become big business, organized by capitalists to ensure the highest profits rather than the greatest art, which would be a desirable by-product. No matter: the same is true of theatre, but on a smaller scale. As Shaw told movie mogul Samuel Goldwyn, ironically reversing their positions, after Goldwyn declared that he was so rich he did not care about money, 'I'm afraid, Mr. Goldwyn, that we shall not ever be able to do business together. You see, you're an artist, and care only about art, while I'm only a tradesman and care only about money.'[4] In dealing with businessmen, Shaw was businesslike, determined to protect his interests.

His terms were simple. He demanded script approval or, if he wrote the scenario, that – as his standard contract said – it be filmed 'without transpositions interpolations omissions or any alterations misrepresenting the Author whether for better or worse except such as the Author may consent to or himself suggest.'[5] Instead of selling world rights, he separately licensed production and distribution in a single country or countries in which the same language was spoken. Instead of contracting for a lump sum or an advance on a percentage of profits, he demanded 10 per cent of the gross sums paid by exhibitors to the manufacturer or to an intermediary, unless the manufacturer were the distributor, in which case he wanted 5 per cent of the gross sums paid by the public at the theatres. 'There may be no profit,' he shrewdly observed, 'but there are always receipts and sometimes it may take ten lawsuits to determine what the profits are but you can always determine the receipts.'[6] Instead of assigning film rights in perpetuity, he did so for five years. If the film were successful, and if it pleased him and the producer, he could renew the licence, which was for one film at a time. If it displeased him, he was not bound to permit the producer to film another play. To sweeten his terms, he did not demand advances. Although producers protested that such demands were outrageous, he had been offered each of them at different times.

British International Pictures made the first movies of Shaw's plays. *How He Lied to Her Husband* (1931), which was little more than a photographed stage play, was a box-office dud. *Arms and the Man* (1932), whose text Shaw helped to cut and for which he wrote new dialogue, received an inadequate budget and, like *How He Lied to Her Husband,* poor direction by Cecil Lewis, who was inexperienced. It was a critical and financial failure worsened by BIP, which cut it severely so that it might earn some money as the bottom half of a double feature.

In 1933 and 1934, Shaw negotiated with RKO to film *The Devil's Disciple* starring John Barrymore and *Saint Joan* starring Katharine Hepburn. He agreed to let *The Devil's Disciple*, but not *Saint Joan*, be trimmed to eighty minutes. Although RKO consented to his terms, the project collapsed when Shaw read the studio writer's screenplay of *The Devil's Disciple*, which he considered hopelessly incompatible with his drama.

Europe beckoned. In 1934, after reading the screenplay, he rejected a French proposal to film *Pygmalion*. If *Pygmalion* were to be filmed, he recognized, it had to be adapted; but since he could not rely on anyone else to do the job as he wanted it done, he would have to do it himself. A proposal arrived from Germany, also for *Pygmalion*. Despite the warning of Augustin Hamon, his French translator, that a faithful German film version would be impossible because the film industry there was no more honest than anywhere else, and because the Hitler regime would not consider itself bound by an agreement with a socialist dramatist whose translator, Siegfried Trebitsch, was Jewish, Shaw cut the text of *Pygmalion*, composed new film scenes, and agreed to a five-year licence for a German film using his scenario. In September 1935, it opened in Berlin and was successful. Four months later, Shaw saw it. The movie used none of his new scenes, introduced new scenes of its own, devised a romantic ending for Eliza and Higgins, altered the Doolittle subplot, and generally changed his work, he charged, beyond recognition. The German *Pygmalion* confirmed the wisdom of his contractual demands: the five-year licence went unrenewed and this *Pygmalion* was distributed only in German-speaking countries.

In March 1937, a Dutch film of *Pygmalion* opened in Amsterdam to great critical and popular acclaim. In May, Shaw saw it and loathed it. Like the German movie-makers, the Dutch flagrantly violated the explicit instructions of their licence and disregarded Shaw's scenario.

In 1934 and 1935, Shaw wrote an adaptation of *Saint Joan*. Elisabeth Bergner, who had played Joan in Berlin, had emigrated to England and would star in the film, which her husband, Paul Czinner, would direct in English. Since *Saint Joan* would be expensive, Czinner recognized, it needed an American market. In July 1934, the Motion Picture Producers and Distributors of America, the movie industry's self-censorship body, created the Production Code Administration, which reviewed a script to determine whether its language and themes were sanitary, requested changes if they were not, and gave or withheld its seal of approval after it was filmed. The PCA prohibited profanity, including 'damn' and 'hell,' 'whore,' and 'fairy.' Unless 'God,' 'Jesus,' and 'Christ' were said reverently, it considered them blasphemous. Religion and the clergy could not be portrayed as villainous or ridiculous; nor could the sanctity of marriage be mocked. Among tabooed subjects were nudity, undressing, and venereal disease.

Since 20th Century Fox would neither finance nor distribute *Saint Joan* without prior Catholic approval, Czinner sent Shaw's script to Catholic Action in Rome, which on 27 August 1935 disapproved it. The reasons included Shaw's view of Joan's trial, which differed from the Church's, and his use of such words and phrases as 'backside,' 'I am damned,' and 'dear child of God.'[7] Czinner continued negotiations. In August 1936, Shaw learned what had happened, refused to submit to any censorship, and withdrew his play from Czinner and Bergner.

In late 1935, in response to the invitation mentioned in the first paragraph of this introduction, a Hungarian émigré named Gabriel, or Gaby, Pascal visited Shaw. A likable, flamboyant, Munchausenlike, self-dramatizing impresario with enormous charm, *élan*, blarney, and chutzpah, Pascal was variously called irresistible and engaging, a charlatan and a megalomaniac, guileless and ruthless. Shaw thought him an adventurer with imagination, but Shaw also perceived that he genuinely venerated his plays. When Pascal announced that he was predestined to translate them into film, he meant it.

To sketch Pascal's background is difficult, since he himself is the source of most information about it and he was unconcerned with contradictions. Born in Transylvania, Hungary, probably on 4 June 1894, his real name was Gabor Lehöl. He claimed descent from Talleyrand, also from Metternich. He was a kidnapped royal child, an orphan, an illegitimate son of a Bulgarian officer. He was Jewish; he was Catholic; he was not Catholic but was raised by Jesuits. He was a shepherd boy who ran off with gypsies; he was abducted by them. A Viennese family adopted him; a Hungarian family did. He attended a military academy, went to an agricultural school, received training in diplomacy. Some of these tales are not mutually exclusive. Some may even be true.

In 1914, Pascal claimed, he worked with Robert Wiene, who later made *The Cabinet of Dr. Caligari*, but filmographies on Wiene fail to list him on the credits of any Wiene film. When war broke out, he became a cavalry officer in the Hungarian Hussars and went off to the Italian front, or perhaps to Russia. In 1921 or 1922, he said, he produced and co-directed *Populi Morituri* (People About to Die, also released as *Sterbende Völke*), in which he acted a leading role; yet credits list Robert Reinert as its sole producer and director and do not list Pascal in any capacity. In Holland, he was supposedly offered financing to make a film in China if he did some spying on the side. He refused, had no money to pay his hotel bill, escaped sans luggage, and went to England, where he produced *The Street of Lost Souls*, starring Pola Negri; yet the only British film she made in England was *The Woman He Scorned*, which Pascal apparently helped to publicize. He moved to Berlin, where, depending on the source, he did or did not co-direct a movie version of Lehar's operetta *Friederika*. Possibly, the only European film he directed was an Italian travelogue. When Hitler came to power in 1933, Pascal fled Germany. In Hollywood, he claimed, he refused to work on a movie unless the star were replaced by an unknown actress, Jean Arthur; yet she had played featured and leading roles for years and was not unknown. He went to India to join Shri Meher Baba, a celebrated mystic, to produce a film on reincarnation; nothing came of the project. He returned to California.

There, according to him, he remembered his encounter at Cap d'Antibes, hid in the toilet of a train to New York, and somehow got to London. To put himself in the right frame of mind to meet Shaw, he went to a barber shop for a shave, breakfasted at the Savoy, and took a taxi to Shaw's flat. With only a half-crown coin in his pocket, he rang the doorbell and, consistent with his tale of skinny-dipping with Shaw, ordered the maid to tell GBS that the brown-buttocked film producer from the Riviera wanted to see him.

Whether or not Shaw remembered the episode, if it happened, he was curious about the foreign caller and saw him. Pascal told Shaw that he was the materialization of Shaw's Richard Dudgeon, the eponymous *Devil's Disciple*, called himself GBS's disciple, and requested cinema rights to *Pygmalion*. He charmed everyone present, Shaw included; but Shaw hedged. He returned; Shaw continued to hedge. On 8 December 1935, he delivered an ultimatum: unless Shaw gave him the rights by four p.m. five days later (Friday the 13th), he would leave England to make a film in China. On the 13th, as Big Ben began to strike four, a messenger rang the doorbell of Pascal's flat in Duke Street. At the fourth stroke, he handed Pascal an envelope with the contract for *Pygmalion*. Allowing for Pascal's usual exaggeration, the story may be true. Shaw's licence to film *Pygmalion* is dated 13 December, and his Engagement Diary records 'Pascal, 11.30' for that date. If he sent a messenger from Whitehall Court then, the messenger had time, and possibly instructions, to arrive at Duke Street at four.

Why did Shaw bypass such established firms as Alexander Korda and Universal Pictures, which sought permission to film *Pygmalion*, and take a chance on an unknown émigré? For one thing, he would have had to take a chance on anyone. For another, Pascal's admiration was sincere. For still another, since established firms in Hollywood, England, and Europe had let him down, he might – and, in the event, did – do better with a producer who sought to establish himself in films by fidelity to Shaw's work. As he confided to Kenneth Clark, 'there is no one else in the field whom I can trust artistically.'[8]

During the almost two years that Pascal struggled to get financial backing for *Pygmalion*, the only bread-and-butter film employment he obtained was as producer of *Reasonable Doubt*, a potboiler. The reasons for his difficulty in financing *Pygmalion* were partly his inexperience and partly the nature of Shaw's licence, which gave him the right to produce *Pygmalion* but not the play's film rights. The distinction is crucial. Whatever agreement Pascal might conclude for his right was subject to agreement by Shaw, who not only was a more astute businessman than Pascal, but also was not so anxious to have a film produced that he would sign a financially disadvantageous or exploitative contract. Although Shaw later modified his terms for Pascal, at this stage he was adamant about them.

Untiringly, Pascal wheeled as he attempted to strike a deal. He sought financing in England and America, France and Italy (with settings and the technical apparatus in place, he could make *Pygmalion* in French and Italian as well as in English). In the summer of 1937, Nicholas Davenport, C.M. Woolf, and Richard Norton (Lord Grantley) joined Pascal Films to produce a British *Pygmalion*. With Wendy Hiller and Leslie Howard as Eliza and Higgins, filming began on 11 March 1938. Except for the first day's shooting, Shaw stayed away, since, as he later told reporters, 'I cannot at my age undertake studio work.' But he advised from afar – often – from casting to costumes.

What emerges from the Shaw/Pascal correspondence is the great extent to which Pascal, in striking contrast to his predecessors, scrupulously in long cables and longer letters kept the 'Maestro' or 'Master,' as he variously called GBS, informed of what he did – whom he negotiated with, advantages and disadvantages of dealing with certain people and firms, contractual problems, behind-the-scenes backstabbing, alternative avenues pursued simultaneously, possible casting, progress during shooting, and so forth – and, particularly important to this dramatist, sought Shaw's approval of script changes. Throughout their relationship, Pascal continued to keep Shaw informed of developments and to persuade him to write new scenes and approve script changes. Shaw revised the *Pygmalion* scenario he had given Germany and Holland, deleting scenes he had created and adding new sequences, notably the ballroom scene and a montage involving Eliza and Freddy. When Pascal, or others through Pascal, suggested changes or additions, Shaw considered them, sometimes acting upon them, sometimes rejecting them, but with reasons.

One significant change on which he was not consulted was the ending, of which three were shot. The directors, Anthony Asquith and Leslie Howard, were dissatisfied with Shaw's conclusion, wherein Eliza explicitly rejects Higgins for Freddy, which Higgins cheerily accepts.[9] Another final scene, which the directors found too inconclusive, collated Higgins's demand that Eliza buy food and gloves for him with her going off with Freddy. The ending they used, in which Eliza returns to Higgins, contravenes Shaw's scenario and his determination to avoid a romantic conclusion. Publicly, Shaw endorsed the film and declared the ending was not worth making a fuss about because the remainder was faithful to his work. Privately, he quipped, the trouble was Leslie Howard's belief that he was really Romeo. Significantly, he blamed unnamed others for sidetracking himself and Pascal, whom he praised.

The American print differed from the British one. Metro-Goldwyn-Mayer, which was affiliated with the distributor, Loew's, had William Axt (under the credit 'Additional Composition') revise Arthur Honegger's score; it used different takes with different camera angles; and it conformed to Hollywood censorship. Out went 'slut' and every 'damn,'

as did all indications that Doolittle was not married to the woman he
lived with or was on his way to his wedding at the end. Pascal fought
against these changes, gave in since the alternative was no American
release, may not have been aware of other studio-made changes, and told
most but not all to the Maestro, who was an ocean away.

Yet *Pygmalion* is a superior film and to date the best film version of a
Shaw play. It was an outstanding critical and box-office success. It won
two Academy Awards, one to Shaw for best screenplay, another for its
adaptation, and its stars received Oscar nominations. In America, it broke
box-office records for an English film. When, in an unexpected turn-
about, Shaw agreed to let Pascal dub it into French and Italian, the film
was financially successful in France and Italy. However, it was the
financiers and distributors who prospered, not Shaw and Pascal. Shaw's
royalties were so high that he moved into the highest tax bracket, which
he said left him a pittance. Pascal's poor business management accounted
for his low income. Since he failed to anticipate how much the film
would cost, he sold parts of his royalties bit by bit to raise more money
to complete it; and each new sum cost him more than the last.

Most significantly, *Pygmalion*'s success cemented the alliance between
Shaw and Pascal. While Shaw did not give Pascal exclusive film rights to
his plays, he proceeded as though he had, even trying to guide Pascal on
contractual dealings. He wrote introductory scenes to *The Devil's Disciple*,
which with *Saint Joan* was on Pascal's agenda, and he encouraged Pascal
to pursue that agenda. John Barrymore was a possibility for *The Devil's
Disciple*; so was Clark Gable. Two GGs were on the list for *Saint Joan*, Greta
Garbo and Greer Garson. Also on Pascal's agenda were *The Millionairess*
with Marlene Dietrich and *The Doctor's Dilemma* with, at one point, Wendy
Hiller and Leslie Howard or Ronald Colman and, at another, Greer
Garson, Cedric Hardwicke, Roland Young, and C. Aubrey Smith. With or
without Shaw, Hollywood tried to entice Pascal, who remained faithful to
his Maestro and did not succumb to its blandishments.

His next Shavian film, which again starred Wendy Hiller, was *Major
Barbara*. Pascal himself directed it. Marjorie Deans became his scenario
editor, with Anatole de Grunwald, without screen credit, helping her to
prepare the shooting script. David Lean, *Pygmalion*'s film editor, assisted
them, received credit for montage, and unofficially oversaw Pascal in
photography and editing, while Harold French, credited as 'Dialogue

Supervisor,' helped Pascal work with the actors. Astutely, Pascal surrounded himself with experts.

He asked, sometimes pleaded with, Shaw for new scenes, which Shaw agreed the film needed. Shaw did not accept every proposal, but when he agreed he wrote with gusto. All the while, they discussed finances, settings, casting, and music; and while Pascal went into great detail over many of these matters, he was reticent when it came to discussing his health, a subject that became paramount some years later. As their correspondence reveals, when Pascal wanted what Shaw recognized to be good – such as a sermon by Barbara, including its themes, at the start of the film, and a scene between Undershaft and Cusins after the Salvation Army meeting – Shaw took Pascal's ideas and embroidered them. When Pascal pinpointed a problem but proposed an inadequate solution, Shaw recognized the deficiency and found the remedy, such as an emotional bridge for Barbara after the apparent loss of Bill Walker's soul. Shaw seldom interfered with visual bridges between scenes, and he willingly authored or authorized changes even while Pascal shot the film; but when Pascal proposed what Shaw considered preposterous, he hurled verbal thunderbolts. Usually, Pascal obeyed Shaw's injunctions, but in one instance – Bill Walker's return at the end – he was so insistent about the validity of his artistic instinct that, as this correspondence documents for the first time, although Shaw wavered, he ultimately agreed to give Pascal his head ('a mistake. But if you are bent on it, try it') – to his later regret, for by the time he changed his mind it was too late to alter the completed film. Partly through Pascal's influence, Shaw became more acutely aware of different techniques for stage and screen. Offering two alterations of a sequence, for example, he recommended one mainly because the other was 'so much more stagey than screeny.'

The chief problem with making *Major Barbara* was beyond the control of either man. On 3 September 1939, while Shaw adapted it to the screen and Pascal did pre-production work, Great Britain declared war on Nazi Germany. The correspondence reveals how the war and wartime restrictions affected financing and directing the film. In some cases, officials provided delayed inductions, but many performers and technical personnel enlisted and many wanted no exemption. As Nazi planes rained bombs on England, Pascal literally filmed *Major Barbara* under fire. Furniture, props, and technical equipment could not be obtained or were bombed. Railways were out of commission, roads unsafe. When a camera crew returned to complete the previous day's location shooting for a London exterior, it would discover the site in rubble. Air raids often interrupted shooting. One day, Pascal completed one take out of seventeen scheduled set-ups. Another problem was Pascal, who frequently lost his temper and bullied people, although he was sweetness itself when his temper subsided. Delays mounted. Pascal tried to follow Shaw's injunctions to limit his retakes to the barest minimum and not to sell parts or priorities of his share in the film in order to obtain more money for retakes; but he was congenitally unable to do so. Shooting was scheduled for ten weeks; it took six months.

Tampering with *Major Barbara* was extensive. Pascal's print ran 137 minutes. When the film opened in London, it ran 121 minutes; in New York, 112 minutes. When it went to neighbourhood and rural theatres all over the world, it was snipped to as few as 95 minutes. Pascal's intentions were honourable. At the start, he refused to make the movie without the speech about 670 fools in Parliament; but the passage survives only in his print, which was not publicly shown until 1977. Yet consider the circumstances. How could one make so antidemocratic a statement when the democracies were fighting the fascists for their very existence? During the war, how could one portray a munitions maker as diabolonian? To ask such questions is to answer them negatively. In Hollywood, Pascal battled the censors, while keeping Shaw informed of his compromises and submissions, or most of them. When Shaw objected to redubbing dialogue, Pascal patiently explained what his compromises consisted of, stressed how minimal they were, and justified or rationalized why they were necessary. Because of wartime filming conditions, the demands of censors, and the practices of distributors and exhibitors, much of *Major Barbara* is botched. What is remarkable is how good much of it is.

Under the title 'Come G.B.S. we have no time to lose,' a full page of the 1941 *Motion Picture Almanac* shows a photograph of GBS and Pascal on opposite sides of a desk. GP tells GBS, 'We have shown them the Guttersnipe Eliza transformed into a duchess in *Pygmalion*. We have shown them the down and out Bill Walker converted by *Major Barbara*. Come GBS we have no time to lose. In the next two years I must bring at least eight more of your best known figures to screen life.' GBS agrees: 'Very well, Gabriel. You are the only man who can do it. What is our next one to be?' GP responds, 'The dream of my boyhood[:] *The Devil's Disciple.*' Shadows tower above them and frame their dialogue. Inside the shadows are titles of the eight plays, plus sketches. The face above *The Devil's Disciple* resembles Gary Cooper, that above *Saint Joan* Katharine Hepburn, those faces above *The Doctor's Dilemma* Greer Garson and Laurence Olivier. Generic Hollywood leading men and women appear above or beside *The Millionairess, Candida, Man and Superman,* and *Caesar and Cleopatra* (but Cleopatra resembles Vivien Leigh). Beside *Arms and the Man* march three toy-like female soldiers.

After filming *Major Barbara* under wartime conditions, Pascal did not want to repeat the experience. He therefore considered shooting his next movie in Hollywood. Another possibility was Western Canada, which was accessible to Hollywood stars and technicians. So were the Bahamas, where he aimed to build studios – a plan Shaw endorsed. Encouraged by the Maestro's approbation, Pascal tried to lure him and Madame Charlotte to fly there for a visit. As Pascal's letters demonstrate, he was indefatigable, if not frenetic, in his efforts to cope with the demands of stars and producers and to nail down financial backing and secure a fair contract that would satisfy Shaw. They also suggest that, with failure following failure, in trying to buoy up Shaw's spirits he was also trying to boost his own morale. To the frustration of both, the Bahaman plans, the Canadian project, and proposals to film Shaw's plays in Hollywood broke down. By March 1943, Shaw told Marjorie Deans, Pascal 'achieved the surprising feat of going to America at the height of his reputation, fortified by a monopoly of my plays for filming, and coming back with nothing done and nothing doing.'[10]

Something was doing in England, however, where by August Pascal arranged, with film magnate J. Arthur Rank, to make *Saint Joan* with Greta Garbo, then *Caesar and Cleopatra* and *The Doctor's Dilemma.* While Shaw and Pascal discussed finances and contracts, the dramatist indicated that he was prepared to write new scenes for *Saint Joan* and to restore portions of what he had deleted for Czinner, including the Saint from Hell in the Epilogue. Because some felt that it would be injudicious for Britain to make a movie about Englishmen burning a patriotic icon of one of her allies, *Saint Joan* was delayed. Replacing it was *Caesar and Cleopatra,* budgeted at £550,000. Rank believed that the prestige it would gain in America would help him to sell other films even if it did not recover its costs – a view he later appeared to forget. He agreed that the screenplay would be by Shaw and no one else, and that Pascal alone would produce and direct. Unstated or understated, since business took precedence, was Pascal's health. As before, Pascal continued to keep Shaw apprised of developments; and also as before, Shaw advised from afar on composers, casting, costuming, make-up, acting, publicity, scenery, budget, and even credits on the final print, while giving Pascal the encouragement he needed. As Shaw did for *Major Barbara*, he suggested and approved cuts and changes, and he wrote new film sequences for *Caesar and Cleopatra*. In his late eighties, however, he lacked the vigour, and perhaps the will, to compose as many new scenes for *Caesar and Cleopatra* as he had created for *Major Barbara*. Does this factor contribute to the new film's lesser quality? Perhaps, but in view of the circumstances of production and of Pascal's directorial ability, one hesitates to blame the writer.

Caesar and Cleopatra was over two years in the making. Rank signed contracts in November 1943, but the film did not open in London until 13 December 1945 – coincidentally, ten years to the day after Shaw agreed to let Pascal film *Pygmalion*. On 12 June 1944, six days after D-Day, shooting began. Four days later, German V-2 rocket attacks bombarded England. In addition to other devastation, they interrupted filming, wrecked a set, destroyed dressmaking workrooms, damaged Pascal's home, and killed several members of the production unit. Wartime conditions caused delays in transporting personnel and materials. Costumes took weeks instead of days to make; then, teenage costume makers were evacuated from London because of the rockets. A film in colour required special, heavier cameras and cranes, which proved impossible to make and difficult to get. Coal rationing meant insufficient fuel for hot-water baths; as a result, the colour of the Egyptians' body make-up varied from day to day. For weeks, the summer sun failed to shine, a catastrophe for a film with so much outdoor footage. What with bombings and the weather, Pascal moved the production to Egypt, where Britannically cool and rainy weather followed him. Shooting ended in September 1945 – fifteen months after it had begun and nine months behind schedule.

Pascal's temper tantrums were worse than they had been on *Major Barbara*. These, plus his failure to make schedules that minimized the actors' time, created delays and deteriorating morale among them and the technical personnel. At its April 1946 meeting, the Association of Cine-Technicians passed a resolution that, because of the inordinate length of time Pascal took to complete *Caesar and Cleopatra*, he 'should be censured and allowed to make pictures in this country subject to special control,' a diplomatic rewording of the original resolution, that he 'should not be permitted to make any further films in this country.'[11]

Critical and public response in both Britain and America was less favourable than it had been to Pascal's other Shaw films. Although *Variety*, before the American première, predicted 'moderately good grosses,' it afterwards revised its forecast to a $3,000,000 loss (with an exchange rate of four dollars to the pound). By contrast, Shaw called the movie a financial success, since it had cost $3,000,000 less than the press said it did. Movie producers are adroit in creative accountancy that raises a film's purported costs, thereby reducing its profits on paper, to the detriment of those whose contracts call for a percentage of profits. Because they can claim excessive studio rental costs (as Shaw wrote to Pascal, the rent for studio space on a balance sheet is as high as a producer wants it to be, and as Pascal wrote to Shaw, Rank's charges were higher than those of others) and can upwardly adjust diverse figures in the expenditures column, it is impossible for anyone but a skilled accountant with access to all the figures and receipts to determine whether a film made or lost money, and how much. For additional calculations, see the headnote to Correspondence number 186.

What did Shaw think of *Caesar and Cleopatra* artistically? He told Cedric Hardwicke it was 'a bad film'; and according to Kenneth Clark, he told Pascal, 'Gaby, you've ruined it.'[12] On 25 March 1947, Pascal too called it bad.

Largely because Pascal's reputation was so low in the English film industry that financing and studio space were unavailable to him, he mainly looked abroad for his next project. He showered Shaw with long explanatory, even pleading, letters and cables, sometimes bewildering Shaw with his imprecision as he changed plans. Professional anxieties and deteriorating health plagued Pascal, who tried to put the best possible construction on both. For *Saint Joan*, he turned to France and America. He tried to sign Ingrid Bergman, but her commitment to act in Maxwell Anderson's *Joan of Lorraine* on stage and screen blocked him. In

Hollywood, he signed an agreement to produce *The Devil's Disciple* for Mary Pickford, who gave him salary advances. Contractual difficulties with Shaw caused delays. When Shaw refused to sign the contract offered to him, despite Pascal's interpretation of his own contract with Pickford (which he later admitted was in error), she successfully sued Pascal. He spent many months trying to establish film-making studios in Ireland, and Shaw put all of his plays at Pascal's disposal for the Irish venture; but since Pascal's Irish partners failed to obtain enough capital, the plan fell apart. He sought backing for *Androcles and the Lion* in Italy and in Mexico. He turned to Malta and to India. As one heartbreaking fiasco followed another, an increasingly desperate Pascal actively pursued new schemes, sometimes in disregard of the advice of his doctors at the Mayo Clinic, where he finally went and fought what would be a losing battle against cancer.

On 2 November 1950, Shaw died. After *Caesar and Cleopatra*, Pascal made no other film in Shaw's lifetime. His cinematic career crested with *Pygmalion* and *Major Barbara*, as did Shaw's. Neither before nor after their collaboration (at least, up to now) has anyone made a better film version of a Shaw play. As producer, Pascal fought for the integrity of Shavian cinema; as director, he tried to create films that were true to their dramatic source. In both capacities, his success varied. Shaw's cinematic writings flourished in partnership with Pascal. He cut, rewrote, and wrote anew when Pascal made him recognize what would have more impact in a different medium; at the same time, Pascal confirmed many of Shaw's ideas about cinema, prompting him to restore passages he had deleted from the *Saint Joan* film and to make other revisions.[13] Their correspondence helps to demonstrate the business, the day-to-day working, and the art of motion-picture making.

NOTES

1 S.N. Behrman, *The Suspended Drawing-Room* (New York: Stein & Day 1965), 65–7; Valerie Pascal, *The Disciple and His Devil* (New York: McGraw-Hill 1970), 65–7

2 Letter to G. Herbert Thring, 10 October 1915 (BL 50627 f 153)

3 Quoted in H.K. Reynolds, 'Shaw in Film Debut Derides Movies, Sees End of Own Career,' *New York American*, 9 October 1926, p. 3

4 Ibid., 1, 3. When I wrote the Introduction to *The Collected Screenplays of Ber-*

nard Shaw (Athens: University of Georgia Press 1980), from which much of this introduction derives, I erroneously called his famous quip 'possibly apocryphal' (p. 19)

5 Files of the Society of Authors in London and of the editor

6 Letter, addressee and date not given, in S.N. Behrman, *The Suspended Drawing-Room* (New York: Stein & Day 1965), 11

7 BL 50633, ff 48–9 (letter to Shaw from Father M. Barbera, SJ) and 50634, ff 169–294 (Shaw's screenplay with marginal notes and crossings-out by Catholic Action). For a published list of the proposed deletions and changes, see *Saint Joan: A Screenplay by Bernard Shaw*, ed. Bernard F. Dukore (Seattle: University of Washington Press 1968), 143–7

8 Kenneth Clark, *The Other Half: A Self-Portrait* (New York: Harper & Row 1977), 38

9 Published in *The Collected Screenplays of Bernard Shaw*, 271–2

10 Letter, 22 March 1943, in Bernard Shaw, *Collected Letters 1926-1950*, ed. Dan H. Laurence (New York: Viking 1988), 667

11 '1945–1946 The Association of Cine-Technicians Thirteenth Annual Report Agenda for Thirteenth Annual General Meeting, Saturday, April 27th & Sunday April 28th,' 7 (Archives of the Association of Cinematograph, Television, and Allied Technicians); ibid., 60–1

12 Letter to Hardwicke, 27 May 1949, in *Theatrics*, ed. Dan H. Laurence (Toronto: University of Toronto Press 1995), 229; Clark, *The Other Half*, 40

13 Compare the screenplay of *Saint Joan* in *Saint Joan: A Screenplay by Bernard Shaw*, which Shaw wrote for Czinner and Bergner, with that in *The Collected Screenplays of Bernard Shaw*, which he wrote for Pascal.

Editor's Note

The 268 pieces of correspondence in this volume (letters, postal cards, cablegrams, and so forth), all by Bernard Shaw and Gabriel Pascal, are divided fairly evenly: 136 from Shaw to Pascal, 132 from Pascal to Shaw. Of the 268, 162 (over 60 per cent) are previously unpublished and 75 (28 per cent) were previously published in truncated form or have had extracts published from them. Thus, 237 of the 268 items in this book (88.5 per cent) are new in whole or in part.

In terms of each writer, 109 of Shaw's 136 pieces of correspondence (80 per cent) have not previously been published (53) or were published only in part (56) – roughly a 50–50 split. Of Pascal's 132 pieces of correspondence, 128 (97 per cent) have not been previously published (109) or were published only in part (19).

Although this correspondence is the fullest between Shaw and Pascal that has been published, there are gaps between a number of items – sometimes of short duration, sometimes of long. One reason is that a letter might have been followed not by another letter but by a meeting or telephone conversation, or by correspondence between Pascal and Blanche Patch, Shaw's secretary. Another is that neither recipient scrupulously filed or catalogued the correspondence, some of which was misplaced, lost, or perhaps stolen.

Furthermore, this volume does not contain all of their extant letters to each other. Want of space, as has been made clear to me on a number of occasions, is the major reason. In making editorial decisions on what to delete, I have followed the principles of relevance, repetition, and reader's interest. As an example of the first, Pascal proposed in one cable not included in this book that, on the basis of meetings he had held with the head of Putnam's, this book-publishing firm might print the text of *Pygmalion* with photographs of the film (in an unpublished letter, he also suggested another firm), to which Shaw replied that his publishing contracts forbade such a venture. As another example, Pascal fills pages with gossip and conjectures about Greta Garbo's love life, diet, and aids to youth and longevity. Since this volume concerns the motion-picture-making activities and plans of Shaw and Pascal, I have deleted pieces of correspondence on these and other subjects, as well as references to them in letters printed here, on the ground of irrelevance. Repetition dictated deletion of some correspondence or portions of correspondence: for instance, a telegram or cablegram by Pascal, followed by a letter that quotes it verbatim; a long cable from Pascal about the need to refilm an address by Shaw, with the complete text of Shaw's address in case Shaw did not have it at hand (a headnote indicates where the text is published); and brief affirmative replies to letters (instead, headnotes indicate replies when the answers are documented). Pascal was so long-winded, whether he dictated a letter or an expensive transoceanic cable, that readers' eyes might glaze and their interest flag at numerous fulsome expressions of thanks and admiration or effusive apologies, or at references to enclosing or being unable to send letters by others or scenarios or still photographs or press clippings, to summaries of what he or Shaw said in a previous letter, to confirmations of receipt or queries about non-receipt of letters or contracts or scripts, to dates or cancellation of dates of screenings and meetings, to film negatives being ready or not ready, to press showings or requests of Shaw for lists of people to invite to them, and to hundreds of similar details. Here, as elsewhere, Pascal's saving graces include self-knowledge and a sense of humour, as revealed in a statement that Shaw's letter 'crossed my 10,000,000 words telegram.' Since enough is enough, I have restricted such statements and references, allowing those that this published correspondence includes to stand as examples of those they exclude. Ellipses indicate deletions within letters and telegrams.

Because English was not Pascal's first language and because he did not completely master it, some readers may be jarred by the contrast between a virtuoso of English prose and one who is not always adept at expressing himself in the language; others, who I hope are more numerous, may be charmed by this dissimilarity. Where italicized letters or punctuation marks may clarify odd expressions, I use them. On all occasions, however, I let Pascal speak for himself, which I submit reveals his personality better than any other course of action would do. Readers should be able to translate 'I like' into 'I would like,' the plural 'versions' into the singular 'version,' and 'a superior meaning because of the organical development for my work' into 'a higher meaning because of the organic development of my work'; to add or interpolate conjunctions, prepositions, and articles, such as 'everybody astonished [but] not myself,' 'he is scared from [of] the long speeches,' and 'I stopped at [the] Mayo Clinic'; to recognize that 'NEWYORK' is telegramese for two words, as is 'MAJOR-BARBARA'; and to make sense of such locutions as 'I was received very friendly in Rome from Com. Freddi Propaganda ministerium,' 'you predicted me,' 'I decided for him he is younger,' 'you approved on it,' 'then arrived your cable,' and 'they recasted Prossy.'

Many pieces of Pascal's side of the correspondence consist of carbon copies and drafts of letters or cables. Unlike original letters, most of them are unsigned. Sometimes 'Gabriel Pascal' appears, typed, below where his signature would be, at other times not. Although I infer that he often signed 'Gabriel' instead of his full name, I do not know how often he did so, but do know that on one occasion he wrote 'G.P.' and on another 'Gabriele.' Rather than guess exactly how he signed the original of each carbon copy, I have, despite the possible appearance of formality, bracketed his full name throughout when I do not know.

Material sufficient to place each item in its context is provided in the form of a headnote preceding it. Annotative matter follows, the subject of each annotation being in boldface type. Certain physical elements of the correspondence, such as the placement of heading information (addresses, dates) and closings, as well as the form of addresses and dates in the headings, have been standardized. Necessary editorial interruptions – where, for example, a word or phrase must be conjectured or a name completed – are placed in square brackets, with conjectured or translated text in regular type and editorial matter italicized.

Acknowledgments

For their help in making this book possible, I thank, first and foremost,

Dan H. Laurence and Mrs Valerie Delacorte. Over the years I have so often thanked Dan Laurence for his generosity that I have run out of new ways to do so, which is a measure of my indebtedness. When I met Mrs Valerie Delacorte, formerly Mrs Pascal, after one letter and one telephone call, she overwhelmed me by lending me hundreds of pages of Pascal's correspondence and giving me permission to publish them. Without her generosity, most of Pascal's side of his correspondence with Shaw would remain unknown.

As on other occasions, I am happy here to acknowledge my debt to the unfailingly helpful Roma Woodnutt and the Society of Authors, acting for the Shaw Estate, and for their permission to print Shaw's correspondence.

To the two anonymous readers of the manuscript of this book, I am indeed appreciative. Often, the quality of such readers seems to be determined by a toss of the dice. In this case, the General Editor and the University of Toronto Press rolled two sevens. Incisive and on target, their advice and admonitions revealed not only conscientiousness, but also an impressive knowledge of Shaw, of writing, and of editing. While I absolve them of whatever errors and infelicities may remain in this book, I respectfully thank them for the errors and infelicities they helped me to remove.

I am grateful as well to other individuals, chiefly for assistance in annotating references: Linda Arnold, Stuart Baker, Barbara Dukore, Martin Esslin, A.W. Godfrey, Harry Lane, Douglas Laurie, Glenn Loney, Christopher Murray, Colonel Eoghan O'Neill, Thomas O'Neill, Anne Paolucci, Michael Saffle, Rakesh Solomon, Harriet Talan, Gordon Taylor (of the Salvation Army, London), and Pat Whelan (of the Abbey Theatre).

For its award of a Fulbright Senior Scholarship in England and Ireland, I am indebted to the Council for International Exchange of Scholars. Other organizations to which I am beholden are the Academy Foundation (Los Angeles, and especially Kristine Krueger), the British Film Institute, the British Library (the Central Library at the British Museum, the Colindale Newspaper Library, and the Westminster Central Reference Library), the Irish Architectural Archive, the Italian Cultural Institute (London), the Mayo Clinic, the National Library of Ireland, Newman Library of Virginia Polytechnic Institute and State University (and particularly to Alex Baer, Joanne Eustis, Anita Haney, and John

Stemmer), the New York Public Library (the Billy Rose Collection at Lincoln Center and the Newspaper Collection at 42nd Street), and the Theatre Museum (London).

For permission to publish letters, I am grateful to the British Library, the Everett Needham Case Library of Colgate University, and the Harry Ransom Humanities Research Center of the University of Texas at Austin.

Last, but not least, I am grateful to Virginia Polytechnic Institute and State University for giving me time and funds to research and prepare this book.

Abbreviations

Type of correspondence

ALS	Autograph letter or letter-card signed
ANS	Autograph note on 'compliments' card signed
ANU	Autograph note unsigned
APCS	Autograph postal card or correspondence card signed
APCU	Autograph postal card or correspondence card unsigned
(c)	Carbon copy
(e)	Extract or truncated text previously published
HD	Holograph draft
(p)	photocopy
SHD	Shorthand draft
TD	Typed draft
TDS	Typed draft signed
TEL	Telegram or cable
TL	Typed letter
TLS	Typed letter or letter-card signed
TPCS	Typed postal card signed
(tr)	Typed transcription or copy
U	Previously unpublished

Sources of the correspondence

Deans	Marjorie Deans
Delacorte	Mrs Valerie Delacorte

Bancroft   Bancroft Library, University of California at
                    Berkeley
Barbara   *Major Barbara* (New York: Dodd, Mead 1941)
BL   British Library (followed by Add. MS folio
                    numbers)
Colgate   Richard S. Weiner Collection of George Bernard
                    Shaw, Special Collections Department, Everett
                    Needham Case Library, Colgate University
Hampden   Hampden-Booth Theatre Library, New York City
HRC   Harry Ransom Humanities Research Center,
                    University of Texas at Austin
Letters   *Collected Letters 1926–1950*, ed. Dan H. Laurence
                    (London: Max Reinhart and New York: Viking
                    1988)
Pygmalion   *Pygmalion* (New York: Dodd, Mead 1939)
Sphinx   *Meeting at the Sphinx* by Marjorie Deans
                    (London 1946)
Unidentified   Unidentified publication in newspaper or
                    magazine

On the set of *Caesar and Cleopatra* at Denham Studios. From left to right: Cecil Parker, Flora Robson, Claude Rains, Vivien Leigh, and Bernard Shaw. Photo courtesy of the Wisconsin Center for Film and Theater Research

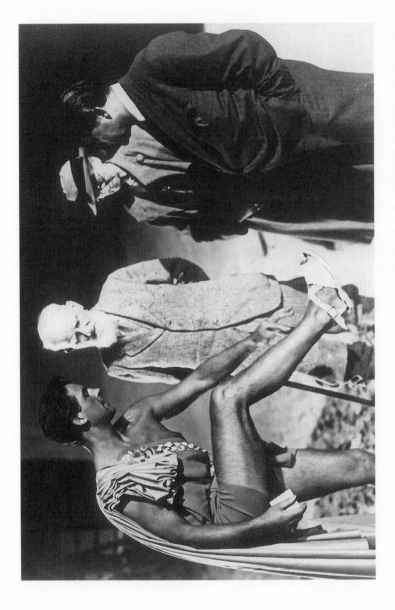

On the set at Denham Studios. From left to right: Stewart Granger, Shaw, Blanche Patch, Gabriel Pascal. Photo courtesy of the Wisconsin Center for Film and Theater Research

Claude Rains, Shaw, Blanche Patch, and Pascal. Photo courtesy of the Wisconsin Center for Film and Theater Research

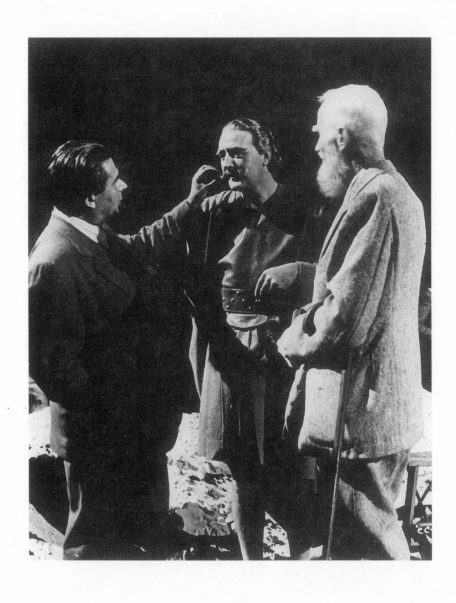

On the set at Denham Studios. From left to right: Pascal, Cecil Parker, Shaw.
Photo courtesy of the Wisconsin Center for Film and Theater research

Caesar and Cleopatra. Pascal and Shaw. Photo courtesy of the Wisconsin Center for Film and Theater Research

Major Barbara. On location at the Albert Hall. From left to right: Rex Harrison,
Robert Morley, Shaw, and Pascal. Photo courtesy of the Wisconsin Center for
Film and Theater Research

Letters

1 / To Gabriel Pascal   4 Whitehall Court
London SW1
13th December 1935

[TLS(p): Delacorte: U(e)]

Appropriately, the Shaw/Pascal correspondence begins with Shaw's cover letter for
a Memorandum of Agreement licensing G.P. Films, which Pascal incorporated,
to produce a British film version of Pygmalion.

Dear Mr Pascal

I enclose an agreement in duplicate. I have put in an additional clause
to safeguard you against the possibility of G.P. Films supplanting you by
another producer. It gives you a personal hold on the film which you
may find necessary. You should be careful to protect yourself in the
same way in any other contracts you may make.

Will you please obtain the signature and seal of G.P. to the second
copy, and return to me? It has to be stamped within fourteen days.

Faithfully
G. Bernard Shaw

2 / To G. Bernard Shaw   Hotel du Cap d'Antibes
Antibes (A[lpes] M[aritimes])
Sunday [25 April 1937]

[HD: Delacorte: U]

Planning to make Pygmalion *in French and Italian as well as in English, Pascal*
tried to obtain financing in Europe. In 1935, Italy's Fascist government took over
the film industry, which it attached to the Ministry of Press and Propaganda, set
up a film section of the Bank of Lavora to finance up to 60 per cent of movie
undertakings it approved, and established a scale of rebates to 25 per cent to pro-
ducers if box-office returns were low. On Wednesday (not Thursday), 21 April
1937, the mythical anniversary of the founding of Rome, the government opened
the Cinecittà *(Cinema City) studios, six miles from Rome, which were equipped*
with Europe's most advanced film-making equipment and facilities, including 16
sound stages.

My dearest Maestro

Confirming my telegramme from Rome, I have arranged in Paris with Monsieur Hamon and in Rome the contract with Mr Castelli for his shares as successor from your Italian translator il signor Agrosti.

I was received very friendly in Rome from Com Freddi Propaganda ministerium and he will give me all the support for the Italian version ... Last Thursday I saw the 'inaugurazione' of the Cinecittà (the Italian Hollywood) in presence of the Duce and all the 'big shots.' I am sending you some snapshots hereby: on the left of the picture a) is the Sicilian popular actor Angelo Musco; in the centre of the picture b) he tries to explain a scene to the Duce and overacts Caesar himself.

I will be back in London next Thursday to start the studio preparations. I could come next Saturday to London and give you a full report with all the happenings and I think you will be very satisfied.

Please give my most affectionate regards to Madame Shaw – thinking always on her lovely motherly looks. I feel myself twice stronger and confident ...

Gabriel Pascal

Pascal often drafted letters, telegrams, and cablegrams to be typed by a regular or temporary employee.

On 17 April Shaw wrote a letter of introduction for him to Augustin **Hamon** (1862–1945), a Socialist-Anarchist author and editor, who with his wife Henriette (née Rynenbroeck) had been Shaw's French translator since 1904. **Agrosti** is an error for Antonio **Agresti** (1866–1926), Shaw's Jewish-Italian translator. Upon Agresti's death, Cesare **Castelli** (b. 1871), Shaw's Italian agent, to whom he also wrote a letter of introduction, became Shaw's translator.

Luigi **Freddi** (b. 1895) was head of the Italian film industry. *Il Duce* (the leader) was Benito **Mussolini** (1883–1945); Adolf Hitler took the title *Führer* (leader) from him. Angelo **Musco** (1872–1937) was a popular Sicilian mime and movie actor. Mrs **Shaw** was born Charlotte Frances Payne-Townshend (1857–1943).

3 / To Gabriel Pascal Sidmouth
10th May 1937

[ALS(p): Delacorte: U(e)]

Dear Gabriel

Here is Eliza *exactly*: hat and feathers, shawl, apron, and above all the basket, so ridiculously misrepresented by a lady's gardening basket in the Dutch & German films.

The picture is cut from this week's Listener, in which an article by Compton Mackenzie throws back to Eliza's period.

Our nerves are improving. You made a tremendous impression on Castelli.

GBS

Sir Edward Montague Compton **Mackenzie** (1883–1972) was a journalist, poet, literary critic, playwright, and novelist.

4 / To G. Bernard Shaw   10 Bolton Street. Piccadilly. London W1

11th May 1937

[TL(c): Delacorte: U]

Having abdicated on 11 December 1936, King Edward VIII (1894–1972) was succeeded by his brother George VI (1895–1952), whose coronation as King of Great Britain took place on 12 May 1937.

My dearest Maestro

Many thanks for your letter of 6th May. I am glad that you have finally had the opportunity to have a good rest after your hard work. For this reason, too, it is much better that I don't bother you with a long letter. I will wait until after the Coronation, or maybe I could come and see you either at Sidmouth or at Whitehall.

I myself have also had a very hard few days, arranging the dates with the Studio. I shall shoot the picture at the Pinewood Studio at Ivor.

Everything is progressing very well, only the Italians would prefer that we made the French version together with the Italian version in Rome, instead of making it here in England together with the English version. I agreed in principle to the terms of the leading part in the French version with Gaby Morlay. She is the greatest French actress of the new generation. She would also like to play the lead in the Italian version as she is a born Sicilian. Her inimitable Sicilian dialect would replace wonderfully the English cockney in the first two reels of the picture. The Italians though would prefer an Italian actress.

The French distributors have already agreed to the French version of the Picture being made in London, so I am sure they will also agree to Rome. I am now making the arrangements to settle all these contracts, and then I hope to start with the rehearsals for the English version in six weeks time. I would like to have at least two weeks rehearsals before I start the actual shooting. I know that it has never been done before, that a picture has been rehearsed like a stage play, but I do not see any other possibility for the actors to have the right style, unless they rehearse their dialogue for two or three weeks.

I would be very glad, as soon as you are really rested, if you could spare me one hour. I would like to show you the letters I exchanged with Castelli and Hamon before I give them any further news.

Wishing you and Mrs Shaw a further restful holiday,

Your always faithfully devoted,

[Gabriel Pascal]

In July 1934 the French stage star Gaby **Morlay** (1890–1964) was considered for 'Elisa' in a French film version of *Pygmalion* adapted by Albert Rièra (b. 1895).

5 / To G. Bernard Shaw   10 Bolton Street. Piccadilly. London W1
13th May 1937

[TL(c): Delacorte: U]

My dearest Maestro

I have just received your lovely card with the picture of Eliza holding the real basket.

Looking at the picture the definite idea came to me, which I have already been discussing vaguely with my art director who has started to design the sketches for the sets, that maybe it would be better to go back to the original period, instead of putting the action in our modern days, which would take away the whole charm of the right atmosphere of the period. I am very anxious to have your reaction on this point ...

[Gabriel Pascal]

John Bryan (1911–69) was **art director** for *Pygmalion*.

6 / To G. Bernard Shaw   10 Bolton Street. Piccadilly. London W1

21st May 1937

[TL(c): Delacorte: U]

... I am sailing on the 'Normandie' on the 26th May and I will be in the States for one week to arrange for the distribution contract of our picture in the States and Canada. As soon as I am back I shall start rehearsals. I have fixed up with the Studios for the 15th August. Before I leave the Board of Directors of my Company desire that the legal position as regards 'PYGMALION' should be cleared up. My solicitors, Messrs J.D. Langton & Passmore, have at my suggestion prepared an agreement to cover a) a licence for the French and Italian rights and b) the prolongation of the licence for the English rights, to which you already friendly agreed at our last meeting in London.

If you agree with the text of the Agreement perhaps you would please sign it and send it to your secretary, Miss Patch, and I will arrange to exchange with her a duplicate duly signed by me on behalf of my Company ...

[Gabriel Pascal]

Blanche **Patch** (1879–1966) had been Shaw's secretary since 1920.

7 / To G. Bernard Shaw   [New York City]

18th June 1937

[TL(c): Delacorte: U]

Frequently, as (c) indicates, Pascal's letters survive in the form of carbon copies, which lack letterheads to indicate where he wrote them. Occasionally, as here, he mentions the location. He was in New York, negotiating with the main officers of Columbia Pictures, whose film-making studios were in Hollywood. Under the studio system, which dominated American movies for decades, executives infrequently signed single-film contracts.

My dear Master

I have practically concluded the distributing contract for 'Pygmalion' with the Columbia Pictures, one of the best American companies, and they insisted that they also distribute the picture in England. They have a much better organization in England than Paramount or the English Company with which I had a preliminary deal, if you remember. They have contracts for Super pictures like 'Pygmalion' will be, with about 1800 theatres in England alone. So this is done.

I am going next week to the coast to see Cecil Lewis – He is working on the technical side of the shooting script – and am sailing back to England on the 14th of July, when I will start immediately rehearsing with the entire cast.

I wish to ask you a favor in our common interest: Please grant me the option on a second play of yours under the same conditions as 'Pygmalion.' You remember I was very anxious to do, after 'Pygmalion' is finished, 'The Millionairess' or 'Candida.' We can decide the play when I return to London, but I have found the ideal actress for the millionairess and a really interesting actor for the Egyptian doctor.

I would be very grateful if on receipt of this letter you would send me a Night Letter Cable – 'Option on second play under same conditions as Pygmalion granted, to be produced after completion of Pygmalion.' My cable address here is WINGFOOT FOR PASCAL NEW YORK. The cable will automatically be forwarded to me to Hollywood, and I could make all my dispositions with my unit also for a second production.

May I also ask you as an indication of your great friendship, that you please postpone a definite decision in the matter of 'Devil's Disciple,' until I return to London and have had an opportunity to speak to you. Ever since I first began picture production it has been the dream of my life to produce 'The Devil's Disciple' for the screen ...

[Gabriel Pascal]

Cecil **Lewis** (b. 1898), one of the four founders of the BBC (British Broadcasting Corporation) in 1922, directed the British film versions of Shaw's *How He Lied to Her Husband* (1931) and *Arms and the Man* (1932).

8 / To G. Bernard Shaw   The Los Angeles Ambassador. California

7th July 1937

[TL(c): Delacorte: U]

My dearest Maestro

Finally last week Cecil received four weeks time from Paramount, to work on our shooting script. I signed a contract with him in name of my company, on the basis of his telegram which he sent me to New York and of which I sent a copy to you two weeks ago.

I bring you the shooting script to London, because I like your definite approval on it before I start the production. Cecil is working very hard and with real enthusiasm and I hope for our sake that you will like what he has done.

I stay in New York until the 14th of July. I bring with me what Cecil has done until this time – the rest he will send us.

My distribution deal is practically settled, but I will not sign it here. I like to show it to my lawyers in London, to be covered for such an important deal.

Certainly I realize, what I knew always: that it is a foolishness to produce important pictures based only on a contract with an English distribution company, without American release ...

[Gabriel Pascal]

9 / To G. Bernard Shaw   10 Bolton Street. Piccadilly. London W1

17th September 1937

[TL(c): Delacorte: U]

The ninth paragraph illustrates Pascal's tendency, in order to obtain a contract, to put the most favourable construction on efforts to undermine Shaw's wishes. Although Shaw's reply to this letter has not surfaced, he may have told Pascal, quoting or paraphrasing Hamlet, that he knew not 'seems,' since the demands of Columbia Pictures actually, not merely at first sight, contradicted his contract with Pascal as well as his standard contracts, and that 'only the right' to make changes in editing and cutting the American print was considerably more than 'only' implies. Since Pascal did not conclude a contract with Columbia, Shaw clearly rejected its contractual revisions, which Pascal urged him to accept.

My dearest Maestro

The reasons for my long silence, for which I apologise, are various.

The first is that my lawyers have been trying to clear up several paragraphs of the draft of the Columbia contract which I did not want to show you until the final draft can be accepted by my firm as being in accordance with my contract with you.

The other reason is that on the 27th July an article appeared in the New York Evening Post – the originator of which must have been connected with Cecil – wherein it was stated that he possessed the exclusive picture rights of 'Pygmalion,' so Columbia, with whom I had been working for two months on the distribution deal, became alarmed and needed all kinds of explanations. However, an old friend of mine, Bill Hillman, the London representative of Randolph Hearst, was going to New York at that time and promised to clear up these mistakes of the Press, which it seems now he has done.

I will try in my modest way to give you a clear picture of the situation. As I told you on my return from America, I was very successful the first weeks in New York with Columbia: everything was agreed on broad lines. Then, when I arrived in Hollywood I heard that Cecil Lewis's literary agents were offering 'Disciple of the Devil' outside of Paramount to each American Company, and that he had stated that he had 'carte blanche' from you to write and make the picture as he liked. The Columbia people asked from me the same carte blanche, and when after the 7th July (the date of my last letter to you) I went back to New York to complete the draft of the contract with the help of my American lawyer, they inserted all kinds of additional paragraphs in the distributing contract in connection with my contract with you, which made it impossible for me to sign the deal.

When I came back to London, I hoped my lawyers could clear up all these paragraphs and bring into accord the Columbia contract with my contract with you, but they were on holiday, and then the Secretary of my Company, Mr Cochrane, who had been working on the corrections and counter-proposals of the distributing contract, had a serious car accident, and it was not until last week that I was able to obtain a clear statement from my lawyers. And now, the General Manager of Columbia – Mr Seidelmann – is arriving in Paris on Saturday morning, the 18th, and I am going there to meet him.

Meanwhile, you remember when I came back to London, you told me that it would be wise to engage a scenarist who has had good stage experience to overhaul Cecil's shooting script, and I have found a very clever man who understands that he must respect your style and spirit, and who is very keen to do so, and who can add several technical improvements to Cecil's shooting script, taking out the dreadful Ascot sequence. He is W.P. Lipscomb – he wrote the play and scenario of 'Clive of India,' and the shooting script of 'Tale of Two Cities.' I hope you will not disapprove of my engaging him for these two or three weeks' supplementary work. He is a real scenario mechanic: for him a shooting script is like a mathematical formula!

Further, I have been approached by London Films who intimated they would be very glad if I would shoot the English version of the picture in their Denham studios: they offer me all the technical assistance I require at a studio rental no higher than that of the other studios with whom I have already a preliminary agreement. They are really doing their best to co-operate with me, but I cannot have the necessary two stages until the second half of December. Therefore, when Castelli arrived here asking for the definitive shooting script for translation into Italian, I communicated with Rome to ascertain if I could have a studio there at once, and after my meeting with Mr Seidelmann (the Columbia General Manager) in Paris I will go to Rome for two days to make sure if I can have studio-space in the Duce's new Cine-Città. I suggest starting at once the Italian and French versions together, and producing the English version immediately after Christmas.

This is the plan, if you would kindly agree to the insertion in our agreement of the supplementary paragraphs which my solicitors have worked out with Columbia's solicitors, because only on this basis could I have the American distributing contract.

At first sight, it seems that their insertions are barbaric contradictions of the main paragraphs in our contract, but if you agree to the principal points, I will fight everything through in such a form that it will be acceptable to you. In any case one of the chief artistic differences between Columbia and myself is that according to my contract with you I will not have any interference by Columbia in the scenario or cutting, and they agree they have no right to change anything at all in the English version of the negative or the prints. They want only the right to make changes in the editing and cutting in the American version if the American censorship asks for it.

If, for some reason, you reject these supplementary paragraphs, it would make it impossible for me to work with Columbia or any other American Company because what they principally require is that the licence which you granted to me should be an 'exclusive and complete grant.' They further require that in my contract with you in addition to the English, French, and Italian versions, you should grant me the Spanish-speaking or dubbing rights and, in the small countries outside the German-speaking countries and Holland and the Colonies, the right of superimposed titles, because in such countries English or American pictures cannot otherwise be exhibited. (When I speak of the 'exclusive grant,' you will remember, my dear Maestro, that you told me at our last meeting that you would write to your American lawyer to enquire if this request is justified and usual with American companies.)

If we cannot find for these insertions such compromise with Columbia as will be satisfactory to you, I would make, as planned, the Italian and French versions immediately in Rome, and come back and make the English version after Christmas for an English distributing company; and after the English version is finished, make a separate distributing contract for U.S.A. in New York with Columbia or another major American distributing Company.

This procedure would mean that we would lose the advantage of the American organisation which is that they book their pictures on the title of the play, the name of the author, and some stars, before the picture is completed, and in the draft agreement with Columbia it is stipulated that they must book our picture as an 'A' class picture, which is the Super-class of each American Company and is booked with about 4,000 theatres to the extent of at least $600,000 to $800,000 before the picture is delivered by the producer. When the picture is finished they make further bookings, so by using the Columbia organisation our picture would be booked by them as one of their own 'supers.' They would give my Company a guarantee of one-third of the production costs on delivery of the pictures, so that practically my Company must provide all the finance, and maybe you have never realised, dear Maestro, that I must give my finance partners a personal guarantee for all the negative costs, and if for some reason I am a commercial failure, the rest of my life must be spent in paying off this guarantee.

It seems a very hard condition, but United Artists, for example, do not give one cent advance on the delivery of the picture to Mr Korda, and they distribute his pictures for the same distributing commission which Columbia is asking from us.

There is another paragraph in our contract which it is important to clarify. In our contract my Company, as manufacturers of the picture, must pay you 10% of all money which we receive from the exhibitors, but here it is necessary to clear up one point: that is, that the money is not received by us direct from the exhibitors – no producer has direct contact with the exhibitors. My chief care with Columbia is to safeguard your interests, and I have insisted that before they have the right to deduct their one-third advance or any other expenses for prints, publicity, etc., they must directly from all income pay you the 10%. Thus, the third line of paragraph 7 in our contract should read, if you agree, 'distributors' for 'exhibitors.'

To give you a definite picture of the frivolous changes Columbia asked in the first draft of their contract, I have asked my solicitors to prepare me a letter for you with each point raised by them and the appropriate legal explanation of it. These points which I have mentioned above, I find justified and necessary if we work with any American company. With regard to the other points, I will fight with Columbia or drop the whole deal with them.

Now about the casting: I am a little bit ashamed, my dear Maestro, that you were again right about Barry Barnes, the actor I presented to you for Higgins. I saw the whole picture which he made, and certainly he is too young, not manly enough and not dynamic enough, and he lacks the real sense of humour without which Higgins would be unsympathetic to the audience, as in the dreadful performance at Buxton by Morley. (A propos, Diana Wynyard was not less dreadful and without any real personality.)

But you must appreciate my position: if I could make the picture only in your spirit, which I will do in any case, not thinking of this stupid box-office question which the distributors ask, I could have cast this picture a long time ago in a way which would please you, and would be worthy of the highest artistic expectations, and also please the genuine cinema audiences of the world. But the mentality of exhibitors and distributors is the mentality of necktie-sellers. They insist on some box-office names for the leading parts: this is my big fight with Columbia about Wendy

Hiller. Her own agent, Harry Ham, has suggested I should give Wendy another picture first before I risk her in such a tremendous part. When I was negotiating with Korda for studio-space, he offered me a selection of all his stars, and he suggested that for Eliza I should have Vivien Leigh, a delightful young actress of whom I enclose some 'stills.'

For Higgins, I have come back to our original idea which seemed to please you, of Laurence Olivier, and Korda is ready to loan this actor to me, but I am not definitely convinced because he is too young and not the real English type. I will however make a test with him as with all the other actors, and show it to you before we go into production.

I heard yesterday that Philip Merrivale has arrived in this country with his newly-wed wife, Gladys Cooper, and will stay here for a few months, so I would like to have him for Pickering, which idea we discussed, if you remember, before I went to Hollywood. I have spoken today with his brother, Bernard Merrivale, and he told me that Philip is very keen to join us because he played this part in New York. If you still like this idea I will sign him up as he is very popular in America also. Roland Young, to whom I suggested Pickering first was crazy, as I told you, to play Higgins, but now his agent asks why we don't cast him for Doolittle. I think however that he is too weak for this type, and I have two or three other good suggestions to make, when you are back, for Doolittle, but the best of them is Edmund Gwenn.

Marie Lohr is definitely fixed for Mrs Higgins, and for Mrs Pearce I suggest either Marie Ney – whom I saw in Buxton and who I think would be better for this part than either Jean Cadell or Irene Vanbrugh. The latter, I agree with you after seeing her again, is too 'vaudeville' for this part, and not simple enough for Mrs Hill. My own choice would be Marie Ney for Mrs Pearce, and Joyce Barbour for Mrs Hill. Joyce Barbour is having a tremendous success in a little comedy 'George and Margaret.'

For Freddie, I have found a much better boy than Romney Brent, who is perhaps a little too high-brow for this part, and this actor is Nigel Patrick. He is the typical Freddie, and I am sure you will like this choice.

I am sorry to bother you with this long letter: if it is too much for you to answer me now, it will be time enough when I get back from Rome at the end of next week, when, as Miss Patch tells me, she hopes you will be back in London, and by that time also I will know the definite situation with Columbia, and your decision about the paragraphs they wish to have inserted in the distribution contract ...

I agree with you that we should not take a French actress for the Italian version, and I think I have found a really excellent artiste for the Italian version – her name is Maria Gambarelli, and she is very much favoured by the Duce. I will bring you back a reel of her last picture from Rome, and I am enclosing her 'stills' herein.

What I would like to express to you, dear Maestro, and what I ask you to appreciate is that it is very hard for a producer who has his own ideas, to serve two masters: on the one side you, my spiritual Master, and on the other this dreadful American company with its cry of 'Box-Office,' whose mentality is killing me, and made me leave Hollywood years ago in misery because I refused to serve them: I realise now that we need them for the distributing contract, and so I ask you to help me to discharge my difficult task with honour and success, so that finally I can start practical production; and after 'Pygmalion,' if you are satisfied, I could produce other plays of yours, which is my greatest ambition, and I am convinced that after 'Pygmalion' has been produced all big American companies will ask for your plays, and we can dictate our own conditions.

But you know how difficult it is to keep one's own personality, small or big, in the presence of your infinite personality, and sometimes even when I am thinking of you (and this I do nearly day and night) I feel that I have an inferiority complex, which I have never experienced in my life – not even in the presence of War Lords, dictators, Popes, or Indian Yogis – since I first set out from my puszta (little Hungarian farm) as a young lad, to conquer the world: and I will lose it again only when I have finished this picture satisfactorily.

Your friendship has greatly heartened me during the fights of these last months, and this friendship is more valuable to me than anything else: with it, I can make the best picture in the world ...

[Gabriel Pascal]

The 27 July **article** was Leonard Lyons's column, 'Lyons Den,' in the *New York Post*. In the 1930s American journalist William **Hillman** (1895–1962) was chief of foreign correspondents for the newspapers of William Randolph **Hearst** (1863–1951). General manager of Columbia Pictures, Joseph H. **Seidelman** (1895–1968), whose name Pascal misspells, later became president of Universal Films. With Cecil Lewis and Ian Dalrymple (1903–89), the veteran screenwriter W.P. **Lipscomb** (1887–1958) collaborated on adapting *Pygmalion*.

Alexander (later Sir Alexander) **Korda** (né Sandor Corda, 1893–1956), Hungarian producer and director who had worked in Paris, Berlin, and Hollywood before he settled in London in 1930, was a major figure in the British film industry. A stage actor, Barry K. **Barnes** (né Nelson Barnes, 1906–65) was a leading man of British adventure films. Pascal may have seen *The Return of the Scarlet Pimpernel* (1937). In Buxton, a city southeast of Manchester, Higgins was played by Robert (later Sir Robert) **Morley** (1908–92), British stage and screen actor who would play Undershaft in Pascal's *Major Barbara*. Diana **Wynyard** (née Dorothy Isobel Cox, 1906–64), a leading lady of the British stage who also appeared in New York, made films in Hollywood and England.

Harry Breden **Ham** (1891–1943), Canadian-born actor, later film producer and distribution executive, was a talent agent in both Hollywood and London. Wendy (later Dame Wendy) **Hiller** (b. 1912), notable stage and screen actress in Great Britain and the United States, would play Eliza. Vivien **Leigh** (née Vivian Mary Hartley, 1913–67), a major English actress of stage and screen, would play Scarlett O'Hara in *Gone with the Wind* (1939). Laurence (later Sir Laurence, then Baron) **Olivier** (1907–89) was one of England's major stage and screen actors.

Pascal misspells the surname of Philip **Merivale** (1886–1946), India-born British stage actor; under Shaw's direction, he played Pickering in the first London production of *Pygmalion* (1914), to the Eliza of Mrs Patrick Campbell (née Beatrice Stella Tanner, 1865–1940); when she took the play to New York later that year, he played Higgins. Merivale's wife, Gladys (later Dame Gladys) **Cooper** (1888–1971), was a beautiful British stage and screen actress; his brother, **Bernard Merivale** (1882–1939), was a dramatist as well as an actor. Roland **Young** (1887–1953), a British actor, was a major Hollywood comedy character actor. A British actor who performed in Shaw's plays at the Court Theatre (1904–7), Edmund **Gwenn** (1875–1959), made many movies, including Shaw's first, *How He Lied to Her Husband*.

Born in Australia, Marie **Lohr** (née Löhr, 1890–1975), a London stage actress since 1901, played Mrs Higgins. Marie **Ney** (1895–1981) was a British stage actress who occasionally appeared in films. The Scottish character actress Jean **Cadell** (1884–1967) played Mrs Pearce. Irene **Vanbrugh** (1872–1949) was a British stage actress. The stage and screen actress Joyce **Barbour** (1901–77) was appearing in *George and Margaret* (1937) by Gerald Savory (b. 1909). A screen actor, Romney **Brent** (né Romulo Larralde, 1902–76) also wrote for the stage. Nigel **Patrick** (né Nigel Dennis Wemyss, 1913–81) was a leading man and character actor of British stage and screen. An American dancer and actress, Maria **Gambarelli** (1900–90), born in Italy of Italian-American parents, was a *première danseuse* of the Metropolitan Opera Ballet; she acted in American and Italian movies, chiefly in the 1930s.

---

10 / To G. Bernard Shaw   10 Bolton Street. Piccadilly. London W1
                                   30th October 1937

[TL(c): Delacorte: U]

My dearest Maestro

Herein I submit to you the definite cast for 'Pygmalion' for your approval: –

Professor Higgins	...	Leslie Howard (the date of his freedom depends on the beginning of the picture 'Lawrence of Arabia')
Mrs Higgins	...	Marie Lohr
Colonel Pickering	...	Philip Merrivale
Alfred Doolittle	...	Wilfrid Lawson
Eliza Doolittle	...	Wendy Hiller or Jean Gilly or Linden Travers (outside Reserve Mabel Poulton) (Definite selection after tests are made of all these artists)
Mrs Hill	...	Jean Cadell
Clara	...	Leueen McGrath
Freddy	...	John Mills
Mrs Pearce	...	Marie Ney

The Bystanders will all be first class actors, such as John Forbes-Robertson, Maltby etc.

I would be very grateful if you would be so kind as to sign the copy of this letter so that I can proceed to make the definite contracts with the artists.

You have already kindly agreed that Mr W.H. Lipscomb is to overhaul the shooting script of Cecil Lewis, and with your permission, I have already made arrangements for this work.

My idea is, if you agree, that Leslie Howard should co-direct the picture.

By the end of next week I shall be able to show you all the tests of the different artists.

Ever your devoted,
[Gabriel Pascal]

Leslie **Howard** (1893–1943), major stage and screen star, played Higgins and also co-directed *Pygmalion*. Wilfrid **Lawson** (né Worsnop, 1900–66), stage and screen actor, acted

Doolittle. The British leading lady Jean **Gillie** (1915–49), whose surname Pascal misspells, first appeared on the London stage in 1932 and entered films in 1937. Linden **Travers** (née Florence Lindon-Travers, b. 1913) was a leading lady of stage and screen. A victim of the talkies because of her cockney accent, Mabel **Poulton** (b. 1905) was a leading lady in films of the 1920s – including *The Constant Wife* (1928), based on the play by W. Somerset Maugham (1874–1965) – but made few pictures thereafter. Leueen **MacGrath** (1914–92), whose surname Pascal misspells, played Clara Eynsford-Hill, her film début; with American comedy playwright George S. Kaufman (1887–1961), she co-authored several plays, including *Silk Stockings* (1955). John (later Sir John) **Mills** (b. 1908), British stage actor, became a major screen star.

The other John is an error for the eminent Sir Johnston **Forbes-Robertson** (1853–1937), for whom Shaw wrote *Caesar and Cleopatra*. H.F. **Maltby** (1880–1963), British comedy playwright and screenwriter as well as actor, acted a Bystander in the opening scene.

11 / To Gabriel Pascal   [4 Whitehall Court. London SW1]
11th November 1937

[ANS: Delacorte: U(e)]

Shaw wrote this note at the foot of Pascal's 30 October letter.

I approve of the first five artists named.

I approve of Miss Jean Cadell only if she plays Mrs Pearce. Her salary would be wasted on the other parts.

I have no objection to Miss Marie Ney if Miss Cadell refuses Mrs Pearce.

The others I know nothing about; but, except for Freddy, they are not important.

I do not propose to interfere in the direction of the picture since I cannot, at my age, undertake it myself.

G. Bernard Shaw

12 / To G. Bernard Shaw   10 Bolton Street. Piccadilly. London W1
13th November 1937

[TL(c): Delacorte: U]

My dearest Maestro

I have been with Mr Henley the Manager of Jean Cadell to see her in her dressing-room at the 'Old Vic,' and she refused categorically to play Mrs Pearce. The only part which she would accept in 'Pygmalion' is Mrs

Higgins, but I told her that we have already arranged with Marie Löhr to play this part. Herewith I am sending you a letter which I received from Mr Henley.

So, in accordance with our last conversation, I have arranged for Marie Ney to play the part of Mrs Pearce, and Joyce Barbour to play the part of Mrs Hill. The latter artiste has a real success in 'George and Margaret': Miss Patch saw her in this play, in the rôle of the mother.

I am awaiting definite information from Mr Harry Ham, the Manager of Leslie Howard – with whom we have agreed all the points regarding his contract – of the date when Mr Howard will be free from his obligation to Korda for 'Lawrence of Arabia.' Mr Ham was obliged to send a long cable to Korda in Hollywood, and every day we are expecting an answer giving us this definite date, so that I can sign accordingly all the other contracts with the different artists, and fix the first shooting date.

I am ... sending you some of the 'stills' of Wendy Hiller.

Your always faithfully devoted,

Gabriel Pascal

David **Henley** (1894–1986), a stage actor in the 1920s, was a talent scout and casting director for films. Jean Cadell was playing Margaret of Anjou in Shakespeare's *Richard III* at the Old Vic, first an affectionate nickname, then actual name of the Victoria Theatre; from 1914 until well past the Second World War, it was established as a home of Shakespeare.

13 / To Gabriel Pascal   4 Whitehall Court. London SW1
18th November 1937

[APCS(p): Delacorte]

The stills are magnificent. She will be the film sensation of the next five years. There is a fortune in her.

GBS

14 / To G. Bernard Shaw   10 Bolton Street. Piccadilly. London W1
23rd December 1937

[TL(c): Delacorte: U]

On 1 January 1938 Shaw confirmed this agreement and also agreed to permit

*dubbing in countries that have no native film industry and have populations so
mixed that most films shown are Anglo-American.*

My dearest Maestro

re 'Pygmalion'

This is to confirm our recent conversation when you agreed that in
regard to the making of the English version of the film my Company is
to have the right to sub-title the English version for distribution outside
the English-speaking countries, in all other countries excepting in those
countries in which the foreign-language versions of the film have been
or will be made and exhibited.

I am happy that these dreadful commercial questions are over and
that I can finally, after Christmas, concentrate all my forces on the making of the picture.

Will you be kind enough to confirm this by signing and returning the
copy of this letter which is attached hereto.

Always your faithfully devoted,

[Gabriel Pascal]

15 / To G. Bernard Shaw   [10 Bolton Street. Piccadilly. London W1]
16th February 1938

[TL(c): Delacorte: U]

My dearest Maestro

I am delighted that you have accepted Anthony's ballroom sequence: I
never dreamt of having a single line in our picture without your trade-
mark, and I would be very grateful if you could receive Anthony and
give him the supplementary dialogues.

I agree with you that the Church will involve the figure of Mrs Doolittle, and I am not afraid of the big salary if she can cover your four magic
words, and I am looking forward to receiving them as soon as possible. I
am sending you also, according to your wish, the script of the sequence
of the church.

Always your faithfully devoted,
Gabriel Pascal

Anthony **Asquith** (1902–68), later the director of film versions of *The Doctor's Dilemma* (1958) and *The Millionairess* (1961), shares screen credit with Leslie Howard for directing *Pygmalion*. According to David Tree (b. 1915), who played Freddy, Howard was nowhere to be seen when he was not acting. Tree is the grandson of Sir Herbert Beerbohm Tree (1853–1917), who played Higgins in the first English production of *Pygmalion* (1914).

The other new scene Pascal proposed, following the lead of the Dutch film version of *Pygmalion*, was at the church, showing the Doolittles' wedding. Since the bride's only words during the ceremony are 'I will,' which are neither Shaw's nor four, and since no correspondence concerning '**your four magic words**' has come to light, what they are is unknown and, at least at present, unknowable. Shaw refused to write this scene.

16 / To G. Bernard Shaw   [10 Bolton Street. Piccadilly. London W1]

24th February 1938

[TL(c): Delacorte: U]

My dearest Maestro

I am so glad that you are pleased with my suggestion of Esme Percy for Cagliostro-Nepommuck. Walking down from Whitehall Court, I turned over in my mind all the faces of the English actors with real personalities (unfortunately there are not many) and suddenly I thought of Esme. After you had approved of him I 'phoned him at Brighton. He came to town yesterday to see me and he is delighted with the part. This morning I arranged for two days' work for him with his Manager, Mr Peacock.

I had a long talk with Anthony Asquith and my other collaborators. I told them how much I liked this unusual figure created by you in such a short time. We are now arranging the shooting script of this sequence so that your new figure will be shewn in the four Reception sets, namely:

(a) in the Entrance Hall,

(b) on the Staircase,

(c) on the top Landing,

(d) in the Ball-room.

I should appreciate your accepting, as technical form, for the entire scene, the arrangement of Anthony's sequence, in so far as the silent action is concerned.

Over the week-end I went through the whole working schedule. With my assistants I arranged to shoot, whatever the ending may be ultimately, the exit from St Paul's Church, Covent Garden, of Doolittle with his bride, and of Mrs Higgins with Pickering. Marie Lohr will leave our unit on the 2nd April and I shall shoot this scene in order to be covered for any eventuality. As soon as the Covent Garden set has been shot, it will be demolished and will be replaced by the reception sets in the Embassy.

Will you let me have, as soon as possible, my dear Maestro, the few words for Mrs Doolittle, so that I may cast the part at once?

I and my whole unit feel rather happy about all the preparations. Like a good old Thespian family, from the stars down to the last prop-man, all share my limitless faith in your play. Guided by your great spirit we are all confident of extraordinary achievements, and in this earnest hour, when our real productive work is starting, I want to thank you for your faith and belief in me, for the great patience you have shewn all through this difficult period of preparation.

The real making of this picture at the studio will be a limitless joy for me and your great heart will guide me to harmonious creation. I feel certain now that you will be pleased with the results. That will be my greatest reward for two years of suffering and fighting with Ibsenian distributor-trolls and picture parasites.

In eternal friendship and devotion,

[Gabriel Pascal]

Esmé **Percy** (1887–1957), well-known actor of Shavian drama, would play Nepommuck, a former pupil of Higgins. The film rechristens him Count Aristid Karpathy. Count Alessandro di **Cagliostro** (né Giuseppe Balsamo, 1743–95), an Italian impostor, travelled through Europe posing as an alchemist.

Monstrous or deformed demons of Germanic and Scandinavian folklore and mythology, who resemble human beings, **trolls** figure symbolically in many plays by Henrik Ibsen (1828–1906) and appear in his play *Peer Gynt* (1867), where they are barbaric, distorted alternatives to the noblest qualities of men and women.

17 / To Gabriel Pascal   4 Whitehall Court. London SW1

24th February 1938

[TLS: Letters]

My dear Gabriel

I have given my mind to the Pygmalion film seriously, and have no doubt at all as to how to handle the end of it. Anthony is a talented and inventive youth; but he doesnt know the difference between the end of a play and the beginning. Just when the audience has had enough of everything except the ending between Higgins and Eliza, to go back to the dirty mob in Covent Garden and drag back Doolittle after he has been finished and done with would produce a boredom and distraction that would spoil the whole affair. As to taking Higgins and Eliza out of that pretty drawingroom to be shaken up in a car it shews an appalling want of theatre sense and a childish itch for playing with motor cars and forgetting all about the play and the public. So away all that silly stuff goes.

Will you impress on Laurence Irving that the end of the play will depend on him? Not only must the drawingroom be pretty and the landscape, and the river if possible, visible through the windows with the suggestion of a perfect day outside, but the final scene on the embankment of Cheyne Walk must be a really beautiful picture. Its spaciousness must come out when the car is driven off. Irving must eclipse Whistler in this.

I am sorry I have had to stick in the flower shop; but it need not cost more than it is worth and you will save by getting rid of the wedding rubbish. It is not a Bond Street shop but a South Kensington one: half florist's, half greengrocer's and fruiterer's with a fine bunch of property grapes for Freddy to weigh for a lady customer. The counters can be made for a few pounds: scales can be hired; and the building can be faked out of any old junk. Everything unsightly can be covered in flowers.

I timed the dialogue in the Nepommuck scenes last night. Actual speaking occupies 68½ seconds, practically nothing.

Our advertising line must be an insult to Hollywood all through. An all British film made by British methods without interference by American script writers, no spurious dialogue but every word by the author, a revolution in the presentation of drama on the film. In short, English *über Alles.*

I am looking forward to seeing you tomorrow.

faithfully

GBS

Laurence (Henry Forster) **Irving** (1897–1988), English set designer for the stage and art director for the screen, designed *Pygmalion.* His grandfather was Sir Henry Irving (1838–1905), pre-eminent actor of his day and the first actor to be knighted (1895). James Abbott McNeill **Whistler** (1834–1903), major American impressionistic painter, would of course be difficult to eclipse. Shaw's reference to *Deutschland über Alles,* the German national anthem, overlooked the fact that the film's producer and prime mover was Hungarian.

18 / To Gabriel Pascal   4 Whitehall Court. London SW1
                                              6th March 1938

[TLS(p): Delacorte: U(e)]

My dear Gabriel

It is charitable of you to turn the studio into a casual ward; but it wont work artistically. Overcast parts are actually more dangerous on the stage than undercast ones; and one stranger stuck into a third act can ruin a play.

The moral of which is that Trouncer must not appear in any of the old scenes of the play.

He can play the big policeman in the scene at the railings. In it he will be tremendous – better than Laughton. In fact he will be worth the fifteen guineas. His appearance in the NBL scene would mean a loss of twenty thousand pounds.

I cannot make a part for the parlormaid for Jean. We implored her to take one of the best parts in the play and be starred in it. It is the only part in the play in which she would be worth two pounds a week. She refused it. She must stand by her refusal. To play the parlormaid would damage her professionally. There are things one must not forgive; and this is one of them.

Who is going to play the ambassadress who receives the guests? Surely Violet would be ideal for that. Why waste her on a walk-on? It is a real part and a dignified one, small as it is. And she isnt like the queen of Roumania. Why not, by the way, a black princess talking Hottentot (all clicks) with Higgins following her and taking down the clicks frantically in his notebook? But she would have to be a really beautiful and dignified negress, which you cannot find easily.

All this took so much consideration that I have not yet had time to look at the first scene and get rid of Piccadilly Circus.

The time elapsing between the acts needs no explanation beyond what Higgins & the Colonel say to Mrs Higgins.

In haste to catch the village post

GBS

Cecil **Trouncer** (1898–1953), one of Shaw's favourite actors, played the First Constable, who interrupts Eliza and Freddy kissing each other at the railings in front of Higgins's house. Charles **Laughton** (1899–1962), major stage and screen star, was Shaw's original choice for Higgins in the film. Pascal may have suggested that Trouncer play one of the dialogueless roles in '**the NBL scene**' (wherein Eliza utters 'not bloody likely'). **Violet** Vanbrugh (1867–1942), sister of Irene, played the Ambassadress.

19 / To G. Bernard Shaw [10 Bolton Street. Piccadilly. London W1]

23rd March 1938

[TL(c): Delacorte: U]

My dear Maestro

I am confirming my last telegram to [you] as follows:

> We finished the whole Covent Garden Saint Paul Church sequences the first week – The sound of the rain takes are excellent and not interfering with the dialogue – Everything going satisfactorily in your spirit –
>
> With love – Gabriel

I am also sending herewith thirty stills of the Covent Garden scenes which we did last week, seven additional stills of the bystanders, and a few other stills of the genuine market types selected by me from Covent Garden.

These stills I hope you will keep, and in future I shall send you at the end of each week the stills of the scenes which have been shot.

Yesterday we made the big scene of the tea-party with Eliza and she will be excellent. I am now really sad that her husband was incorrect and broke the five years agreement which we made with her agent when we definitely decided, as you remember, to give her Eliza's part.

With my kindest regards to Mrs Bernard Shaw,

Yours faithfully devoted

[Gabriel Pascal]

Wendy Hiller's **husband** was Ronald Gow (1897–1993), best known for *Love on the Dole* (1934), which he and Walter Greenwood adapted from the latter's novel (1933), and in which Hiller made her London stage début.

20 / To Gabriel Pascal   [4 Whitehall Court. London SW1]
                                                    24th March 1938

[APCS: Pygmalion]

The stills are wonderful; and Wendy is perfect.

But Higgins is fatally wrong. He should have a topper (cylinder hat) badly in want of brushing, stuck on the back of his head, and a professorial black frock coat and black overcoat, very unvaleted. This is the only way in which he can make a unique figure in the crowd. And it is this rig-out which should be reproduced in the final scene.

If the scenes are shot it cannot be helped; but it starts Leslie frightfully on the wrong lines.

                                                    GBS

21 / To G. Bernard Shaw   [10 Bolton Street. Piccadilly. London W1]
                                                    1st April 1938

[TL(c): Delacorte: U]

My dear Maestro

I am sending you herewith the stills of the tea party and of other scenes in Mrs Higgins's drawing room.

Wilfrid Lawson is a real knock-out. Leslie Howard and I believe that he will be a greater actor in pictures than Emil Jannings was in the days of the silent screen. He certainly cannot be surpassed by any actor in the world as Doolittle, and I am glad that I insisted fanatically in casting him ...

                                                    [Gabriel Pascal]

Born in Switzerland, Emil **Jannings** (né Theodor Friedrich Emil Janenz, 1884–1950) was an internationally famous German film star, best known today for *The Blue Angel* (1930).

22 / To G. Bernard Shaw   [10 Bolton Street. Piccadilly. London W1]

14th April 1938

[TL(c): Delacorte: U]

One may infer what is contained in the letter on censorship, which has not been
located but is probably from the MPPDA (the Motion Picture Producers and Dis-
tributors of America), the self-censorship body of the American film industry, from
Shaw's response two days later.

My dear Maestro

Herewith I am sending you the letter received from the American organization about the Censorship. Will you be so kind as to return it to me
after you have been through it.

In the meantime I am sending you 57 stills of action and portraits of
the stars.

The work is progressing very well. I hope in three weeks' time to have
finished the shooting, and in another five weeks the cutting, editing,
and synchronising of the picture.

In order to give Cecil Trouncer a bigger part as the policeman we
have made from the two policemen in the Freddy scenes, pp. G-18–22,
Scs. G-42–48 (Cecil's script), only one. I hope you agree with this.

I wish you and Mrs Shaw a happy Easter holiday.

Yours always faithfully devoted,

[Gabriel Pascal]

23 / To Gabriel Pascal   [4 Whitehall Court. London SW1]

16th April 1938

[TLS(p): Delacorte: U(e)]

To secure Hollywood's agreement to finance or distribute a film version of Saint
Joan, to star Elisabeth Bergner (1897–1986), Paul Czinner (1890–1972), Hun-
garian stage and screen producer-director, agreed to 20th Century Fox's demand
for approval by the Vatican before concluding a contract. Czinner therefore sent
Shaw's scenario to Catholic Action, which disapproved and recommended major
changes. As defined by Pope Pius XI, Catholic Action provides for 'the participa-
tion of the laity in the apostolate of the Church's hierarchy.' Although Catholic
Action, headquartered in Rome, is not an official Church body, its examiners

were priests whose viewpoint represented that of the Vatican. When Shaw discovered what Czinner had done, he refused to let him film the play. Like Catholic Action, the MPP, Shaw's shorthand for the MPPDA, refused to authorize the filming or distribution of a movie that had words or subjects it considered improper or indecent. Shaw refused to submit to such censorship.

My dear Gabriel

No: I must have two policemen, one aged forty and the other aged twenty, and two scenes, because I must produce the impression of the two lovers having run at least as far as Cavendish Square from the first policeman and to Hanover Square from the second.

We must get all these stars into the bill by naming them, thus. The Rector, O.B. Clarence; Rogerson P.C. Cecil Trouncer; Ventimore P.C. Raymond Novarra; Chelsea Rose, Eileen Beldon &c.

I did not know that you intended to send the script to the American amateur censors, who have no legal status whatever. If I had known I should have locked you up until the film was finished. It was by doing this that Czinner messed up the Bergner-Joan film. It is entirely impossible for any serious dramatist to work under the M.P.P. regulations or subject [himself] to the lists of words and subjects compiled by the Catholic Action for the guidance of their office boys. There is only one course for you if you want to do serious work in film drama, and that is to make your film and let M.P.P. attempt to boycott it if they dare. They wont dare.

The stills are all right, and the scenes beautiful; but it is amazing how hopelessly wrong Leslie is. He ought to change parts with Trouncer. However, the public will like him and probably want him to marry Eliza, which is just what I dont want.

Dont worry about Scott. Above all, dont waste time trying to coach him. You will only worry him and drive yourself mad. You might as well try to teach the differential calculus to the umbrella stand.

The amazing thing is that he nearly always gets away with it, even when he does everything wrong from beginning to end. The part of the Elderly Gentleman in my Methuselah is one of the most difficult and important on the modern stage. He was perfect in it. I dont expect ever to see anything better, or *hear* anything better, than Scott and Eileen Beldon in that play. So let him alone and take what the gods send you.

I think I have a copy of Lewis's scenario of The Devil's Disciple in the country, but am not quite sure. If I have I will send it to you.

This afternoon I go down to Ayot St Lawrence, Welwyn, Herts until Thursday, when I have to do a ceremony for the National Theatre, and a broadcast in the evening.

a rivederci
GBS

O.B. Clarence (1870–1955), who acted the Inquisitor in the first London production of *Saint Joan* (1924), played the Rector. **Raymond Novarra** may be an error for Ramon Novarro (1899–1968), Mexican-born star of American silent movies. The British actress Eileen **Beldon** (1901–85) played the Parlor Maid. **Scott** Sunderland (1883–1952) was a veteran English stage actor.

After *Arms and the Man*, whose scenario its director Cecil **Lewis** wrote and submitted to Shaw for comments and suggestions, which he gave, Lewis prepared a screen treatment of *The Devil's Disciple*, for which he tried to secure backing. The former scenario survives in the Berg Collection of the New York Public Library; the latter has not surfaced. On 21 April, Shaw participated in a **ceremony** in which he handed the deeds of a site in South Kensington, London, to representatives of the National Theatre, for which he spent years trying to raise funds.

24 / To G. Bernard Shaw   [10 Bolton Street. Piccadilly. London W1]

21st July 1938

[TD TEL(c): Delacorte: U]

MY DEAREST MASTER, OUR PICTURE PRESENTED YESTERDAY TO ENGLISH CENSORSHIP IT PASSED WITHOUT ANY CUT OR REMARKS. EVERYBODY ASTONISHED NOT MYSELF. STOP. DISTRIBUTORS OTHER PRODUCERS BIG AMERICAN MAGNATES WHO SAW PICTURE DECLARED IT GREATEST EVER MADE IN BRITISH STUDIO. SEVERAL DECLARED IT ONE OF THE GREATEST OF ALL AND THE FIRST PICTURE WHERE THE GENIUS OF A GREAT AUTHOR IS FAITHFULLY FOLLOWED. I AM GLAD TO GIVE YOU THESE REPORTS. STOP. AM LEAVING NEXT TUESDAY FOR NEW YORK TO PRESENT PICTURE TO AMERICAN CEN-SORSHIP HOPING WITH SAME RESULT. STOP ... OUR PICTURE IS SELECTED FOR VENICE FESTIVAL IN INTERNATIONAL CINEMA COMPE-TITION FOR WORLD PREMIERE HOPING TO GET FIRST PRIZE. AM PROUD AND GRATEFUL THAT YOU HAD FAITH IN ME. AM CERTAIN OUR NEXT PICTURE WILL BE EVEN BETTER AND WITHOUT SMALLEST COMPROMISE ... GABRIEL

25 / To G. Bernard Shaw [Los Angeles]

12th August 1938

[TD TEL(c): Delacorte: U]

Pascal went to New York, then to Los Angeles, with a print of Pygmalion *to nego-tiate its distribution in America.*

PRESENTATION OUR PYGMALION CREATED ARTISTIC REVOLUTION
ON THE MARKET HERE ALL BIG EXECUTIVES DECLARED IT IS THE
BEST PICTURE EVER MADE IN ENGLAND CLOSING NEXT WEEK MOST
IMPORTANT DISTRIBUTING CONTRACT NOT ONLY FOR PYGMALION
BUT FOR OUR FUTURE PRODUCTIONS DISCIPLE AND CAESAR STOP
FLYING TODAY HOLLYWOOD CONTRACTING FREDERICK MARCH FOR
CAESAR STOP HOW RIGHT WAS YOUR JUDGMENT ABOUT HOWARD
WENDY IS FORTUNATELY DOMINATING THE WHOLE PICTURE I
CABLED TO HER LAWYER TO CONFIRM ME THE SIX YEAR AGREEMENT
STOP ... SAILING 20TH FOR VENICE TO ATTEND WORLD PREMIERE THE
29TH STOP THANKS TO YOUR FAITH IN ME WITH OUR NEXT PICTURE
CAESAR WILL CHANGE THE STYLE OF PERIOD PICTURE MAKING STOP
YOUR GENIUS AND THE ANGELLIKE HEART OF MRS SHAW GUIDING ME
TOWARDS NEW ARTISTIC ACHIEVEMENTS WISHING YOU BOTH HAPPY
HOLIDAYS IN ETERNAL AFFECTION.   GABRIEL

Frederick **March** (né Frederick McIntyre Bickel, 1897–1975) was for many years a promi-nent American star of stage and screen.

26 / To G. Bernard Shaw [Los Angeles]

15th August 1938

[TD TEL(c): Delacorte: U]

THE ICE IS BROKEN SCREENED TODAY WITH GREAT SUCCESS YOUR
PYGMALION TO THE MOST IMPORTANT PEOPLE IN HOLLYWOOD WE
WILL HAVE THE BEST DISTRIBUTION AN ENGLISH PICTURE EVER HAD
STOP FEEL PROUD THAT THROUGH FUTURE PICTURES OF YOUR
PLAYS FOR MILLIONS OF PEOPLE ALL OVER THE WORLD DIVENTO

VOSTRO FEDELE MESSAGGERO [becoming your faithful messenger] IN ETERNAL LOVE AND DEVOTION ... GABRIEL

27 / To G. Bernard Shaw [Los Angeles
August 1938]

[TD TEL(c): Delacorte: U]

METRO AGREED THAT DISTRIBUTION RIGHTS ARE NOT IN PERPETU-ITY BUT FOR FIVE YEARS FROM 22ND AUGUST 1938 I NEVER INTENDED TO MAKE THE CONTRACT OTHERWISE WOULD BE GRATEFUL IF I COULD HAVE THE CORRECTED LETTER TOMORROW – MUST MAIL IT TO NEW YORK BEFORE SEPT 28TH ... WITH LOVE GABRIEL

28 / To G. Bernard Shaw [*no address*
before 26 August 1938]

[TD TEL(c): Delacorte: U]

CONCLUDED TODAY DISTRIBUTION FOR OUR FILM PYGMALION FOR NORTH AND SOUTH AMERICA CANADA AND SOUTH AFRICA WITH THE METRO COMPANY STOP PICTURE WILL BE RELEASED AS THE BEST ENGLISH PICTURE EVER MADE IN EUROPE STOP WENDY SENT ME A VERY DISAPPOINTING CABLE TELLING THAT SHE WILL NOT SIGN WITH ME A LONG TERM CONTRACT I THINK THIS IS VERY UNGRATE-FUL TO YOU WHO DISCOVERED AND ME WHO CREATED HER AS A FILM STAR STOP METRO IS READY GIVE ME GRETA GARBO FOR YOUR ST. JOAN STOP TAN[T] PIS [so much the worse] FOR WENDY STOP I CAN ALSO HAVE HELEN HAYES OR CATHRINE CORNELL FOR CANDIDA WHICH I WOULD PRODUCE AFTER CAESAR WHILE PREPARING DISCI-PLE STOP AM 29TH VENICE THEN FOR TWO DAYS ROME ARRANGING EXTERIORS FOR CAESAR THEN ABOUT 10TH SEPTEMBER LONDON HOPING FIND YOU AND MRS SHAW IN GOOD HEALTH I PRAY FOR IT TO THE MADONNA STOP EMBRACING YOUR ALWAYS FAITHFUL DISCIPLE   GABRIEL PASCAL

Born in Sweden, Greta **Garbo** (née Gustafson, 1905–89) went to Hollywood and became an international star of silent and talking movies. Helen **Hayes** (1900–93), American stage star, occasionally appeared in films. Like Shaw, but in a different manner, Pascal misspells the first name of Katharine **Cornell** (1893–1974), American stage star whose Shavian roles included *Candida*.

29 / To Gabriel Pascal The Impney Hotel. Droitwich. Worc.
26th August 1938

[TLS(p): Delacorte: U(e)]

On 6 August 1938, Elisabeth Bergner, using Max Reinhardt's heavily cut version, which Shaw loathed, played the first of seven performances of Saint Joan *at the Malvern Festival. Shaw, who saw her on 20 August, felt she misrepresented the role.*

My dear Gabriel

We must not quarrel with Wendy because she has a good business head on her, or else has a good adviser. I should do the same in her place.

Garbo is quite out of the question: we must stick to English films and English stars and never let a Hollywood sex appealer within two thousand miles of the studio.

Katherine Cornell refuses to be filmed, and must be ruled out for Candida until she changes her mind, which she would be very unwise to do until she retires; for Candida is one of her trump cards on the stage; and a film would kill it dead so that it would pay neither her nor me to have it screened. Besides, as it lasts two hours without a change of scene and has no visual interest it is not suited to the cinema.

H.H. is no use to us: she is an American speciality. Elisabeth Bergner has been such a complete misfit as Joan that I told her positively that she must not film it; so the way is clear for Wendy, who is as much tied to us as if she had signed ten contracts.

As this place is agreeing with me pretty well I shall not be back in town when you return from Italy or wherever you are; but Miss Patch will know where I am and forward everything.

sempre a te
G. Bernard Shaw

30 / To Gabriel Pascal

The Impney Hotel. Droitwich
1st September 1938

[TLS: Letters]

My dear Gabriel

Now is the time to be careful – extraordinarily careful. The success of
the Pygmalion film will set all Hollywood rushing to get a rake-off on
the next Shaw film. Where the carcass is, there will the eagles be gathered. No American feels safe until he has at least five other Americans
raking him off, most of them contributing nothing except their
entirely undesirable company. They get so settled in that way of doing
business that they do not understand how a European with a cast iron
monopoly under his own hat can play his game singlehanded. So
again I say be careful, or the film will make a million and yet leave you
with a deficit.

Elisabeth Bergner, though she drew full houses at Malvern, was such
a hopeless failure as Joan that I told her she must drop the film project.
The play is therefore free; but the Californian suggestion of Miss Garbo
for Joan is – well, Californian. If the heroine of the play were the
Blessed Virgin they would probably have suggested Miss Mae West. We
must have Wendy. There is no gratitude in business; and it would be
the height of folly to quarrel with her after we have made her a star of
the first magnitude. Somebody else would get her and exploit the work
you have done with her. She cannot refuse the part, which is unique;
and even if she did, or if she dropped dead, I could produce two young
English provincial Joans who would be better than any Hollywood
siren.

As to Caesar, the difficulty is to find an actor capable of filling the
part. Robert Donat is far too young. The best heavy on the English stage
is Trouncer, who played the policeman in Pygmalion, and ought to have
played Higgins. He has just had a tremendous success as Bombardone
in Geneva. The sole objection to him is that he has not Caesar's beak
and shape of head. But he is our only big gun. His Inquisitor in Joan is
first rate. Caesar must not be a *primo amoroso* [romantic leading man].

As to conciliating the Vatican, that is utter nonsense. What Czinner
calls the Vatican (that is how he lost the film) is some petty official who

has a list of words which must not be used by film actors. He objected to 'halo' because it is religious, and to 'babies' because it is sexual. I make it an absolute condition that the Catholic Action shall be entirely ignored, and the film made in complete disregard of these understrappers of the Church. Really responsible Catholics will not object to the film; but it is not fair to consult them about it, as it is one thing to welcome a film and quite another to guarantee it as orthodox. When the play is filmed it will be irresistible. The Hollywood simpletons say that none of the twenty million American Catholics will go to see it. When the Catholic Action can keep these Americans out of the saloons and gambling casinos and Ziegfeld Follies I shall believe in its power to keep them away from St Joan. Until then, we go ahead.

Do not approach Monsignor Gonfalonieri; but if you happen to meet him you can explain to him the utterly silly and impossible objections, grossly insulting to me, which were made in America, and say that the play led to great hopes in England among Catholics of my conversion to The Faith. The play practically wiped out the scurrilities of Mark Twain and Andrew Lang which were formerly the stock-in-trade of Protestant writers on the subject. But whatever you do, do not ask him for any official expression of approval. Say that nobody, not even the Pope, could be made answerable for Shaw.

Is it really necessary to trouble Messrs Whitney and Selznick? Why not ask your British bankers to back you on the strength of Pygmalion's succès éclatant [brilliant success]? Failing them there are lunatics in London who, excited by the press notices, will back anything filmable to any amount if it has our names attached. We must shew the Hollywood distributors that we are independent of them as far as capital is concerned. They threaten not to distribute, as they did in the case of Pygmalion; but when it comes to the point they MUST distribute, not only for the immediate profit but because we are insuppressible and they would be unwise to quarrel with us. They will always hope to land us next time, and feel foolish if they are left out this time.

I shall be at this address until after the 24th September: possibly a week or two longer. Meanwhile I am in no hurry to see the film: it will be quite time enough when it is released and on show at the picture palaces.

Scott Sunderland could play Burgoyne in the Devil's Disciple[;] the rest of the cast can be as American as you like. Scott has played Britannus in Caesar very satisfactorily.

That is all for the present – and quite enough too.

Congratulations on the conquest of Venice!

G. Bernard Shaw

The third sentence, which Lomax quotes in *Major Barbara*, is from Matthew 24:28. Mae **West** (1892–1980), stage and screen actress, was both a sex symbol and a parody of one; there is no evidence that Shaw had seen her films. Robert **Donat** (1905–58) was a British stage and screen actor. *Geneva* opened at the Malvern Festival on 1 August. The character **Bombardone** is based on Benito Mussolini.

Shaw's **list of words** is not an exaggeration: those he cites were forbidden by Catholic Action. Whatever its influence on American Catholic moviegoers, the disapproval of Catholic Action persuaded American distributors and exhibitors not to show *Saint Joan*. In the **Ziegfeld Follies**, which began on Broadway in 1907 and ran for 24 editions, Florenz Ziegfeld (1867–1932) perfected the opulent American theatrical revue, a combination of musical specialties, comic sketches, and gorgeous women. The Catholic prelate Carlo **Confalonieri** (1893–1986), whose surname Shaw and Pascal misspell, was personal secretary to Pope Pius XII (1876–1958) for 19 years. Among the works of American writer Mark **Twain** (pseudonym of Samuel Langhorne Clemens, 1835–1910) is *Personal Recollections of Joan of Arc* (1896); among those of the Scottish writer Andrew **Lang** (1844–1912) is *The Maid of France* (1908).

The financial enterprises of John Hay (Jock) **Whitney** (1904–82), publisher of the *New York Herald Tribune*, included films. David O(liver) **Selznick** (1902–65) was an American film producer.

31 / To G. Bernard Shaw [*no address*]

13th September 1938

[TL(c): Delacorte: U(e)]

My dearest G.B.

I am back in London, and as I wired you from Castelgandolfo my visit to Monsignor Gonfalonieri was very successful, and Venice was very successful.

The Volpi Cup is not as the Press stated for Leslie Howard, but to 'Pygmalion' by George Bernard Shaw, produced by Gabriel Pascal, stars Leslie Howard and Wendy Hiller. I received the document from the jury in this way.

I told them that if they did not give recognition to Wendy Hiller, I would not accept any 'coppa' or any mention of the picture. So after the foolish British delegate (who devoted his time to whisky drinking and flirtation, instead of being diplomatic and keeping the intrigues of German delegates away from the Italians) he left Venice protesting because we had not received the Mussolini Cup, which was not the way to get it.

Freddi, at the reception by the Minister Alfieri in the presence of Conte Volpi, made a speech stating that our picture was the best of all, and that it was thanks to the British delegate that we did not receive the Mussolini cup, but all the Ministers said that the 'Coppa' Volpi had more artistic value than the Mussolini Cup which has only a political significance.

I was in the private villa of Mussolini in Riccione visiting his son Vittorio, and I procured my permission from the Government for the externals, and they assured me the greatest cooperation for everything.

The German Minister asked me to send a print [of] the picture to the Fuhrer – he will see it this week. Mussolini's son asked to send a print to the Duce, and the same print will be presented – after the Duce has seen it – to the Pope. So this will help tremendously for the income in Italy and Germany.

About the German version of 'Caesar,' I had a long telephone conversation from Paris with our friend Trebitsch, and he will be in Paris on the 15th of this month, which is the day after tomorrow, and I promised to ring him in Versailles on the evening of the 15th. I would like therefore, before speaking to him and making a deal with him for the German version, to see you for 15 minutes, so if you like, I could come out tomorrow Wednesday afternoon at tea-time, and bring you all the Italian criticisms, and talk over the whole future position, because I agree that I must be extraordinarily careful in all the next artistic steps, because now the whole world is watching my next decisions.

I cannot put in writing the tremendous victory we had in New York and Hollywood, I must tell you personally. Certainly we changed the whole face of picture-making, and before I decide my next steps I should like to see you, my dearest master, and have a few minutes with you. I am dying from the desire to embrace you, and to kiss the hands of Mrs Shaw, so please telephone MAYFAIR 0605, or send me a telegram if I can come tomorrow.

[Gabriel Pascal]

The **Volpi Cup** was an award of the Venice Film Festival, the first of its kind. Giuseppi Volpi, Conte di Misurata (1877–1947), Venetian financier and statesman under Mussolini, founded it in 1932 as a prestige tourist attraction; it became a showcase for Italian and German propaganda films. A Jewish-Austrian writer, Siegfried **Trebitsch** (1869–1956), was Shaw's German translator. **Vittorio** Mussolini (b. 1916), thanks to his father, became prominent in the Italian film industry and had his name inserted as director of some films.

32 / To Gabriel Pascal   The Impney Hotel
                                                    Droitwich. Worcestershire
                                                    14th September 1938
[TLS: Bancroft]

My dear Gabriel

Dont think of coming down here; it will be a waste of a whole day and no fun of any sort for you here. We shall be back in London soon now; and then you can tell us all about it at your ease. I know everything that has been made public. You have had a tremendous triumph, on which I congratulate you and myself. Also I congratulate several other gentlemen who would have spoilt the film if you had not prevented them, but are in the bills as the presiding geniuses of the production.

I am still supposed to have no exciting visitors and to be a bit of an invalid; but there is really nothing the matter with me now except 82 years.

                                    sempre astuto ed infidele
                                    [always crafty and faithless]
                                    G. Bernard Shaw

33 / To G. Bernard Shaw   [*no address*]
                                                    17th September 1938
[TL(c): Delacorte: U]

My dear G.B.

I have received your letter of the 14th and 16th September. Regarding that of the 14th I thank you for your congratulations and thank you for the last lines of the first paragraph of your letter about the other 'gentlemen.'

Strangely enough one Italian paper 'Il Messaggero' states in its criticism 'Di chi il merito di questo mezzo miracolo?' [Who should get credit for this modest miracle?] I will send you translations of the criticisms from Germany and other countries after I have received them next week ...

About the political situation I agree with you one hundred per cent, and I have sent today a very diplomatic letter to the Banco di Lavoro which is backing Vittorio Mussolini, telling them that I would only make the exteriors of 'Caesar & Cleopatra' for the English version, in Rome, and I must make the studio work at the Pinewood studios, so nobody could criticise us in England, because anyone with any common sense will know that there is never enough sunshine here for ten weeks at a time to make the important exteriors for this picture.

Castelli sent me a long letter saying that he is at our disposal for the translation work of 'Caesar' but poor man he is not doing it himself because neither he or his wife understand more English than Chinese. So I think it is better we give to the poor Cesare his 5% and we do not let him do any work.

A propos of your question, he is one hundred per cent Jew, but no harm will happen to him, as I have already spoken to the authorities about him. They love and admire you so much in Italy – as you know – that they would never harm your translator. Apart from this, Castelli is known as a very honest and respectable old man, and they will never handle the Jewish question in Italy, as the crazy Hitlerians did in Austria.

A propos Trebitsch, I spoke to him yesterday on the phone, and he tried to convince me to pay out his 5% as your German translator for 'Caesar.' I told him that I would not do anything until I had seen you, and the fact is that we will receive German marks for the German version, so how could I pay him in good sterling, but if he is in misery and needing money, I would give him some advance on his 5%. This is the only concession I could promise him.

I was so glad you suggested to me a new talented girl, because I don't believe that Wendy Hiller is a loyal person. She will always be influenced by her dishonest and stupid husband.

So I telephoned at once to Mr Prentice and he asked me to come down next Tuesday to Birmingham. I will let you know my opinion about Miss Myrtle Richardson.

It would be fine to have a new girl for Apollodorus. Cecil Trouncer in my opinion would be better as Rufio. He is much too heavy for Caesar. I agree that Donat – after I saw his new film – is lacking in spiritual quality for it, and Howard is out of the question as he is too weak and effeminate. So I hope to see you next week in London and then we can talk over all future plans.

Don't be afraid, my dear master, that I will sell myself to American interests. Whitney offered me the highest salary ever offered a Producer, and Metro offered me a blank contract, but I told them that I must be artistically one hundred per cent independent, and money does not mean anything to me.

The only thing Metro asked me was that they could distribute our pictures in America, to which I agreed, and I reserved one picture a year for our English distributors.

I will explain all this much better to you at our next meeting.

Give my most devoted and affectionate regards to Mrs Shaw, and embracing you,

> my dearest 'infedele' maestro,
> [Gabriel Pascal]

In September, Myrtle **Richardson**, an English actress, joined the Birmingham Repertory Co. for its 1938–9 season. The 'new girl' refers to the person who would play Cleopatra, not Apollodorus, who is male. Robert Donat's new film was *The Citadel* (1938), adapted from the 1937 novel by the Scottish doctor A.J. Cronin (1896–1981).

34 / To G. Bernard Shaw

[*no address*]
23rd September 1938

[TLS(c)(tr): Delacorte: U]

My dearest Maestro

Re: 'PYGMALION'

I am sending you a copy of our Metro Distributing contract for your information.

I would be glad if you would approve on the copy of this letter that your royalty of 10% of the gross receipts from the picture will be paid by the Westminster Bank Ltd., 26 Haymarket S.W.1, on the certificates of the Chartered Accountants, Messrs. Finnie, Ross, Welch & Co.

The first advance payment of Metro will be one hundred & fifty thousand dollars, on which you will receive your 10% as soon as the advance is received, which in the contract is specified as being fifteen days after the approval of the negative.

I ask you also to approve the dubbing of the artists' voices in Spanish, because in all South American countries all great pictures are presented in this way.

I myself will also supervise the whole editing of our picture in America, and I will also supervise the dubbing of the artists' voices in Spanish.

The distribution rights of Metro are for five years from 22nd August 1938, so that there is a difference of about three months from our last Agreement dated 22nd May 1937, so I ask you to approve the terms and period of my Distributing Agreement with Metro, and the consequential extension of the period of my Company's rights under our supplemental Agreement.

Always yours,

faithfully devoted,
Gabriel Pascal

35 / To Gabriel Pascal

The Impney Hotel
Droitwich. Worcestershire
26th September 1938

[ALS(p): Delacorte: U]

Dear Gabriel Pascal

I approve of your arrangement with The Westminster Bank as to the Pygmalion percentages, and have advised them accordingly.

I shall not object to the dubbing of the voices in Spanish for South America provided it is done under your personal supervision.

I agree to the extension of the term of our agreement to the 22nd August 1943.

I have read a copy of your agreement with Loew's Inc. and disapprove

of it violently. In particular the last three lines of paragraph (d), page 5
are *ultra vires* [*beyond the scope of Pascal's legal power or authority*], as you
have no power under our agreement to go beyond the date 22nd August
1943. Unless you have power to break with L's Inc. completely on that
date I must break with you then.

I will not okay any document. You have our agreement to exhibit to
L's Inc.; and beyond it I will not go.

I return the copy of the Loew agreement, revised as it should have
been in your interest. Better let me draft the next one.

faithfully
G. Bernard Shaw

PS Bon voyage! Shew this letter to Metro-G.

36 / To G. Bernard Shaw   [*no address*]
Thursday 29th September 1938
[sent by express delivery on 1 October]

[TL(c): Delacorte: U]

*Trying to avoid war, British Prime Minister Neville Chamberlain (1869–1940)
pursued a policy of appeasement. At the Munich Conference on this date, he and
French Premier Edouard Daladier (1884–1970) agreed to Hitler's dismember-
ment of Czechoslovakia; the result, said Chamberlain, would be 'peace in our
time.' On Tuesday, 4 October, Pascal met Shaw at a special press showing of*
Pygmalion. *The next day, Pascal sailed for America.*

My dear G.B.S.

... In regard to the points you raise as to the last three lines of paragraph
D on page 5 of your copy of the Distribution Agreement with Loew's
Inc. – the rights granted to Loew's are in fact only for five years from the
22nd August, 1938, which you agreed to, and any possible extension
beyond such period can only be with your express consent, and in accordance with your wish I will not enter into any discussions for any extension of this period.

Loew's Inc. have already been sent by me a photostatic copy of each
of the Company's Contracts with you in regard to the film, and when I

am in New York next week I will show your original letter to the executives of Loew's Inc. and Metro-Goldwyn-Mayer.

I would also remind you that in our conversations at Stratford-on-Avon I told you that in regard to an Italian version of the film, the Italian distributors after seeing the picture at the Venice Exhibition declared that it would not be possible to find any actress comparable to Wendy Hiller's portrayal of the part of 'Eliza' and equally no actor could be found to replace Leslie Howard's portrayal of the part of 'Higgins,' and that accordingly it was undesirable for an Italian version to be made and that it was preferable to have the English film dubbed in the Italian language, for the purpose of which your translator Mr. Cesare Castelli has already prepared a translation of the dialogues for the picture. In order that the necessary arrangements for the dubbing can now be proceeded with I would ask you to formally give my Company the right to authorise the dubbing in the Italian language to be done.

I hope to see you Tuesday morning.

Always your faithfully devoted,
[Gabriel Pascal]

P.S. I am glad that your and my prognostications about the War were right, and that old Musso stepped in at the last moment to support Chamberlain. Certainly the peace with Musso would cost some money to the City of London, but we have also some advantage from it, because in this way we can make the exteriors for 'Caesar and Cleopatra' in Rome as proposed. I received yesterday a letter from young Musso confirming all our agreements. I will bring it to you on Tuesday ...

37 / To G. Bernard Shaw   [French Line, S.S. Normandie]
13th October 1938

[TLS: BL 50522 ff 158–60: U]

Shaw filmed a spoken preface to American audiences of Pygmalion *that was used as a trailer.*

My dearest Maestro

I thank you for making the speech again to the American audience. I received a cable from Mr Boxall (from the English Metro Studio) telling me that the first take was wrong because the negative was scratched. I hope that the whole second tape will be as brilliant as I believe the first would have been if the cameraman had done his work conscientiously. Unfortunately it was not my own cameraman; otherwise this mistake would not have happened. Metro is making great preparation for the opening of our picture and they decided to have its premier in four weeks at the Astor Theatre on Broadway following their own picture Marie Antoinette with Norma Shearer.

I was so touched with the kindness of Mrs Shaw towards me and it was one of the greatest moments in my career when you read the lines of Caesar to Maria Dea, our little Cleopatra. I think she is a Godsend to us for this part. I am going to the Coast at the end of this week and will speak with John Barrymore to let you know at once. There was a big controversy in the press after I left about Clark Gable. They are fools because I never gave them any definite statement about Clark Gable. I told them only that there was a discussion with Louis B. Mayer in which I hoped to get Clark Gable. Meantime I received on the boat a cable from my Hollywood manager stating that if we desire Clark Gable we can get him for Devil's Disciple.

I had a very rough crossing but I had a marvelous comfort being the whole days with Maestro Toscanini who is sending his regards to Mrs Shaw and to you. I enclose a postcard upon which his regards is written. I selected this card because it shows the chapel which has a unique delightful architecture. Toscanini told me the whole inside story of his fight with Mussolini and it is really a shame how Italy and the Government behaved itself towards him. I asked him if he will have free time would he make the music for one of our pictures Devil's Disciple, Saint Joan, Caesar or Cleopatra, but he is like you, my dearest Maestro, he never says a definite Yes, but he was really very much impressed with my plans; and I have a legitimate hope that he will do it for us if in principle he ever agrees to make the music for a picture. He spoke very highly about Honegger who made the music for Pygmalion. As I told you I had a long conversation with Wendy Hiller and her husband and she agreed to make a deal with me for two pictures to be made after she has her baby, one picture a year, from these two pictures one should be Saint Joan.

I thank you also for your permission which you gave me last Wednesday to dub the voices of our English Pygmalion in Italian and French and distribute it in Italy and France in this form and make a genuine Italian and [French] version with Italian and [French] actors separately on a later date ...

Gabriel

Film executive Harold Granville **Boxall** (b. 1898) would become managing director of MGM British Studios. Canadian-born Norma **Shearer** (née Edith Norma Shearer, 1900–83), a Hollywood star whom Shaw admired, played the title role in MGM's lavish *Marie Antoinette* (1938). Marie **Déa** (née Odette Deupès, b. 1919) was a French stage and screen star, whose roles included Eurydice in Jean Cocteau's film, *Orphée* (1950). John **Barrymore** (1882–1942), stage and screen star, and a member of an American theatrical dynasty, was in *Marie Antoinette*; as previous negotiations for him to play in *The Devil's Disciple* came to nothing, so did these negotiations for him to play in *Caesar and Cleopatra*. One of America's most popular film actors, Clark **Gable** (1901–60) did not act in a film or play by Shaw. Louis B. **Mayer** (1885–1957) was general manager and head of Metro-Goldwyn-Mayer.

The Italian conductor Arturo **Toscanini** (1867–1957) was internationally pre-eminent. Born in Switzerland, Arthur **Honegger** (1892–1955) was one of France's outstanding composers of the between-wars period.

38 / To G. Bernard Shaw   New York City
13th October 1938

[TLS: BL 50522 ff 156–7: U]

My dearest Maestro

I presented your letter of September 26th, 1938, as you desired, to Metro-Goldwyn-Mayer and am very glad to tell you that these people were delighted to accede to your wishes in respect to the changes that you indicated in that letter. As a result, our distributing agreement now provides that it is to be for a term of five years only – ending August 22, 1943 – and the Spanish version is to be made under my personal supervision. So I have plenty to do in the next few weeks before I start on the preparations for our next picture.

I was much pleased to find out that there was great enthusiasm on the part of the executives and staff of Metro for the release of our picture in America. I am encouraged to say to you, as a result of the talks that I have had with quite a few of the important personalities in the Company that there is every reason to feel that the success of 'Pygmalion' in America will equal that which it is having in London – if indeed it may not be even greater ...

Gabriel

39 / To Gabriel Pascal [*no address*]
received Beverley Hills, 29th October 1938

[TEL (p): Delacorte: U]

... LEICESTER SQUARE CINEMA STARS HOWARD AND SUPPRESSES WENDY WHOSE PRESS NOTICES ARE OVERWHELMING AM REMONSTRATING STRONGLY.   BERNARD SHAW

40 / To G. Bernard Shaw [Los Angeles
29 October 1938]

[TD TEL(c): Delacorte: U]

The previous summer, Pascal asked Ian Dalrymple to prepare a film scenario of The Devil's Disciple. *On 3 November, Dalrymple had a telephone discussion with Shaw, who urged him to add new scenes. The same day, he sent Shaw a list of new scenes and indicated where they would be interpolated in the play text.*

... METRO GOING TO USE INFERIOR TAKE IN ANY CASE ... STOP DALRYMPLE CABLED ME THAT HE IS READY WITH OTHER TWO-THIRDS DEVIL'S DISCIPLE AND ASKED ME TO BE PERMITTED TO VISIT YOU AND SUBMIT HIS WORK TO YOU ... LOVE GABRIEL

41 / To G. Bernard Shaw [Los Angeles]
31st October 1938

[TD TEL(c): Delacorte: U]

CABLED PUBLICITY MANAGER GENERAL FILM DISTRIBUTORS AND MANAGER LEICESTER SQUARE THEATRE TO STAR WENDY HILLER WITH HOWARD STOP THIS WAS MY ORIGINAL INSTRUCTION BEFORE I LEFT STOP I AM DISGUSTED MYSELF WITH MANAGEMENT OF PUBLICITY STOP I SENT A CABLE FROM THE BOAT TO LEICESTER SQUARE

THEATRE ON OPENING NIGHT TO BE READ TO AUDIENCE WHERE I
EMPHASIZED MY GRATEFULNESS TO YOU FOR YOUR FAITH IN ME
STOP THEY SUPPRESSED THE CABLE AND LET LESLIE HOWARD HAN-
DLE THE SPEECH STOP I HEARD LAST WEEK THAT IN HIS SPEECH HE
OMITTED MENTIONING THE AUTHOR AND TRIED TO PUT HIMSELF AS
ONLY RESPONSIBLE PARTY FOR THE SUCCESS GIVING WENDY A SEC-
ONDARY PLACE STOP I HOPE MY TWO CABLES WILL HAVE YOUR KIND
CONSIDERATION STOP   LOVE GABRIEL

42 / To G. Bernard Shaw

[Los Angeles
c. 23 November 1938]

[TD TEL(c): Delacorte: U]

Pygmalion *opened in New York on December 7th. Shaw's full address, deleted here,
is published in his* Collected Plays with Their Prefaces, *Vol. IV (London: Max
Reinhart 1972 and New York: Dodd Mead 1975) and* The Collected Screenplays
of Bernard Shaw *(London: Prior and Athens: University of Georgia Press 1980).*

MY DEAREST MAESTRO THESE FOOLS OF BRITISH FOX MOVIETONE
ALSO RUINED THE SECOND TAKE OF YOUR SPEECH AM ASKING YOU
TO ACCEPT MY OWN UNIT AND MY OWN CAMERAMEN WHO PHOTO-
GRAPHED PYGMALION TO TAKE AT PINEWOOD STUDIOS YOUR
SPEECH AGAIN IN A PROPER WAY DIGNIFIED AND WORTHY OF YOUR
WONDERFUL SPEECH STOP MR MAYER AND ALL EXECUTIVES OF
METRO THANK YOU FOR YOUR KINDNESS TOWARDS THE AMERICAN
PUBLIC STOP TO BRING NEARER TO YOUR MEMORY ALL THAT YOU
SAID AM SENDING YOU COPY OF YOUR SPEECH AS FOLLOWS ... MY
PRODUCTION MANAGER SAMUEL AT YOUR CONVENIENCE WILL CON-
TACT MISS PATCH TO MAKE ARRANGEMENTS TO SHOOT IT WEDNES-
DAY OR THURSDAY ... GABRIEL

43 / To G. Bernard Shaw

[Los Angeles]
24th November 1938

[TL(c): Delacorte: U]

*Audiences at film previews filled out cards indicating their reactions. Pascal mis-
quotes the first paragraph of Shaw's letter of 1 September.*

My dearest Maestro

... As I cabled you yesterday, we had a preview in Santa Barbara to try out the strength of the sound and the audience's reaction and definitely time the sound according to the laughter. We had about two hundred laughs and some of them were so strong that we were obliged to raise the sound of Eliza's lines in the tea-party.

The cards from the audience which they sent to Metro after the previews were very interesting and I will send you photostatic copies of each of these answers from the audience as soon as I arrive in New York.

As you know by my cable of yesterday, I am flying to New York today where the premier will be next week and I hope that my New York lawyer arranged all the difficulties about the contract. From what I have experienced in the last three weeks I have come to the conclusion that – apart from Nicholas Davenport, who is an old friend of mine – the other people in my company are not loyal and they would like to take not only my shirt but also the skin away from me. So, I will ask the New York head office of Metro to pay from all the income to the Westminster Bank your ten per cent directly without interference of the chartered accountant because their behavior while I was away was not satisfactory. The picture will gross great money here and everywhere. I am glad that you will be satisfied with the final results also.

About the future: They offered me Greta Garbo again for Saint Joan. I told them that we both agree that Wendy Hiller will play or nobody, otherwise I do not make the picture. Certainly it is necessary as soon as I arrive that we clear up Wendy's contractual situation. However, Saint Joan cannot be done before next summer because Wendy told me before I left London not to count on her before next June or July.

For Caesar and Cleopatra – the political situation with Italy is so uncertain that I prefer to postpone this also – approximately until the Spring of 1940.

There remains THE DEVIL'S DISCIPLE which I would like to do about next May and I would like very much to do a picture at once before Devil's Disciple in London for the same English distributing company, General Film Distributors, and as I told you in my cable, I would like to do DOCTOR'S DILEMMA.

Metro made a picture 'THE CITADEL.' It is a very great success and I am certain that I can make an even better picture from Doctor's Dilemma. I think the Scotchman, Ian Dalrymple, would be the right man to wr[i]te the continuity and the screen adaptation. If you agree on it, please cable me at the Hotel Ambassador and I will cable to Dalrymple to visit you and discuss with you the screen adaptation. He wr[o]te the adaptation of 'The Citadel' also. Please, My Dearest Maestro, receive him. He is one of the few honest and talented scenario writers in England.

All these rumors Miss Patch told Dalrymple are without any foundation. Certainly, they offered me here great salaries. One company offered me $250,000 salary a year but I am not a salary man. I must be independent – must make our pictures according to our own visions. I am certain that you agree with me on this point. I must be more careful of my own interests in 'Doctor's Dilemma' because you were right in one of your letters: 'Pygmalion will make millions and great profit for everybody, but in the end nothing will be left for you.' But I don't mind, because we both proved to the world what we wanted to prove and now we can continue on this Indivisible Invincible ...

[Gabriel Pascal]

Nicholas **Davenport** (1895–1979), a member of Pascal Film Productions Ltd, was a financier, writer, and Pascal's economic adviser. **Dalrymple** was one of the screenwriters of *The Citadel*, as was Emlyn Williams (1905–87), Welsh actor and dramatist, who played Snobby Price in the film of *Major Barbara*.

44 / To G. Bernard Shaw   [Los Angeles]
                                        21st December 1938
[TD TEL(c): Delacorte: U]

... THE NATIONAL BROADCASTING COMPANY ASKED ME IF YOU COULD SPEAK NEW YEARS EVE FROM LONDON TO NEW YORK ABOUT PYGMALION PRECEDING SCENE PLAYED BY WENDY HILLER AND LESLIE HOWARD WENDY BROADCASTING FROM LONDON AND HOWARD BROADCASTING FROM HERE RE-RECORDING THE MATCHING SCENE IN NEW YORK ... GABRIEL

45 / To Gabriel Pascal   [*no address*]
                                    [received] 23rd December 1938
[TEL(p): Delacorte: U]

BROADCAST IS BAD ADVERTISEMENT FOR FILM ITS ONLY EFFECT
IS TO PREVENT PEOPLE GOING TO SEE IT BUT DO AS YOU PLEASE
SHAW

46 / To G. Bernard Shaw   [Los Angeles]
                                             29th December 1938
[TD TEL(c): Delacorte: U]

MY DEAR MAESTRO I AGREE AS ALWAYS WITH YOU AND CANCELLED
FOR THE MOMENT THE BROADCAST STOP THERE IS NO DANGER THAT
ANY BROADCAST COULD KEEP THE PEOPLE AWAY FROM SEEING THE
PICTURE BECAUSE EVERY DAY HUNDREDS OF PEOPLE STAND IN CUE
BEFORE THE CINEMA STOP METRO PREDICTS AT LEAST THREE
MONTHS FIRST RUN IN NEW YORK AND HOLLYWOOD ... GABRIEL

47 / To Gabriel Pascal   [4 Whitehall Court. London SW1
                                      received 5 January 1939]
[TD TEL(p): Delacorte: U(e)]

PRESS CAMPAIGN AFOOT HERE TO REPRESENT DILEMMA AS AMERI-
CAN FILM WITH HOLLYWOOD STARS AND HOLLYWOOD DIRECTORS
STOP OUR AGREEMENT MUST BAR ALL AMERICAN ARTISTIC COLLAB-
ORATION YOU MUST BE SOLE DIRECTOR AND CONTROL PUBLICITY I
HAVE RECEIVED 10% OF METRO ADVANCE   SHAW

48 / To G. Bernard Shaw   [Los Angeles]
                                             5th January 1939
[TD TEL(c): Delacorte: U]

*As Pascal indicates on 10 January, illness prevented him from writing the long
letter he promises would follow. On that date, he again promises a long, explanatory letter which, if he wrote it, has not been found.*

MY DEAREST MAESTRO I AM ASTONISHED THAT YOUR GREAT MIND DOESNT RECOGNIZE THE WHOLE BLUFF AND IDIOCY OF THE ENGLISH CINEMA PRESS STOP OUR DOCTOR'S DILEMMA WILL BE AS PYGMALION ONE HUNDRED PERCENT ENGLISH CAST AND ONE HUNDRED PERCENT ENGLISH UNIT STOP WE DONT NEED ANYONE FROM HOLLYWOOD BECAUSE WE PROVED TO THEM THAT OUR ARTISTIC SYSTEM IS BETTER THAN THEIRS STOP I WILL BE ACCORDING OUR AGREEMENT THE PRODUCER DIRECTOR OF THE PICTURE AND NOT ONE FRAME WILL BE IN THE PICTURE WHICH IS NOT MADE BY ME AND INSPIRED BY YOUR GREAT SPIRIT STOP LONG LETTER FOLLOWS STOP OUR TRIUMPH WITH PYGMALION IS CONTINUING ALL OVER THE COUNTRY AND WENDY HILLER'S PERFORMANCE IS DECLARED BY THE WHOLE AMERICAN PRESS AS THE BEST OF THE YEAR   AFFECTIONATELY GABRIEL

49 / To G. Bernard Shaw   [Los Angeles]
                                               6th January 1939
[TD TEL(c): Delacorte: U]

IN MY CABLE YESTERDAY I FORGOT TO TELL YOU THAT PASSING THROUGH NEW YORK I ENGAGED JEAN CADELL FOR THE HOUSEKEEPER EMMY AND THIS MORNING I CONCLUDED WITH C. AUBREY SMITH FOR SIR PATRICK DAVID TREE FOR REDPENNY AND ROLAND YOUNG FOR BONINGTON AS WE AGREED UPON IN OUR LAST CONVERSATION STOP LESLIE HOWARD CAME TO ME IN HIS SWEET SNEAKY MANNER AND ASKED FOR THE PART OF DUBEDAT STOP THE YOUNG ENGLISH ACTOR LAWRENCE OLIVIER IS HERE STOP ALSO ANXIOUS TO RETURN TO ENGLAND AND PLAY THE PART STOP GREER GARSON WHO IS PLAYING THE LEAD WITH ROBERT DONAT IN THE PICTURE GOODBYE MR CHIPS FOR JENNIFER   [GABRIEL]

C. Aubrey (later Sir Charles Aubrey) **Smith** (1863–1948), a well-known character actor in films, was in the first professional production of *The Admirable Bashville* (1903). Greer **Garson** (1908–96), Anglo-Irish leading lady in films, with stage experience, went to Hollywood, where she was a star.

50 / To Gabriel Pascal   [4 Whitehall Court. London SW1
received 9 January 1939]

[TEL(p): Delacorte: U]

CADELL WILDLY WRONG FOR EMMY NOT UGLY ENOUGH CLARE
GREET INIMITABLE ORIGINAL STILL AVAILABLE FOR BOTH EMMY AND
RUMMY IN BARBARA OLIVIER PROBABLY ALLRIGHT BUT I NEVER SAW
HIM DO NOT GIVE CADELL OR TREE UNATTRACTIVE PARTS   SHAW

Clare **Greet** (1871–1939) played these roles in the first productions of *Major Barbara*
(1905) and *The Doctor's Dilemma* (1906).

51 / To G. Bernard Shaw   [Los Angeles]
10th January 1939

[TD TEL(c): Delacorte: U]

MY DEAREST MAESTRO YOU PREDICTED ME BEFORE I STARTED YOUR
PICTURE THAT THE AUDIENCE WILL SEE IT FIVE TIMES AND I PRE-
DICTED YOU THAT IT WILL BE AN HONOR FOR THE BEST ACTORS IN
THE WORLD TO PLAY A PART WITH ONLY A LINE FROM BERNARD
SHAW WE WERE BOTH RIGHT SO WHY GRUMBLE STOP JEAN CADELL
ASKED ME HERSELF FOR THE PART OF EMMY SHE IS READY AND ANX-
IOUS TO PLAY IT BUT I WILL TRY ACCORDING TO YOUR WISH TO GET
IN TOUCH IN [*i.e.,* for] BARBARA WITH CLARE GREET STOP CEDRIC
HARDWICK DESIRES TO PLAY THE PART OF WALPOLE WHICH I
AGREED KNOWING THAT YOU BOTH LOVE HIM STOP THANK YOU FOR
ADVICE REGARDING OLIVIER I DECIDED FOR HIM HE IS YOUNGER
AND MORE SINCERE ACTOR THAN LESLIE STOP I WAS VERY SICK
THESE THREE WEEKS HAVING HEAVY COLD AND WAS NOT ABLE TO
WRITE POSTPONED IT EVERY DAY AS SOON AS RECOVERED SENDING
YOU LONG EXPLANATORY LETTER STOP PLEASE BE PATIENT WITH
YOUR JUDGMENT ABOUT CASTING UNTIL YOU RECEIVE MY LETTER
AFFECTIONATELY GABRIEL

Cedric (later Sir Cedric) **Hardwicke** (1883–1964), veteran actor of Shavian roles, was a
transatlantic stage and screen star.

52 / To Gabriel Pascal   4 Whitehall Court. London SW1

24th January 1939

[TLS(p): Delacorte: U(e)]

Dear Gabriel

I enclose the Dilemma agreement. Please execute the counterpart and return it to me. Insert the date in both copies.

You will find a couple of new clauses at the end.

When you return I must have a word with you about players with big reputations in little parts. It makes an imposing *affiche* [poster]; but it disappoints and exasperates the public. They expect a big part from a big name and if they dont get it they feel cheated. Besides, it disgraces the players, which is always bad for business.

I am sorry to hear that you have been ill. Take care of yourself: my film career depends on you.

More when we meet.

Faithfully

G. Bernard Shaw

53 / To G. Bernard Shaw   [Los Angeles]

4th February 1939

[TD TEL(c): Delacorte: U]

In a cablegram sent the previous day, Pascal promised to telephone Shaw the next morning between eleven and twelve London time (three and four a.m. Los Angeles time). 'Last night' may refer to the small hours of the same day.

IT WAS VERY DIFFICULT TO HEAR CLEARLY LAST NIGHT. CERTAINLY WE MUST AND WILL HAVE A FULL ENGLISH CAST FOR DOCTOR'S DILEMMA OUTSIDE OF THE PART OF THE JEWISH DOCTOR WHO MUST BE A FOREIGNER STOP HAPPY TO RETURN AND WORK ON THE SCRIPT. I THINK YOU DID NOT UNDERSTAND THAT MARLENE DIETRICH WOULD LIKE TO PLAY THE MILLIONAIRESS NEXT YEAR AND IF YOU LIKE THE IDEA I WILL INCLUDE THE MILLIONAIRESS IN OUR PROGRAM. ARRIVING THE FIFTEENTH   LOVE GABRIEL

Born in Germany, where she had acted Hypatia in *Misalliance* (titled *Parents and Children*) and Eve in *Back to Methuselah*, Marlene **Dietrich** (née Maria Magdalene Dietrich, 1901–92) became a glamorous international screen star. After rejecting an offer to return to Germany to make films for the Nazis, she became a United States citizen, entertained American troops during the Second World War, and made anti-Nazi radio broadcasts in German. At this time, her career was at a low ebb; but providentially, she was soon offered the female lead in *Destry Rides Again*, which once more made her a star.

54 / To Gabriel Pascal   [4 Whitehall Court. London SW1]
20th February 1939

[APCS(p): Delacorte: U]

Charles Graves rang me up last night as a friend of Marlene. She wants me to cable her some token of my interest in her. Apparently she wants to be able to tell the press that she is coming to Europe at my invitation to discuss a film of The Millionairess.

Without this she thinks she will have to sign up for several years with a Hollywood corporation.

She is a naturalized American, by birth echt [genuine] Berliner. The foreign touch would suit the millionairess very well, if she can act. Graves says she very decidedly can.

Jean Cadell was my original selection for the other woman. For the millionairess I selected Edith Evans, who, however, is not keen on an unsympathetic part, and, failing her, Leonora Corbett, who was *very* keen.

I expect to be here all this week, as our house in the country is ravaged with influenza.

GBS

The journalist Charles (Patrick Ranke) **Graves** (1899–1971) was the brother of the poet and novelist Robert (van Ranke) Graves (1895–1985). Edith (later Dame Edith) **Evans** (1888–1976), British stage star, was a veteran Shavian actress. Like British stage actress Leonora **Corbett** (1907–60), she made few films.

55 / To G. Bernard Shaw   [Los Angeles]
                                               12th May 1939
[TD TEL(c): Delacorte: U]

At the end of March, Pascal and Laurence Irving arrived in New York from London. On 6 April they went to Hollywood. On the date of this cable, Shaw received the Oscar trophy he had won for Pygmalion. The Doctor's Dilemma *and* Major Barbara *were front runners for Pascal's next film, but Wendy Hiller's signature settled the matter in favour of the latter.*

... LAURENCE AND MYSELF COMPLETED PREPARATORY TECHNICAL WORK AND RETURNING BEGINNING JUNE WILL START PRODUCTION JULY RECEIVED NEWS THAT WENDY HILLER CONTRACT DEFINITELY SIGNED SUGGEST MAJOR BARBARA HER NEXT PICTURE ... GABRIEL

56 / To G. Bernard Shaw   [Los Angeles]
                                               24th May 1939
[TD TEL(c): Delacorte: U]

CEDRIC HARDWICKE IS VERY ANXIOUS PLAY UNDERSHAFT IN MAJOR-BARBARA PLEASE CABLE IF YOU AGREE ON IT BECAUSE CEDRIC HAD TERRIFIC SUCCESS HERE IN TWO PICTURES AND HE WOULD LIKE TO COME BACK TO ENGLAND UNDER TWO PICTURE CONTRACT WITH ME FOR DOCTOR'S DILEMMA AND MAJORBARBARA STOP SAILING HOME MIDDLE OF NEXT MONTH WITH LAURENCE LONG LETTER FOLLOWS AFFECTIONATELY GABRIEL

57 / To Gabriel Pascal   [4 Whitehall Court. London SW1
                                         received 1 June 1939]
[TEL(c): Delacorte: U]

WHY TIE YOURSELF UP CEDRIC IS NOT INDISPENSABLE IN EITHER PLAY   SHAW

58 / To Gabriel Pascal   Ayot St Lawrence. Welwyn. Herts.

23rd July 1939

[ANS(p): Delacorte: U]

Determined that others would not circumvent their intentions, as they had done with Pygmalion, *Shaw and Pascal collaborated more closely on* Major Barbara. *Shaw cut passages and wrote numerous new sequences. As he had confirmed in his cable of 5 January, Pascal would direct as well as produce their next film.*

Dear Gabriel

Can you come hither on Tuesday? If you start at 10.45 you will arrive here at 12. We can then talk about Major Barbara for an hour and a half until lunch at 13.30. You will be back in London easily by 16 or earlier if you wish.

We shall be alone, as Mrs Shaw is still unable to travel.

I will have the nationality letter ready for you.

G. Bernard Shaw

59 / To Gabriel Pascal   Ayot St Lawrence. Welwyn. Herts.

24th July 1939

[ALS: Letters]

This 'nationality letter' is a testimonial to help Pascal's application for British citizenship.

Dear Gabriel Pascal

Now that you have shifted the artistic centre of gravity of the film industry from Hollywood to Middlesex I hope you will shift your nationality in the same direction.

You have your choice of all the world except the place where you were born. The operations of Herr Hitler have closed that to you. The next best place for you is the British Empire with residence in London. It would be a calamity for British films and for me and for yourself if you chose California. England is the place for you: your work and all the employment it gives are there; and the new departure you have made so successfully in film drama would have been impossible in America.

Besides, you will be far more at home with us. California is not suited to a Magyar de la vieille roche [of the good old stock].

always yours

G. Bernard Shaw

60 / To Gabriel Pascal   4 Whitehall Court. London SW1

9th August 1939

[ALS(tr): Delacorte: U]

Shaw wrote a new scene to be inserted after Barbara and Peter Shirley leave the West Ham shelter. On a riverside wharf, she throws her Salvation Army bonnet into the waters. A watchman rushes to her and grabs her arm, fearful that she might commit suicide. When she faints, he blows his whistle. An ambulance arrives and two stretcher bearers carry her into it.

Dear Gabriel

... The bridge between Acts II & III must not switch off from Barbara to Undershaft: it must follow up her despair at the sale of the Army to Bodger & Undershaft.

I enclose the script. You will see how I have done it. It will involve a scene down the river on location; but it will be worth it. You will have to wait for a full moon and choose a reach of the river that runs north and south.

Wendy on a stretcher will be irresistible.

The next scene, which I have not yet completed, will be next morning at breakfast with plenty of eating and drinking at Lady B's.

GBS

61 / To Gabriel Pascal   4 Whitehall Court. London SW1

21st August 1939

[TLS: Letters]

My dear Gabriel

I enclose the breakfast scene to follow the river scene. I expect I shall have a lot of new scenes to join the 3rd and 4th acts.

I have read the Undershaft-Sardanapalus scenes you and Laurence mapped out. You and he must have got frightfully drunk in Hollywood to conceive such a thing. Stephen and Cusins playing baccarat and Undershaft living like a second lieutenant just come into a legacy, with nautch girls all complete, is beyond the wildest dreams of Sam Goldwyn. I cannot put on paper the imprecations with which I hurled it into the waste paper basket; so unless you kept a copy it is dead. However, never mind: I shall give you plenty to do in the Perivale scenes.

I hope I did not seem too impossible on Saturday; but I had given that agreement long and careful consideration and made up my mind like granite. If I give way an inch you give way a foot, and everyone else gives way or grabs all over the place until the whole business goes to pieces. There must be a rock somewhere in the shifting sands; and I have decided to be that rock.

It is of the first importance that the money for Barbara shall be advanced on Barbara and for Barbara alone. I know the artistic value of your indifference to money; but if I gave you more than one agreement at a time you would raise the last penny on the whole lot and spend it on the first, leaving yourself penniless for the rest, whilst I should be tied up for years. I want you to have these great successes without utterly ruining you. Hence my obstinacy on the point of one agreement at a time.

your adamant

G. Bernard Shaw

The '**3rd and 4th acts**' are Act III, Scenes 1 and 2. A luxurious, sensual, and indolent way of life was attributed to the legendary King **Sardanapalus**, who was mistakenly identified as the last Assyrian emperor. Samuel **Goldwyn** (né Goldfish, 1882–1974), American film producer, employed eminent novelists and dramatists to write screenplays. The previous year he produced a lavish, spectacular musical, *The Goldwyn Follies*.

62 / To G. Bernard Shaw

[*no address*]

30th August 1939

[TL(c): Delacorte: U]

The apparent ellipses in the following are typographical devices.

My dearest GBS

I have written you several letters, answering yours of the 21st instant, but I destroyed each one. I feel strongly now I must answer to you.

First, thanks for the new breakfast scene included in your letter of the 21st, and the new staircase scene you gave me last Thursday. Both are wonderful and have the freshness and rhythm of the Mug Todgerfairmile sequence which I admire as a unique masterpiece. I am so glad that in the breakfast scene you put in Barbara's line, 'The uniform would be out of place there,' which line gives us a marvelous suspense for the [P]erivale scenes, leaving it open, Barbara's final decision.

The river scene I love more and more and I am sure it is an ideal way to bridge the second and third acts. But I must, with my usual frankness, repeat, that this scene is so strong that it could stand a simultaneous action between Undershaft and Cusins at Undershaft's home ... and a short Club scene between them.

The great superiority of the screen dramaturgy over the play dramaturgy is (and this is the reason why the screen technic can produce better results than the stage technic) that we can intercut in two series of events, and when it is done in the right way, and motivated with the right suspense, each parallel action supports the other and the result is a higher note for the leading artist ... in this case Barbara.

I agree with you, that the gambling scene is a Sardanapalad, and I was never keen on it. It would be wrong of me to place it entirely on Laurence, but certainly as art director, he favored building up the night sequence which next day Cusins is mentioning in a similar technic as we did in Pygmalion, and I had enough polemics with him about it. But ... in honesty, I must say that as I mentioned above, I also, like Laurence, very strongly believe that a short scene intercut in the right rhythm, after the river scene, between Undershaft and Cusins, would help the average audience enjoy more visually the sequence on page 304 in the play.

I am looking forward with great interest to the promised new scenes in the [P]erivale sequence, and the new end scene.

I reflected very much about your suggestion to use, in the montage scenes, when we show the several sides of the munitions factory, Tschaikowsky's '1812' as background music.

I would be very grateful also, if you would work in, in the new end, one scene in the choral society, and a short scene with Peter Shirley's arrival in the factory which I suggest to cut in on page 319 before the Bilton scene.

Now about the casting. I followed your advice and got out from my obligation with Cedric Hardwicke, and I made a deal yesterday with the manager of Robert Morley. I believe destiny helped us, because I feel I can do miracles with this great promising character actor.

Also, to avoid overcasting, I got out of my obligation with Gordon Harker, and will take a less known player for it ... one who will be Peter Shirley and not remain Gordon Harker.

I am attempting to use the same policy in replacing Ralph Richardson (who is cast for Bill Walker) with a very talented actor, John Clement.

I also found the right actress for Mog. Her name is Sophie Stuart. I will show her photos to you, and I think you will like my selection.

So, there is really no danger of overcasting – but I maintain my policy, that the smallest part in your play, when I am producing the picture, must be played by the best talented actors in the country. The highest salary of great stars cannot be as expensive as a weak actor in a smaller part (principally in wasted negative material).

And now, my dear Rock, I would like very much to whisper to you a few words, being myself, since the creation, a Whirlwind who I am sure was sent by the elements, through their wise forethought ... to you. Did you not feel, during all these days, the rush of my wings – how much and how happily I rejoiced that your decisions you have made only to protect me from further financial mistakes. Please be, and keep on being, my Rock for many many years here, and in all eternity – later, on the other shore, where I shall follow you in my devotion, my crystal clear Rock, as your [T]ill [E]ulenspiegel.

Don't think for a moment that I was sad because of your firmness. On the contrary ... I was jubilant and I was proud that we both are more logical than weaker people, who try to come between us.

I don't mind that you changed your mind, and don't want to sign future agreements, but I must remind you, my dearest Master, on existing old agreements, and that on the basis of them I made with your knowledge several commitments in America and here.

I have bothered you enough with business. I feel spiritually it cannot exist ... anything like a business agreement between the Rock and the Whirlwind. The elements have them destined for each other since many thousands of years, based on higher purpose, and no human law can dissolve it.

I know the high privilege to produce your plays, but I know I can do it only if I am faithful to myself as to my dear Rock, and I have my spiritual harmony; this I have only if your spirit is brightening me.

Please don't take away from me this spiritual harmony whatever happens, which is my life breath. You know, my dear Master, how I adore you, forever and ever, and no material matter can influence my devotion and love.

[Gabriel Pascal]

The **new breakfast scene** is in Act III, Scene 1. The staircase scene is in Wilton Crescent, with Barbara, Cusins, and Morrison, before Undershaft arrives. The new '**Mug Todger-fairmile**' film sequence is between Mog Habbijam and Todger Fairmile, neither of whom appears in the play.

In the 1930s Gordon **Harker** (1885–1967), a British actor, was known for his portrayal of cockneys. Ralph (later Sir Ralph) **Richardson** (1902–83) was one of Britain's great stage and screen actors. John (later Sir John) **Clement** (error for Clements, 1910–88) was a distinguished British stage and screen star. Sophie **Stuart** (error for Stewart, 1908–77) was a Scottish actress. A German peasant's son born about 1300, Till **Eulenspiegel** was a scapegrace who committed outrageous pranks against nobles, priests, tradesmen, and innkeepers.

63 / To Gabriel Pascal

Hotel Esplanade. Frinton-on-Sea. Essex
31st August 1939

[ALS(tr): Delacorte: U]

Shaw, who with Charlotte was on holiday at Frinton-on-Sea from 29 August to 29 September, eventually wrote a sequence between Cusins and Undershaft, although he did not set it in a night club. The new scenes culminate in Undershaft's London apartment, where Cusins gets drunk and passes out.

Dear Gabriel

Get that notion of following the scent of Undershaft out of your head. You and Laurence were drunk, like Cusins, when you conceived it. One horse at a time is enough except in a circus. A club scene would be a return to Hollywood at its stalest.

Also Shirley is dead after the shelter scene. A mistake to revive him. And there is no room for much more of Bilton than in the play. Edmund Gwenn, by the way, 'created' Bilton.

I am not at all anxious *now* about overcasting. You promised me Hardwicke, Harker & Richardson: you now offer me a string of nobodies. But never mind. I am used to such changes; and if you can make them act I shall not complain.

The change of air has, so far, done me nothing but good. I feel delightfully lazy; but I will tackle the remaining sequences presently.

G. Bernard Shaw

PS Tell your people that this place is Frinton, not Trinton

64 / To Gabriel Pascal　　　　　Hotel Esplanade. Frinton-on-Sea. Essex
5th September 1939

[ALS(tr): Delacorte: U]

On 1 September Hitler invaded Poland; two days later Britain and France declared war on Nazi Germany.

My dear Gabriel

I enclose another sequence with a rough sketch of the scene. It will be followed by two scenes which must be either taken on location (if Imperial Chemical Industries will allow it) or at all events studied on the spot, preferably the latter, as the artist can always improve on nature.

After these a series of architectural scenes with Undershaft as compère [master of ceremonies] – Indian temples and the like – which will cost some dollars and knock Hollywood into a cocked hat.

I have a furious letter in The Times today against the closing of the theatres, and claiming exemption for actors from war service. You and all the people with studios must back me up by claiming exemption for film workmen as essential for the entertainment of soldiers on leave and evacuated children.

There are no shelters in Frinton; and I refused to leave my bed on Sunday when the false alarm came.

Cecil Lewis is in control at Gillingham, Kent, No 10 Group, R.A.F., a very hot spot close to Chatham Dockyard.

Mrs Shaw has had a bad relapse today; so dont come until I sound the All Clear. Meanwhile I peg away at Barbara.

G. Bernard Shaw

The **sketch** was of a green hill on which one could see the names Undershaft and Lazarus on a white wall. Under wartime conditions, **Imperial Chemical Industries** may not have permitted a camera crew in their plant. The **series of scenes** is in Undershaft's factory and village. Shaw was trying to persuade Cecil **Lewis** to claim conscientious objector status so that he could work at the B.B.C., in films, or in another area of public entertainment. Charlotte **Shaw**, who had grown very bent, was afflicted with painfully crippling lumbago and arthritis.

65 / To G. Bernard Shaw

[*no address*]

11th August [*error for* September] 1939

[TL(c): Delacorte: U]

My dearest GBS

I received your two letters dated the 31st of August and the 7th of September, and have been waiting a few days to give you definite good news, which I can do now.

Thanks for the two sequences and the sketch of the Green Hill, which I gave yesterday to Laurence, who was delighted with the idea and will work on it. He was very excited also about the possibility of the Buddhistic temple in the factory. I am waiting anxiously for this sequence before I can explain to Laurence what we want.

Before I report to you about the whole situation, my dearest GBS, don't be scared that I undercast the picture. I can never do this, because nothing is so much hated by me as bad actors, and I will as I promised you when we started our cooperation, always cast each part in your plays with the best existing actor for the part.

I had a long talk with Ralph Richardson, and if he is not called as a pilot instructor, he will be in our picture. Unfortunately John Mills, our Cusins, is already in uniform, so I am negotiating by cable with Maurice Evans, who is very anxious to come over. Cedric Hardwicke is a coward and doesn't want to come back, but Gordon Harker will be in the picture, so practically I will keep my whole original cast suggestions.

Now let me give you a short report of the happenings in the last week.

First, I have a great surprise for you. It is an idea for a short prologue in connection with Dürer's drawing, the Four Horsemen, which I prefer to explain to you personally. Don't be afraid, it is not a Hollywood proposition. It will be a real Shaw-Pascal touch, considering the actual world situation.

In the hour war was declared, I sent you a telegram, 'War or no war, I will go on with our program.' The next day, I sent to the Minister of Information, Sir Joseph Ball, who is the director of picture productions, my readiness to cooperate in any service of propaganda, and I was put on the list with Korda and the others. Then a day later, I had a board meeting and arranged to put all my people on half salary, instead of sending them away, for an interregnum of the next two weeks. While the Pinewood studios were taken away from me by Lloyds, we arranged that Laurence can continue work on the sketches at home, keeping the art department with him.

Our distributor, like all distributors, lost his head and instead of telling us that he is scared from the war, his lawyer sent to my lawyer, Sidney Wright, a letter informing us that they cannot continue financing the picture because our MAJOR BARBARA contract has not the same conditions as our Pygmalion contract. They refer to the supplementary letter on Pygmalion, where you gave me the world rights, exclusive of the German version, and the dubbing rights. I think it is better, when it is calm, that Sidney explains to you this legal position. I am enclosing herewith a copy of the letter from distributor's lawyer to Sidney Wright, which letter arrived one day after the war declaration.

So, all these days I was fighting with a few courageous friends of mine for the continuation of production, the opening of cinemas and theatres, and the creation of new spirit. Fortunately Sir Joseph Ball, who controls the situation, is an intimate friend of one of my partners, Nicholas Davenport, and we are working now on a plan to continue production with the help of the Treasury, if my distributor and Rank should fail us.

Failing all this, I would be obliged to make the picture in New York at the Astoria studios. I had a long talk yesterday with Wendy and the other artists, and Wendy declared, 'It is always better to make the picture in New York than not at all.' But I prefer to do it here, having the right vibration, the local atmosphere, and your guiding spirit, and New York would be only a last emergency. So, this week Davenport and myself will meet Sir Joseph Ball, and I will let you know at once the result ...

[Gabriel Pascal]

Born in Wales, Maurice (Herbert) **Evans** (1901–89) became an American citizen in 1941; Shakespearean and Shavian roles highlighted his stage career. German artist Albrecht **Dürer** (1471–1528) painted The Four Horsemen of the Apocalypse. In politics, war, and business, Sir (George) Joseph **Ball** (1885–1961) was a quintessential *éminence grise*; at this time he was head of the motion-picture production area of the Ministry of Information. Possibly, Lloyds of London would not insure Pinewood Studios. In the next letter, Shaw wonders how Pinewood was lost, but the letter with Pascal's explanation has not been found. On 29 September, Pascal is uncertain whether Pinewood would be opened. He filmed *Major Barbara* at Denham Studios.

66 / To Gabriel Pascal   Hotel Esplanade. Frinton on Sea. Essex
                              12th September 1939

[ALS(tr): Delacorte: U(e)]

Although Shaw would write a scene in which Toscanini conducts a chorus from the opera Moses in Egypt *(1818) by Gioacchino Antonio Rossini (1792–1868), with new lyrics, Pascal would have neither time nor money to film it.*

Dear Gabriel

Here is a champion effort, the musical part of which will probably cost at least £3000, and involve the co-operation of Toscanini. The name of the quartet from Mose in Egitto is 'Dal Tuo Stellata soglio.' I shall not compose the new words for it until I hear your reaction – and his.

If La[u]rence likes travelling let him fly to Dublin. There he must take the Harcourt St train to Shankill. Thence he must walk or drive (if he can get a conveyance) to Ballycorus smelting works, where he will see the chimney up the hill and the tower on the top, unless their ruins have totally disappeared, which suggested my scene.

At Faringdon in Oxfordshire Lord Berners has built a campanile with a view of the white horse which is much more English than desolate Irish Ballycorus.

I have three more pictures in Blanche's hands (I write in shorthand) before the film lands in the final act in the book finally.

The new Jain temple in Bombay contains two shrines with the wonderful figures. The priest assured me that they are still made in India as Undershaft describes, and that I could buy one. I am sorry I didnt.

The old Jain temple, of which I have seen only the photographs, is one of the wonders of the world.

Maurice Evans is the best available Cusins.

Cedric has 'given his proof,' as he was the last man to be demobilized in the last war and can remain *embusqué* [a shirker] this time without reproach. Trouncer, having only one lung, is probably exempt.

Give Davenport exciting descriptions of the Barbara scenario, and say that it is a pity that it is all off, as my agreement is unalterable.

When the present disgraceful blue funk is over, with its black-outs and its shut-up-everything and its family prayers, the studios will be working overtime. But how has Pinewood been lost? That is serious.

GBS

PS Mrs Shaw is worse as to the lumbago – cannot walk. That raid alarm did her no good, damn it!

The scene that the **smelting works** suggested to Shaw is of Perivale St Andrews. Gerald Hugh Wyrwhitt-Wilson, fourteenth Baron **Berners** (1883–1950), was a composer, novelist, painter, and aesthete.

67 / To Gabriel Pascal   Hotel Esplanade. Frinton-on-Sea. Essex
15th September 1939

[ALS(tr): Delacorte: U(e)]

Dear Gabriel

I enclose the missing sheet.

You are now complete with a surfeit of pictures and billions of expenditure, quite enough without Albrecht Durer or anything medieval. Everything must be modern and contemporary or else in the future.

Do not let your time be wasted by attempts to get the agreement altered and the affair put on the old Hollywood basis. There will be no alteration and no side lines of any sort: they must take it or leave it as it is.

The more outrageously expensive it is the easier it will be to get the money. On the other hand, all the new scenes can be discarded and the film restricted to the printed text. But it will pay to outdo Korda in extravagance.

And now what is the next film after Barbara to be? I want to know before I begin a new play.

Do not consider shooting in America. We must keep All-British. Otherwise we shall not get any extra petrol.

GBS

68 / To G. Bernard Shaw   [Hawkeswood. Gerrards Cross. Bucks.]
21st September 1939

[TD TEL(c): Delacorte: U]

DEAR GBS RECEIVED YOUR LAST LETTER ONLY THIS MORNING BECAUSE WAS WHOLE WEEK IN TOWN WAITING NEGOTIATIONS WITH MINISTRY OF INFORMATION FOR PERMISSION TO GO ON WITH PRODUCTION MAJOR BARBARA STOP HAVE SPOKEN YESTERDAY TO SIR JOSEPH BALL WHO IS VERY FAVOURABLE TO OUR GOING ON STOP MY CABLE TO TOSCANINI WAS NOT DELIVERED LAST MONDAY BUT THIS MORNING WESTERN UNION CONFIRMS THAT HE ARRIVED IN NEW-YORK YESTERDAY AND RECEIVED CABLE STOP HAVE SENT MY CAMERA-MAN OVER WITH LETTER TO HIM AND THE COPY OF YOUR NEW SCENE FOR HIM STOP PROPOSE NEXT PICTURE AFTER BARBARA SAINT JOAN PLEASE LET ME KNOW HAWKESWOOD IF I COULD COME SATURDAY HAVING LAST CHANCE USING MY CAR   AFFECTIONATELY GABRIEL

69 / To Gabriel Pascal   Hotel Esplanade. Frinton. Essex
21 September 1939

[APCS(tr): Delacorte: U]

My wife is still so ill that the slightest incident frightens and upsets her. I dare not ask you to come; for she *must* be well enough to return to Ayot on the 29th; and I fear a relapse. So dont come.

You must apply for extra petrol for your film work, stating the amount of capital at stake and the number of persons employed. They can hardly refuse.

Many thanks for your telegram, which tells the whole story up to date.

GBS

The close-ups of Arturo and the soloists will be great fun if he will consent. If not, Albert Coates would be the next best.

The Russian-born composer Albert **Coates** (1882–1953) conducted the orchestra of the Imperial Opera House, St Petersburg, from 1910 until the revolution. From 1919 to 1946, he lived in England. He and Shaw were good friends.

70 / To G. Bernard Shaw [*no address*]

29th September 1939

[TL(c): Delacorte: U]

My dearest GBS

Thanks for your last letter.

I was not wasting my time as you believed, about the contract, but in contrary have been working on constructive things, because the old financing set-up with the distributor failed, when they refused the terms of my contract with you. So, with my friend Davenport, I worked very hard the last two weeks to get Government support and Treasury support, and only after these negotiations were very successful and Sir Joseph Ball, who is head of the picture department in the Ministry of Information, gave formal assurance of his support to my future picture productions, Mr. Arthur Rank came back to me and started new negotiations. Now I am not worried about this side.

More important is, as you can see from Davenport's correspondence with the Ministry of Information, that Sir Joseph Ball is ready to free any actor which we need from Military service.

I am negotiating now for Ralph Richardson, who is already somewhere in uniform. If this should fail, what is your reaction to take Wilfrid Lawson for Bill, who arrived last week back from America? Unfortunately Maurice Evans definitely refused, under the war circumstances, to come back. So I must go back to John Mills, who is very good for the part. You approved on it once, and I engaged him, but he is already with his Regiment. I hope that the Ministry of Information will free him for eight weeks. More difficulty is with Ralph. The agent of Gordon Harker telephoned me yesterday that Gordon will be back from his tour by the middle of November, and he is ready to play Peter Shirley. I found a perfect Snobby Price in Marius Goring. I made the deal, as I wrote you last month, with Robert Morley for Undershaft. His manager called me that he has a great offer from Hollywood, and wants a definite starting date. But Morley assured me personally that he will be faithful and wait for my decision. This decision will depend on the following facts:

Is Mr Rank ready to open the Pinewood Studios or not. If not, I must transfer my unit to the Denham Studios, where the Government left four stages open, and these four stages would have to be shared between Korda and myself. This would not influence my independence at all, and is the only way that I could start at least by the beginning of November. All the small studios are busy with all kinds of junk of stupid propaganda pictures and their usual lowbrow food, which my idiotic colleagues believe suit the English audience in wartime. I am determined more than ever to prove to England and America that we must make in wartime even better pictures than in peacetime, because the spiritual desire of the masses are more awakened when they are facing great events, as today. I am certain you agree with me, my dear Master, and I hope I can give you definite news next week.

I hope that Mrs Shaw is already recovered, and I can visit you soon at Ayot St Lawrence.

[Gabriel Pascal]

P.S. I am enclosing a copy of a letter from Davenport to Sir Joseph Ball, and his answer.

I have received no answer yet from Toscanini. It would help very much if you would write him a letter. His address is: Hotel Astor, Broadway, New York – telling him how delighted you would be if he would accept my offer.

J. Arthur (later Baron) **Rank** (1888–1972), head of the Rank Organisation, became a titan of the British film industry. Marius **Goring** (b. 1912), stage and screen actor, is best known for his performance as the composer in the film *The Red Shoes.*

71 / To Gabriel Pascal   Ayot St Lawrence. Welwyn. Herts.
30th September 1939

[APCS(p): Delacorte: U(e)]

We are back at Ayot safely; but we are stuck there until the 12th, almost inaccessible except to people with extra petrol. Mrs Shaw is better, and can bear a visitor for lunch without being any the worse for it.

The Ministry of Information is abolished virtually. How does that affect Sir Joseph Ball?

I have written a long letter to the Home Office in reply to their inquiry about your eligibility for naturalization.

No use writing to Tosca: I cut no ice with him. My invention of the scene shews the value I set on him.

As you are handling the affair with consummate ability I just dont think about it.

GBS

72 / To Gabriel Pascal   Ayot St Lawrence. Welwyn. Herts.
                                         30th September 1939
[APCS(tr): Delacorte: U]

On 17 September, the troops of Joseph Stalin (1879–1953), dictator of the USSR, invaded Poland.

I had not room on the other card to say that W.L. would overdo Bill. He is too old for it. The part of Shirley is definitely not worth his salary.

At present, by the way, nobody is worth more than £3 a week.

But the war is over. It was over the moment Stalin crossed the Polish frontier. The only question left for us to consider is how soon the order to cease Fire will be given.

GBS

73 / To G. Bernard Shaw   Hawkeswood. Gerrards Cross. Bucks.
                                         26th October 1939
[TL(c): Delacorte: U]

My dearest Maestro

I am pleased to tell you we have now received the statements on the returns from General Film Distributors up to the 30th September, as a result of my having conveyed to them your views on the matter. My threats worked very well indeed, because they sent me back an alarmed letter, apologising for their two months' delay, and saying that I have certainly not explained the full facts to you, which is ridiculous because, as you know, I did. But at their wish I now pass on to you their own explanation of the delay:

> The facts are as follows: with regard to accounting, we use, as is well known in the trade, a mechanical system of accounting involving the operation of electrically driven Powers machines. These were installed at Sydmonton Court, near Newbury, on the outbreak of the war; but owing to the fact that the motors required adapting to a different voltage and to direct current, and the necessity of rewiring the house, they were not in working order until a fortnight ago, and even now are not working with normal efficiency.

I don't believe a word of this, but the fact remains that our threats worked very well, and I am very grateful to you. I realise now that your system is much better than twenty thousand lawyers' shrewdness and cleverness.

At the same time I would like to confirm the arrangement which we made at our last meeting in the presence of one of my directors, Mr Davenport; namely, that you, dear G.B.S., would extend the time of payment of the future 'Pygmalion' royalties until after the production of 'Major Barbara,' when we shall be able to repay you from the advances made to us on delivery of that negative.

We hope to clear up the accounts with G.F.D. very quickly now, and as soon as we have done so we will send you a copy of the returns showing the amount due to you, for which you are giving us the extra time for payment, thus permitting us to utilise these funds to help us with the production of 'Major Barbara' until the several advances become due.

I have made definite arrangements now for the distributorship with United Artists, and have told Wolfe and Rank that if they have not the money they promised to me they cannot have the distribution of the picture. United Artists have given me a stock-holder deal: this means that the distribution will cost us about half of what we pay to Metro.

Sir Joseph Ball was very anxious to have lunch with you, so that when Blanche told me that you are not coming into town this week, I postponed it again to next week. He wanted very much to influence me to make 'Geneva' as a quickie; at once, before 'Major Barbara.' I told him that I believed you would not mind if I produced this picture between 'Major Barbara' and 'Doctor's Dilemma'; but that I must go on at once with 'Major Barbara,' because all commitments are made accordingly.

Wendy tried to get my permission to allow her to make a picture with another company before 'Major Barbara.' It is a dreadful play, 'Gaslight,' which I refused, because we start production latest in December; so if she tries to approach you please be adamant. We have not created our star to give the value to some crooked company.

I hope Mrs Shaw is well again, and that you feel better yourself. Please let me know – or tell Blanche to do so – whether you are coming up to town next week or not.

I liked Antony Eden's speech yesterday evening. It was the first decent English speech I heard during the war. What is your opinion about it?

[Gabriel Pascal]

Wolfe is an error for film financier Charles Moss **Woolf** (1879–1943), managing director of General Theatre Corporation. **Gaslight** (1938) is by Patrick Hamilton (1904–62). (Sir) Anthony **Eden** (1897–1977) would become Secretary of State for Foreign Affairs 1940–5 and Prime Minister 1955–7.

74 / To Gabriel Pascal   [Ayot St Lawrence. Welwyn. Herts.]
                                27th October 1939

[TLS(tr): Delacorte: U]

My dear Gabriel

Dash it all, I did not say I could wait until Barbara was on the market. The date I gave was the 31st December next, when I have to make monstrous payments to the Commissioners of Inland Revenue. So keep up the pressure if possible. Tell them I am not in the least surprised to learn that they cannot add two and two together without a machine.

Tell Sir Joseph Ball that a production of Geneva before Barbara might mess up both of them. We must get our grip of the public with Barbara before we touch anything else. It is not yet certain that Geneva is not quite out of date. The results of the tour must settle that question before we decide. Geneva is not technically good film stuff anyhow.

I have great doubts as [to] being able to come up to town next week. Mrs Shaw is much better today; but until she is able to move about for three or four days in succession I can promise nothing.

Nobody but an incorrigible Magyar militarist aristocrat could have enjoyed Eden's speech. He declared that the whole empire was with us heart and soul without ever mentioning India: and he guaranteed victory for us on the strength of a survey of the forces in operation without mentioning Russia. What are you to do with such people? However, he delivered the speech well and self-conceitedly, which would have been all right on the stage. Off it he ought to have been shot.

How is your health? Ought I to insure your life?

In great haste, the post in this village being at sixes and sevens occasionally.

GBS

On 30 October, Maurice Colbourne (1894–1965), an English actor who appeared in many Shavian plays, who was Sergius in the film version of *Arms and the Man*, and who frequently toured Canada, began a Canadian **tour** of *Geneva* before its Broadway opening on 30 January 1940, with new scenes that brought the play up to date. It was unfavorably received in New York.

75 / To G. Bernard Shaw   [*no address*]
4th November 1939

[TL(c): Delacorte: U]

My dearest G.B.S.

I gave your message to my board, and we will reserve a certain amount of money which you must fix with Davenport the next time you are coming to town, for the 31st of December.

I received finally two stages at the Denham studio for the first week after Christmas, and with the help of Sir Joseph I hope to get the half of my unit for three months free from their military service.

I gave Sir Joseph, who I saw two days ago, your message, that you prefer that I proceed with MAJOR BARBARA and we do GENEVA between MAJOR BARBARA and DOCTOR'S DILEMMA if the tour is successful. I am not myself sure if it is good picture material, but I would like that you listen to Sir Joseph the next time you come to town, because he has definite propagandistic ideas in connection with your play, and I would like to know your reactions. So Blanche will let me know as soon as you are ready for a lunch.

Thanks for your offer to the incorrigible Hussar I am, for the life insurance. I think it is not a bad idea, because as I predicted to you, you will live to the age of at least one hundred years, and a Gypsy woman predicted to me that I will die when I am fifty-five, so it is only decent that you take out a life insurance for me in your own interest. But let's use these few years we play our guest role here to our common spiritual joy.

With my most affectionate regards to Madame Charlotte.

[Gabriel Pascal]

76 / To Gabriel Pascal Ayot St Lawrence. Welwyn. Herts.
7th November 1939

[APCS(p): Delacorte: U]

Do not make any *personal* sacrifice to secure the stipulated result.
Strictly between ourselves, I can manage this time if necessary.

GBS

77 / To G. Bernard Shaw [*no address*]
13th November 1939

[TL(c): Delacorte: U]

My Dearest GBS

Thanks for your little note. I kept it for myself without telling them of your kind gesture. So I work hard to get everything settled in your sense, and I think I will have success.

Two days ago Walter Hudd came to see me and I decided to give him the part of Stephen. He played it many times, and he is so anxious to play it, that for an actor of his sincerity who has this great desire, the half battle of his part is already won. He looks a little bit old for the part, but I think a clever make-up will help him through. He has a solemn face, which we need for Stephen.

I must ask you, my dearest Master, a great favor. You remember we agreed that I start the second act with the marching of Barbara's army with Jenny to the Shelter before we start the scene between Snobby Price and Rummy. It would be wonderful if before Barbara is marching away, we show the last phase of the meeting, where they convert Peter Shirley. I would need practically no dialogue – only the end of the meeting where Barbara is asking Jenny to pray. I have a clear vision of this scene, and what I am asking you, if you feel the same inspiration, is to write the prayer of Jenny, praying for the new convert, Peter Shirley, praying for the other souls in the listening crowd, praying for the struggling humanity, the soldiers and also for our enemies, that God inspire their mind for the good. I would let Jenny, with closed eyes, say this prayer, then the army band starts their hymn and they march on to the shelter, and we continue with page 266 as in your play. The whole scene should not be longer than a printed page. I feel that it is necessary as a binding scene between the first and second acts. It would be a wonderful link for Barbara, exactly as the river scene of Barbara is now between the second and third acts.

My health is much better now. I found a very good Doctor, I think you met him years ago – Professor Plesch, and he asked me to go for two weeks away to Devon to have some rest before I go into production. My nerves are down from all this stupid struggle and financial negotiations, and I will work out there my book of mise-en-scene with all the technical camera angles, etc.

Laurence definitely resigned from the art direction, and I engaged Vincent Korda. I was first nervous about the change. Now I am very glad, because Vincent has much more understanding for your conception of the factory. He realized your vision of the Undershaft-Lazarus giant letters over the green hills, and we will have a very agreeable surprise from this sincere hard-working artist.

I am leaving Thursday for Salcombe, and I would be glad to see you for a few minutes Wednesday, if you are coming to town.

I hope Mrs Shaw and you are well again. We must postpone our meeting with Sir Joseph Ball until I am back from my short holiday which I need, according to my Doctor, very badly.

[Gabriel Pascal]

Walter **Hudd** (1898–1963), who played Private Meek in *Too True to be Good* in 1932, did look younger than his age. Vincent **Korda** (1897–1979) was Alexander's brother.

78 / To Gabriel Pascal   Ayot St Lawrence. Welwyn. Herts.
                                                     21st November 1939

[ALS: Letters]

Dear Gabriel

I am much relieved to have you safe in Salcombe instead of worrying yourself to death here. You needed the change; and the news that it has been a success rejoices me.

Your notion of a scene representing the conversion of Shirley by Barbara is the very worst I ever heard. Shirley is not converted: the bitterness of his lot is that being an atheist sacked as 'too old over forty' he is driven by starvation to beg a crust from the Salvation Army. Get Shirley out of your mind: there is just enough of him in the play. Beware of the temptation to overdo every good effect. Enough is enough: another word and enough becomes too much: the fault of Hollywood.

Besides, such a scene would collide with the Mog Habbijam – Bill Walker scene, and wreck both, besides spoiling Barbara's conversion scene with Bill. Big effects must not be repeated.

Why does Hudd want such a disagreeable part as Stephen, on which he would be thrown away? Why not give him Lomax? Scott Sunderl[an]d, by the way, would be an ideal Cholly; if only he could *act* him instead of *being* him.

I dont believe that links and bridges are needed to connect the acts for filming. The audience will make the jump exactly as they do in the theatre.

I left undone an important bit of Barbara: the words for the Rossini quartet. I have now done them and will send you a fair copy when Blanche types it. It has been a horrid job. Nothing would have been easier than to write a few pretty verses; but to fit them to Rossini's notes and accents, and to provide for the big recurring portamento [glide from one note to another] was the very devil; and the result is queer, but singable. I almost drove my wife mad bellowing it over and over on Sunday night. Stephen must be a complete prig – the dictionary gives saputello;

but I dont know whether that is the real equivalent. It is always bad economy to waste an agreeable actor on a charmless part: that is why I think a better use might be made of Hudd.

Who is your Shirley now?

I must stop. Stay as long as you can in Salcombe.

Katherine Cornell now wants to play Barbara with Maurice Evans in the spring in New York; and this, I think, will be good business for us; so I have told her I am enchanted.

> Whoosh!
>
> GBS

'Smart aleck' would be closer to **saputello**. Katharine **Cornell** did not play *Major Barbara* or any other Shaw play the next spring, but she starred in *The Doctor's Dilemma* in 1941.

79 / To G. Bernard Shaw [*no address*]

22nd November 1939

[TL(c): Delacorte: U]

... I think I explained myself badly over the Shirley scene, through having to dictate hurriedly. I never intended to make an idiotic conversion scene. When I said: 'The scene where Shirley is converted' I meant the scene where Shirley is picked up by Barbara on the road. I never intended, either, to make another real meeting scene, as the Mog scene, which is so masterly, would kill any second scene of a meeting by making it fall flat. But I have something in mind which I had better explain to you verbally on Saturday, when I am in London.

Please don't worry about Walter Hudd. Stephen is a very difficult part to play, and it is exactly for these more difficult parts that I need good actors, and not these young sissy idiots who always play these kind of parts on the London stage.

For Peter Shirley I have definitely called off the deal, as you wished, with Gordon Harker. The old rascal had the impudence – because he played centuries ago in your play – to ask for a script to approve, a new invention of this Cockney Pagliacco [clown]; so to hell with him! ...

For poor Scott I have a part in mind which I will submit to you on Saturday also. For Lomax I think he must await another reincarnation, and then maybe the Muse will blow some talent towards him in the moment of his creation. The most perfect Lomax in this and all reincarnations is and remains David Tree. I hope you agree on this point at least.

I am so glad you gave permission to Katharine Cornell and Maurice Evans for 'Barbara.' Certainly it will be a wonderful preparation for the arrival of the picture in America. I don't remember if I told you that I was negotiating for weeks with Maurice Evans for Cusins; but when the war broke out he cancelled the whole business. Now we have a very decent English actor for this part, David Niven, who is maybe much better than our original decision, John Mills, who is in uniform. I needed the protection of the War Office and the Ministry of Information to have Niven freed for the next three months ...

[Gabriel Pascal]

In 1929 Gordon **Harker** had played Bill Walker in London. David Tree played **Lomax** in the film. David **Niven** (né James David Graham Niven, 1909–83), born in Scotland, was a star of British and Hollywood films for decades.

80 / To G. Bernard Shaw

[Mumford's Farm
Chalfont St Peter. Bucks.]
6th December 1939

[TL(c): Delacorte: U]

Pascal's proposed opening scene begins with a close-up of Dürer's 'Four Horsemen.' A government official orders anti-aircraft guns from Undershaft, whose employees, Bilton and Pettigrew, then discuss the Undershaft inheritance, which Lady Britomart and Stephen do in the play. Act I follows.

My dearest G.B.S.

I arrived here last Saturday morning and unfortunately again became sick, which is why I have not written to you before. Today is the first day I feel more human-like, and sitting in my little cottage in the sun: I think in a few days, if this nice weather remains, I will be well again.

Hereby I am sending you a short outline of the first scene, which I hope you will write for me. In the whole of the third act now, with all your new magnificent supplementary scenes, the factory has become so dominating that in my conception it is essential to start the picture with a short scene introducing Undershaft, in a mysterious way, in the factory. Thus we get the audience interested in him at once, more so than the invisible suspense which we have at present in the Lady Britomart Stephen scene, which works wonderfully on the stage, but which creates nervousness from the picture audience.

The picture audience is interested only in a person when they see him – they are never interested in one we only talk about. So the off-stage technique cannot be applied to the picture audience.

This short opening scene which I am asking for, would also be a compromise of the Ministry of Information's requirements. I must be grateful to them because they influenced the Treasury to give me some financial protection and it was the Treasury who called upon Sir Martin Holland, the Bank of England man, to ask my Bank to discount the distributors' minimum guarantee, which made it partly possible to make our picture. I would also like to put the audience familiar at once with the foundling story. I have engaged for Pettigrew, O. B. Clarence, and our old friend Scott Sunderland I would like to play the Official at the War Office.

Lying here in my bed my spirit is clearer than ever that we must have a prayer from Barbara. I do not mind if this prayer scene is a kind of monologue before or after the Bill Walker–Jenny Hill scene; or perhaps we could have it at the beginning of the second act, ending a meeting with the prayer and then Barbara marches off to the shelter, where, as in the play, we start with Snobby Price and Rummy.

In your play, on page 339, Barbara says: 'Oh, did you think my courage would never come back? did you believe that I was a deserter? that *I, who have stood in the streets, and taken my people to my heart, and talked of the holiest and greatest things to them,* could ever turn back and chatter foolishly to fashionable people about nothing in a drawing room? Never, never, never, never: Major Barbara will die with the colors.'

You yourself, my dear Maestro, suggest such a scene with Barbara, so please, for Heaven's sake, write me a prayer!!!

You told me once, when I was with the foolish, red-headed Irish girl, Greer Garson, at lunch, that you believe in prayers and in dreams. Now, how do you like this? Last night I was again in the Vatican in the cause of our future picture 'Saint Joan,' but this time in my dreams. I have spoken with Cardinal Pacelli, the present Pope, and with the old Pope, for whom I had not a very great admiration, but he was touchingly human and send[s] you messages that we must make the picture as soon as possible. So you see, my Master, what dead and living spirits are working for us and we *must* have a marvellous prayer ...

I will ask Davenport to visit you and give you a report about the financial situation; I will make him also to bring you a telegram from the young Mussolini in which he asks us to re-consider our old plan of shooting 'Caesar and Cleopatra' in Rome.

If, as I hope, the political situation between our country and Italy is eased, I think after 'Doctor's Dilemma' is the time to do this picture, and if Morley is successful as Undershaft, I think he is the ideal Caesar for us. For the moment, however, it is better that I concentrate all my forces on our present picture, 'Major Barbara.'

I stay here only until the 10th of this month and then I go back to Denham. I do not know if I have told you that I have bought 'Mumford's Farm,' and as soon as 'Major Barbara' is ready, I will build there from one of the old barns, a theatre with a real stage, and a recording room. I will rehearse all our plays there and do only the actual shooting at the studio; all the recording, dubbing and cutting business I will do at my own place, far away from the mad-house atmosphere of a big studio.

Maybe we can use the theatre during the summer for a kind of Festival Theatre, which I hope to open with one of your plays and try out all kind of young talent which we can use later in pictures. I hope that your spirit will encourage me in this enterprise and slowly I can free myself from any picture studio and make our pictures in my own workshop.

Now I have said enough nonsense, but from these injections I am physically so weak that I cannot concentrate.

Awaiting anxiously the new beginning and the prayer,

[Gabriel Pascal]

Eugenio **Pacelli** (1876–1958) was Pius XII, elected in 1939 after Pope Pius XI died that year.

81 / To G. Bernard Shaw

[TL(c): Delacorte: U]

Dearest G.B.S.

As I told you yesterday, it would close the 'General' episode at the Shelter very nicely if you could write me a scene in the corridor at the Albert Hall. For this I need nothing as set-background beyond a door in the round corridor so well-known to music-lovers all over the world. Undershaft and Cusins are coming out, Undershaft mopping his forehead with his handkerchief. I took the provisional dialogue for this scene from the breakfast-room:

> CUSINS: Why did you insist on remaining anonymous?
> UNDERSHAFT: If I gave my name, all the charitable institutions would be down on me like kites on a battlefield.

It would certainly be better if you could write special dialogue for this short scene, ending with Undershaft inviting Cusins to dinner at his own house.

You remember that you yourself once put it into my mind that it would be fine to have, instead of the cursed idea of the night-club, a short scene between the two men in Undershaft's home, following the dinner with the Spanish Burgundy, and ending with Undershaft putting Cusins in a taxi. This would be followed without interruption by the riverside scene, so that we leave the audience with Barbara.

For this so-called 'Dining-Room Scene' I suggest taking over pages 284–286 in the play, starting with the poem, and ending with Cusins' line:

> Mr Undershaft: you are, as far as I am able to gather, a most infernal old rascal; but you appeal very strongly to my sense of ironic humour.

I enclose a copy of the scene as I have worked it out; but it would certainly be fine if you could re-edit my modest effort to put this sequence in the right style. The advantage of changing the position of this scene is that it gives a much greater suspense of a continuation of the Shelter episodes, but separated from them; and the discussion about Barbara, starting: 'May I ask, as Barbara's father ...' lead[s] us straight to her, in the riverside scene.

All the rest of Act II remains unchanged; but if we put this scene at the end of the Shelter sequence we have a lightening of the atmosphere, and a more personal touch between Cusins and Undershaft, bringing us in a more intimate way, for the popular audience, to Barbara when she is deserted by the river.

What I need very badly, after the line: 'You appeal very strongly to my sense of ironic humour,' is a line or two from Undershaft when he puts Cusins into a taxi.

I have asked Vincent Korda to prepare you a sketch of my idea of Undershaft's dining-room.

About my coming to Ayot St Lawrence next Monday – a week to-day – would suit me very well.

Embracing you with
affectionate love,
[Gabriel Pascal]

82 / To Gabriel Pascal   [4 Whitehall Court. London SW1]
                                                    7th March 1940

[TLS(tr): Delacorte: U(e)]

My dear Gabriel

Tell Mog that she must on no account call herself by a name which could be mistaken for that of an already celebrated actress. She must find a new name: if possible unlike any other on the stage or elsewhere, but with the same initials so that she need not have her clothes re-marked. I suggest Kate Cordant. There is no such name in the telephone directory nor have I ever met with it: it is a new invention and is as easily said as Ellen Terry. There are 21 Corbells in the directory.

Now as to all these agreements that the distributors want. Well, they can't have them. You say, very truly, that money is nothing to you. So much the better from the artistic point of view, but it throws on me a moral obligation to prevent you from ruining yourself. On every agreement I give you you can raise, say, £50,000 per play. But there is no limit to what you may spend on each play. You are generous and reckless instead of having, as you need to have in this business, a heart like the nether millstone. And you have mad fancies for introducing Chinamen, in colors which you cannot photograph, into all-British films. If I give you contracts for nine plays you will raise £450,000 on them, and spend it all on a single Chinaman. Then, having nothing left for the other films, you will have to borrow at 50% from hysterical serpents and others who will bleed you white. I shall get nothing; and you will get worse than nothing: that is, ruin, bankruptcy, disgrace, despair and suicide.

Now there is only one way in which I can make you set a limit to your expenditure on each play; and that is to give you one agreement at a time. It is no use telling me that United Artists must have their announcements ready three years ahead. They may also want the moon and the stars. The reply is that they can't have them.

When Barbara is finished it will be time enough to think of her successor.

GBS

The name taken by the American actress who played **Mog** Habbijam was Cathleen Cordell (née Kelly, b. 1917). Pascal cast the Chinese dramatist S(hi-i) I. Hsiung (b. 1902) as a laundryman ('**Chinaman**') in one of the Salvation Army scenes.

83 / To Gabriel Pascal

[4 Whitehall Court. London SW1]
16th March 1940

[APCS (p): Delacorte: U]

Dear Gabriel

I enclose an agreement for Blanco Posnet. Please keep the copy I have signed, and return the other with your signature across the stamp and duly witnessed. Fill in the date in both copies.

You now have agreements for The Devil's Disciple, Blanco, and Caesar, which is enough for these uncertain times.

Man & Superman in its entirety seems to me a crazy adventure. Have you ever thought of filming Byron's Don Juan? Somebody will do it someday.

The other plays in the program must wait until we have settled the cast. Candida, St Joan & The Millionairess are inseparable from the title parts. Katharine Cornell would be all right for Candida, the Lunts for Arms & the Man, and ????? for The Millionairess; but I am not so sure about St Joan: I should like to see the Barbara film first.

Somehow I cannot take the Italian project for Caesar quite seriously. Do you think it will really come off? I cannot get a centesimo out of Italy at present.

G. Bernard Shaw

Don Juan (1819–24) is the unfinished satirical poem by George Gordon, Lord **Byron** (1788–1824). Alfred **Lunt** (1893–1977) and his wife Lynne (née Lillie Louise) Fontanne (1887–1983), American stage stars who played in *Arms and the Man* in America in 1925, were America's greatest acting couple for over three decades.

84 / To G. Bernard Shaw

[*no address*]
18th April 1940

[TL(c): Delacorte: U]

My dearest G.B.S.

'*Major Barbara*'

I have at long last settled the finance difficulties for 'Major Barbara,' for which purpose it has been necessary to have a Supplemental Agreement with my British Distributors, General Film Distributors, copy of which I enclose and I am sure that you will have no objection to its terms.

With kind regards,
Affectionately yours,
[Gabriel Pascal]

85 / To Gabriel Pascal

[4 Whitehall Court. London SW1]
27th April 1940

[TLS(tr): Delacorte: U(e)]

My dear Gabriel

The supplementary agreement puzzles me. I want to know who is providing the capital for the Barbara film. I understood that *I* was, by waiting for my royalties, several millions of which are long overdue. But the supplementary agreement declares that the National Provincial Bank, and Korda are in it, and that G.F.D. have a call, although it is not clear that they have contributed anything. How does Korda come to have a finger in the pie? They all are to be paid first: that is the gist of the agreement. But where do I come in? As to you, you will be left with nothing, though you are in complete command of the situation. You should have a prior claim to at least £25,000, win, lose or draw.

I should have written this before; but I thought you were coming to see me this (Saturday) morning, and have only just learnt that you are in Devon.

G. Bernard Shaw

G.F.D. is General Film Distributors. Pascal was in **Devon**, investigating background locations for Undershaft's factory town.

86 / To G. Bernard Shaw   [10 Bolton Street. Piccadilly. London W1]

29th April 1940

[TL(c): Delacorte: U]

My dear G.B.S.

Thank you for your letter which I received this morning. I sent a copy of it at once to Mr Davenport, who is concerned with the finances of my Company, and asked him to state clearly whether what I have always intended is actually the case: that your 10% royalties should be protected whatever happens.

Concerning Korda, he is 'in the pie' because he is an executive of United Artists, and he covered the United Artists' income for our Bank here with a minimum guarantee. Secondly, he transferred his studio facilities to me without any financial interest; otherwise it would have been really impossible to get studio space at all for many months to come. This is the reason why he is indirectly in our deal, but he has nothing whatever to do with my production. As executive partner for United Artists, he has a common interest in making as much money as possible through United Artists in America.

As soon as I have Mr Davenport's answer, I will send you a further explanation about the whole deal.

I am ashamed to tell you that you are partly right in criticising me for not being able to protect my own financial interests. After I sent you the letter with the copy of the supplementary contract, the Bank and the Distributors started to grumble again, and, to save the continuity of production and prevent an unexpected withdrawal of support, I was obliged to give up the remaining half of my salary for the picture. So I decided to work during the picture without a salary as it was the only way to get the production going.

The last line of your kind letter sounds like a sweet fairy-tale: 'You should have a prior claim to at least £25,000, win, lose, or draw.' You do not know, my dear noble friend, these so-called English financiers, but believe me, I will make this picture such a masterpiece that these Parasites of the City will not be good enough to polish our shoes.

[Gabriel Pascal]

87 / To G. Bernard Shaw Location address: Chateau Bellevue
Totnes, S. Devon
24th May 1940

[TL(c): Delacorte: U]

Pascal filmed scenes of Undershaft's village at Dartington.

Dearest G.B.S.

I know you will have sensed that my long silence must have had very serious reasons. When I came back from Dartington ten days ago, the main reason for doing so was that after the invasion of Holland and Belgium the Bank made all kinds of difficulties, and tried to persuade me, with the distributors, to postpone the whole picture. I flatly refused any further postponement; and after a week's fight, I convinced them that it must go on.

I then came back here with the troupe, to finish the whole sequence of Piety Square, Jain Temple, and all the new scenes written by you, for which I have these wonderful backgrounds here. Unfortunately, a few days ago we found that the Kodak negative stock was faulty (one result of the war being that no American stock, the so-called 'Rochester

Kodak,' can be imported any longer); and I am obliged to retake the whole sequence, which I shall finish by the end of this week.

I could then come back to London for a day or two if you would like to see me, to talk over our future plans in the light of what is happening now. Apart from that, my idea is to stay on down here with my Shavian 'Thespis car' and rehearse for a further week, before I start shooting at the studio. By the end of next week we shall know whether it will be possible to start the studio work at all, or not; and in the meantime I believe it will be the wisest course for me to hold my players together here until I have definite news from the Denham Studios that I can continue, rather than to go back to London, and face the danger of their dispersing all over the place in this emergency, so that I lose my control of them ...

[Gabriel Pascal]

88 / To Gabriel Pascal Ayot St Lawrence. Welwyn. Herts.
26th May 1940

[APCS(p): Delacorte: U(e)]

Pascal began location shooting in Devon on this date. From 26 May to 3 June, 900 British ships evacuated 340,000 out of 400,000 British and French troops from Dunkirk. Pascal began filming at Denham Studios on 17 June, three days after the Nazis entered Paris.

Dont bother about me. How can we talk in the light of what is happening when nobody knows what is happening? Stick to Dartington until you are through with it.

You were naturalized just in time. That was a piece of luck to begin with. All I hear now is that officers who can really command are so valuable that you will be conscripted.

GBS

89 / To Gabriel Pascal Ayot St Lawrence. Welwyn. Herts.
23rd June 1940

[APCS(p): Delacorte: U(e)]

On 10 June, Italy declared war on Britain. On 22 June, France concluded an armistice with Germany.

I should have written to you a week ago about the Barbara scenes had I not expected a call from you – God knows why! – on Thursday.

I considered the suggestions very carefully but found them unworkable. It is of the utmost importance in Barbara that there should be none of the old theatrical game of making fun of religion and introducing pious characters only as Tartuff[e]s. To set Miles and Lomax clowning at family prayers would be fatal. We must resist these temptations.

There is nothing that I can put in at the end that will not be out of date a week hence. A broadcast that cost me many days' work was completely knocked out by Musso and the Armistice. Better let well alone. Le mieux est l'ennemie [*sic*] du bien [The best is the enemy of the good].

GBS

Tartuffe, a religious hypocrite, is the title character of the play (1664) by Molière (Jean-Baptiste Poquelin, 1622–73). **Miles** Malleson (1888–1969), British actor, dramatist, and screen writer, played Morrison. The quotation is from *Dictionnaire Philosophique* (1764) by Voltaire (François Marie Arouet, 1694–1778).

90 / To Gabriel Pascal   4 Whitehall Court. London SW1
                                              28th February [*error for* June] 1940
[APCS: Letters]

My dear Gabriel

Don't give way to fancies about my moods. I am a proper tra[de]sman and not a gentleman-amateur with moods. When there is a job to be done I do it, as you know, without waiting for moods. But this thing that you want is

W R O N G

and mustn't be done. The play must begin with two people, rousing interest in two *new* couples, all six piling up the interest in Undershaft, the protagonist. Then they must go away one after the other until even Lady Britomart goes and leaves Stephen to finish the sequence *alone*. It would be utterly spoilt if you introduced the two couples before Brit & Stephen have prepared their appearance. The unity of place must be kept unbroken throughout: a change to the nursery would break it, and cost a new scene which would do nothing but mischief. So put it out of your too active mind.

The stills are splendid. Barbara must keep sunny – no Maiden's Prayer business – until the blow of Bodger's Whiskey falls.

I expected the trouble about Cusins. Stephen Murray is, I suppose, unobtainable; but there is a young actor named Guinness whom you ought to see. L.H. is quite out of the question: be adamant on that. If you cannot get the right man, take the bull by the horns and cast Hudd to Cusins. He is wasted on Stephen, who is much easier to cast.

In great haste to catch the post: therefore brusque,

GBS

The film's distributors wanted Leslie Howard (**L.H.**) to act Cusins, thereby reuniting the stars of *Pygmalion*. From the outset, Shaw and Pascal opposed Howard in the role. Pascal cast Andrew Osborn (1912–85), who resembled Howard, and filmed some scenes with him on location in Devon; but he became dissatisfied with Osborn and dropped him. Stephen **Murray** (1912–83), a veteran of Shavian roles, was the Second Constable in *Pygmalion*. After the war, Alec (later Sir Alec) **Guinness** (b. 1914), a stage star, would have a spectacular movie career.

91 / To G. Bernard Shaw [*no address*]
3rd July 1940
[TL(c): Delacorte: U(e)]

My dearest G.B.S.

I received your letter of the 28th June, with its Mene Tekel inscription: 'WRONG.'

I agree dramatically with what you say about the unity of place; but leave it to me, without going into polemics, to keep my faithfulness to you as artist, and at the same time to cut away when that is demanded by the iron law of movement, which is the basic element of the cinema (and the reason why it is also called 'movies'). So please have faith in my judgment where to intercut short movements, always respecting your dialogue. I do it in extreme necessity.

I am glad you like the stills. I will send you another batch at the end of this week. I agree with you that Wendy should be sunny, and I am keeping all the scenes before her breakdown in this mood.

I saw Alec Guinness weeks ago, but it is uncertain whether we could get his exemption; so I decided definitely on Rex Harrison, who is excellent, as you will see from the stills. I certainly had a great fight with the distributors over the whole L.H. question, and I am happy it has turned out this way ...

[Gabriel Pascal]

Mene Tekel is part of the handwriting on the wall (Daniel 5:25–7): 'God hath numbered thy kingdom, and finished it. Thou art weighed in the balances, and art found wanting.' The **iron law of movement** may pun on the English economist David Ricardo's (1772–1823) 'iron law of wages' which, ironically, Shaw had repudiated. Rex (later Sir Rex) **Harrison** (né Reginald Carey, 1908–90), handsome and debonair, became internationally renowned on stage and screen. His most famous role was Higgins in *My Fair Lady* (1956), the musical adaptation of *Pygmalion*.

92 / To Gabriel Pascal   4 Whitehall Court. London SW1
                              6th July 1940

[TLS: Letters]

Shooting for Major Barbara *was scheduled for ten weeks. About six had passed and, with time-consuming retakes, which the actors thought were endless, Pascal was behind schedule and over budget. Fearful of how much this novice director might cost them, his financial backers tried, unsuccessfully, to supplant him with the director of* Pygmalion. *The war also created delays and would soon create more. On 10 July, the Battle of Britain began, with the Nazis bombing English cities as well as military targets. Chiefly as a result of wartime catastrophes,* Major Barbara *took six months to shoot. As he had done on* Pygmalion, *Pascal sold portions of his share or priority on his return to obtain more funds.*

My dear Gabriel

As I feared, you have made a worse financial mess of Barbara than you did of Pygmalion. Things have now come to a crisis at which the film has already cost twice what it should. Yet it is still unfinished. The financiers wont go in; the cast is exhausted and sulky; and you have lost your head. And the financiers' notion of saving the situation is to call in Anthony Asquith, L.H. having opened his mouth too wide!

Now here are my instructions, which you must obey like a lamb. You will finish screening my script, *without a single retake*, until you have it complete. When it is finished, and not until then, you will go through the rushes and be satisfied with what is good enough, no matter how much better you could make it if you had another hundred thousand pounds and another six months. Any sequences that are really unpresentable you can then retake. Nobody with any artistic or technical pretensions is to be allowed to interfere with you; but Woolf and Davenport must stand over you with revolvers and stop you ruthlessly if you waste a penny or a foot of film by attempting to take anything twice over. The cast must absolutely refuse to do anything twice over. You must finish, finish, finish at all sacrifices until a Barbara film is ready for release, no matter how far it may fall short of *the* film of which you dream.

If you do this Woolf and the bank will recover their lost confidence in you; the cast will recover their spirits; and Davenport may be able to induce them to go on when they see that they are no longer throwing good money after bad.

This is clear and exact: will you do it or wont you?

If you would like to come to Ayot St Lawrence on Sunday at 12.30, so that we can have an hour before lunch for a glorious row, do so (let me know tomorrow); for I can stand up to you and none of the rest can. The situation is desperate; and you alone can retrieve it by doing seriously what I tell you.

Ring up Whitehall tomorrow.

> Your thoroughly alarmed
> and now iron jawed
> GBS

---

93 / To G. Bernard Shaw [*no address*]
16th July 1940

[TL(c): Delacorte: U]

Dearest G.B.S.

... The only thing that is hindering us from finishing the last scenes of Act II is that poor Donald Calthrop died very suddenly yesterday morning, just when we were supposed to start shooting his final scenes in the picture. I was called early in the morning by a doctor, who said Calthrop had been unwell for two days. I was suspicious that he was not the right doctor for me, and sent at once for Professor Plesch; but ten minutes before Plesch arrived, the poor sweet soul ran away from his years of sufferance.

So the problem is as follows: I am missing five lines of dialogue from the final scene of Act II (pp. 300–302 of the play).

> 'Don't you hit her when she's down.'
> 'Ain't you? You'd sell yourself to the devil for a pint of beer; on'y there ain't no devil to make the offer.'
> 'And dear at the money!'
> 'You make too much of him, miss, in your innocence.'
> 'You've youth and hope. That's two better than me.'

That is all, provided I sacrifice your supplementary scene outside the eating-house, which is really not so essential.

For these five lines, I must either find an actor who can copy Donald's make-up, and play the scene principally on Wendy; or ask you to re-write the scene between Bill and Barbara, keeping Peter Shirley as much as possible in the background for one or two lines, or giving his lines to Rummy. I know this is a barbaric suggestion, but I am so confused for the moment until I find the right double that I cannot make a better one. To re-take all Donald's previous scenes – as the financiers, strangely enough, proposed to me – would be madness, and treachery against poor Donald's spirit; because he played his scenes so perfectly that no actor in the world could repeat his performance.

So please speak to Miss Marjorie Deans, my scenario-editor, and give her your instructions as to what you suggest I should do.

[Gabriel Pascal]

Donald **Calthrop** (1888–1940) played Peter Shirley. To film his final scene, another actor was made up to look like him and was photographed from the rear in a long shot; still another actor, imitating Calthrop's voice, dubbed dialogue. Shaw agreed to transfer to Rummy Mitchens the third and fourth speeches quoted by Pascal. The dubbing actor spoke the first and fifth speech, and the second was transferred to a separate scene. Marjorie **Deans** (1901–82) worked closely with Pascal as his assistant on this film and on *Caesar and Cleopatra*.

94 / To G. Bernard Shaw   [*no address*]

24th July 1940

[TL(c): Delacorte: U(e)]

My dearest G.B.S.

I have some good news for your birthday. Yesterday the representatives of the Ministry of Information, Sir Kenneth Clark and Mr Beddington, saw a rough cut of half of the second act. Mr New, our banker, Oscar Deutsch, the greatest exhibitor in this country, who has contracted our picture for all his Odeon cinemas, and the distributor, C.M. Woolf, were also present. In the evening I had a short meeting with Oscar Deutsch, who embraced me, and declared, in the presence of the manager of a great American company, that what he had seen was the greatest piece of art he ever saw on the screen. And Davenport, who was also at this screening, reports that Mr C.M. Woolf was beaming with joy, Mr New moved to tears, and that the rest of those who were present went into superlatives of praise ...

Today was to have been our last day on Act II. Unfortunately Wendy became ill, and I was obliged to send her home at lunchtime and now her doctor has asked us to give her three or four days' sick-leave, or it may mean three or four weeks. She has a bad throat. This is a new delay, but I will manage it somehow; and I hope it will in any case be covered by the insurance, so don't worry about it.

Thank you for the few lines for Rummy and Barbara, which saved the end of the second act for me. As you will see from the stills (P.2-115), I was able, through this new scene of yours, to make good the sad loss of Donald Calthrop, whose double is so good that nobody will discover in the end that Calthrop is missing. You can see him in the stills numbered P.2 97 and 99, in the background.

Now, my dear archangel, as you have already refused to accept a birth-day-present from me, I am, on this birthday of yours, going to ask for a birthday present from you. As we always foresaw, the best part in this play is that of Bill Walker; and the actor, Robert Newton, as you can see from the stills, has surpassed everything we ever expected from an actor of the young generation in England. His last scene in the second act is so powerful, and leaves such an expectation in the minds of the audience, that it would be a crime to deprive them of a further scene with Bill in the third act.

So please, for once in your life, be patient with me and yourself. Don't jump from your desk, but have a real Shavian inspiration, and bring Bill back in the picture. What I suggest is that in the Shelter, after Bill's line: 'There it is! Take it or leave it!' when he flings down the pound, Undershaft should take him aside, give him his visiting-card, and tell him to come and see him at his factory. This would mean only one line. We could then have a real scene between Barbara and Bill at the factory, to come somewhere between the end of the bargaining scene, with her line: 'Is the bargain closed, Dolly?' and her final scene with Cusins, beginning: 'Barbara: I am going to accept this offer.'

My idea is that the same morning when Barbara and the rest of the family visit the factory, Bill has also gone there himself, and been given a job, with the result that he is a happy, changed man; in one word converted – through Barbara – to a new life, and certainly one day he will be the Bilton of the Factory.

Believe me, dear G.B.S., it is not madness that I am asking, and it will not disturb the structure of your play. On the contrary, it will bring a future workman of the factory of the future nearer to the heart of Barbara and Cusins, and nearer to the hearts of the audience. Your whole life, as you told me at our last lunch at Ayot, you were fighting for the people, the English workers; so let it be shown clearly in 'MAJOR BARBARA' that the good-hearted young man of the people, put in the right way, will be one of the best co-operators in the new Undershaft factory, when it is re-organised by Barbara and Cusins. Such a scene will have a great meaning in these hard times, where our only hope is towards the working-classes; and this genuine fellow of the gutter will be a symbol for thousands of young people who need a Major Barbara.

So whatever happens, don't throw away this suggestion in your youthful birthday mood. If you don't like it at once, wait another twenty-four hours, when you will feel forty years younger again, and then give me this new scene. I am begging for it not only for myself, as your faithful producer, but in the name of millions of people who will see our picture, and will enjoy this new scene written by you together with the other new scenes you have written with such admirable youthfulness for the film. Don't tell me as an excuse that this will add to the cost of the picture. I have the sets there, and this one scene won't cost me a cent more. It will mean a few hours' work, and the actor who plays Bill is at my disposal under his contract.

Believe me, my dramatic instinct is right. We can't leave Bill out of the third act. His part is perfect in the play; but in the cinema we must bring back such an important character in the last third of the picture ...

[Gabriel Pascal]

Sir (later Lord) Kenneth Mackenzie **Clark** (1903–83), author and art historian, was director of the National Gallery 1934–45. John **Beddington** (d. 1959, age 66) was director of the films division of the Ministry of Information. Mr **New** was with the National Provincial Bank. Oscar **Deutsch** (d. 1941, age 48) was chairman of the board of Odeon film theatres. As Bill Walker, Robert **Newton** (1905–65), British character actor, was a big hit.

95 / To Gabriel Pascal

Ayot St Lawrence. Welwyn. Herts.
28th July 1940

[TLS(tr): Delacorte: U(e)]

My dear Gabriel

It is not possible to bring back Bill unless you are prepared for his marrying Barbara and becoming the hero of the play in place of Cusins. He is finished and done with in the second act. To drag him back merely to give the actor another turn because he is so good is one of those weaknesses which an author must resist: to bring an actor on the stage with nothing to do after he has made his effect in scenes where he was all important is to spoil his part and make a disappointment of him instead of a success.

I say nothing about the impossibility of his becoming a model citizen with a new suit of clothes in a single night: audiences accept such impossibilities, as they do in the case of Shirley.

What you really miss is a more complete reassurance of Barbara as to the loss of Bill's soul. But the only way to mend that is by enlarging Undershaft's speech to her before they go to the factory when she reproaches him with having turned her convert into a wolf, like this –

'Did he not spit in Todger's eye to save his honor? Did he not give up his hard earned pound to save his soul? Do you not know what a pound means to such a man?: more than ten thousand pounds to me! Will he ever strike a woman again as he struck Jenny Hill? It is your faith that is failing, not his. You have set him on the road to his salvation: it may not be your road; but he will not turn back. You have finished with Bill: your work is done in the Army. So put on your hat and come and have a look at *my* work.'

You can put that patch into the reel if you like: it will give Barbara a better cue for recovering her joyousness; but that is all that can be done.

You know I would change the last act if I could; but it will not work.

My apologies for interfering on Friday. I tried to keep quiet; but I suddenly felt 20 years younger, and couldnt.

GBS

On Shaw's birthday, **Friday** 26 July, he visited the Albert Hall, where Pascal shot the large Salvation Army meeting, and was an enthusiastic extra in the crowd.

96 / To Gabriel Pascal

Ayot St Lawrence. Welwyn. Herts.
[28 July 1940]

[APCS (p): Delacorte: U(e)]

The flourish for the brass is in B flat; so the conductor told me.

Ask him to try the effect of a single trombone sounding G flat quite quietly after the others have stopped, Undershaft pretending to play it. It ought to have the effect of a question.

It must not be harsh or ugly. The band is first rate, and should not be asked to do anything inartistic or comic. The more you have of it at its best the better.

I forgot to say this in my letter to Denham, which unfortunately missed the village post this afternoon.

GBS

Muir Mathieson (1911–75), British **conductor** and musical director of hundreds of films, conducted the music for *♪ ajor Barbara*.

97 / To G. Bernard Shaw　　　　　　　Denham Film Studios
Denham. nr. Uxbridge. Middlesex
31st July 1940

[TL(c): Delacorte: U]

My dearest G.B.S.

Thank you for your letter of the 28th July, and your card the following day. First, about the flourish for the brass: I gave your message to the conductor, asking him to try the effect of a single trombone sounding G-flat; and I am grateful for your suggestion, as I myself felt after you left that the discord would be vulgar. I think the conductor will now be able to put it right, according to your advice.

Now about Bill: I agree with you that to bring Bill to an important issue in the third act would upset the balance of the relationship between Barbara and Cusins. But I will surprise you with a little scene at the end of the picture, to prove Barbara's success by letting Bill appear, clean and shaven, and giving him two of your own lines re-echoed. Please let me surprise you with this little scene when you see the picture.

I am really delighted with the supplementary lines enlarging Undershaft's speech to Barbara, and I think these will be a very great help for the short scene between them. I would be very grateful if you could give me some supplementary lines for Barbara also at this point, before her line: 'Oh, you are right: he can never be lost now: where was my faith?' because her metamorphosis seems to be too abrupt ...

[Gabriel Pascal]

As the last paragraph of Shaw's card indicates, he wrote it the same, not **the following**, day.

98 / To Gabriel Pascal　　　　　　Ayot St Lawrence. Welwyn. Herts.
[4 August 1940]

[APCS(p): Delacorte: U]

I forgot to say that the real difficulty about Bill is that he would never come to a tall hat and hymnbook: that is not how his conversion would take him. You should have made him shadow Barbara until she threw herself into the river (instead of her hat) and then jump in and rescue her ...

Bergner, still persistent, says the film will not be out until 1945. The sooner we get it and the Disciple out the better.

GBS

99 / To G. Bernard Shaw   [*no address*]

15th August 1940

[TL(c): Delacorte: U]

My dearest G.B.S.

... About Bergner, I also received a note that she is anxious to do the play, and I heard at the same time from the Theatre Guild about Katharine Hepburn. Certainly if you change your mind about allowing the play to be produced before the picture is ready, it would be preferable to give permission to Hepburn. Little Elizabeth is a fool, because I shall have produced at least twelve of your stories by 1945.

Anyway I agree with you that our next two pictures will be 'ST JOAN' and 'THE DEVIL'S DISCIPLE.' I will start on 'ST JOAN' as soon as Barbara is finished.

I hope you and Madame Charlotte will be able to see, in two weeks' time, the whole of the second act in the definite cut, but without the final music, which I will re-record with William Walton at the end of the picture.

Yesterday I again saw Bob Donat in 'DEVIL'S DISCIPLE.' He told me that you had been there in the afternoon, and he was very pleased that you had told the Manager you like his performance. He is keen to play the part in our picture, but he believes that it should be an American actor to do it perfectly. What is your opinion? We once together selected Gary Cooper for the part, from his photos. Give me your reaction, because I will make my dispositions accordingly ...

Bob Donat asked me whether, if I screened the second act for you, he might be present. The best thing would be if you and Madame Charlotte could come to lunch, a week on Monday, at my house near the studio, and have the screening afterwards; because it would make great difficulties to have it in town. My house would be at your disposal, and you could have your afternoon rest there. So please let me know your decision about this.

I forgot to remind you last time about my suggestion for the introductory titles of the picture. I think we discussed it once, and you liked the idea; which is, that after the title 'GABRIEL PASCAL PRESENTS' you should appear on the screen, seated at your desk. You take your pen in your hand; then I have a Close-up of your right hand as you start to write the following titles, each one on a separate sheet, which you turn over as it is finished: Scenario and Dialogue by yourself; the names of the three stars; my name as producer and director; William Walton for the music; then, on one page, the names of the technical staff, for which I will give you a list in due course. Finally, on a separate page, you write the following lines with your own hand, the camera showing each word as you write it: 'This play of mine, Major Barbara, is, I hope, both true and inspired; but whoever says that it all happened, and that faith in it and understanding of it consist in believing that it is a record of an actual occurrence, is, to speak according to Scripture, a fool and a liar, and is hereby solemnly denounced and cursed as such by me, the author, to all posterity.'

This last page will be accompanied by William Walton's heavenly music, and I think it will be the most dignified introduction for our picture. I hope you like the idea. I shall put the full cast of the picture at the end this time, so that we don't waste too much time before we come to the action.

[Gabriel Pascal]

The **Theatre Guild,** founded in New York in 1919 to produce non-commercial plays, was very influential in American theatre, especially during its early years. It presented so many works by Shaw that it was sometimes known as 'the House of Shaw.' Katharine **Hepburn** (b. 1907), durable star of American films and stage since 1932, greatly admired Shaw. After his death, she had a great success in the title role of *The Million-airess* in London and New York (1952). William (later Sir William) **Walton** (1902–83), British composer of symphonies, concertos, operas, and oratorios, wrote film scores, including that of *Major Barbara. The Devil's Disciple* opened in London 24 July 1940. Gary **Cooper** (né Frank James Cooper, 1900–61), an American film star for decades, did not act in any of Shaw's films. By **titles,** Pascal means credits. Pascal's proposed **lines** are from Shaw's preface to the play.

100 / To Gabriel Pascal   4 Whitehall Court. London SW1
                                      16th August 1940
[TLS: Letters]

Dear Gabriel

I think it would be unwise to give the Americans a Hepburn impression of Joan immediately before Wendy. It might make Wendy quite unacceptable. The present impression is one left by Cornell, which will be on the whole helpful. I shall therefore not license any American Joan until the film is safely established.

I saw The Devil's Disciple on Wednesday. The production is so outrageously bad that if I could have done so without breaking my neck I should have jumped from my box on to the stage and rehearsed it before the audience. On the screen it would be quite impossible. The minister's wife, instead of being a pretty nonentity, is a raving madwoman. The whole affair is provincial, and second-rate at that. The final scene with the gallows is ridiculous. I wish I had seen it earlier: I would not for worlds have let you get an impression of the play from it.

The secret of its success is plain enough. Richard, instead of being a tragic figure and a complicated character, is played by Donat as a good-natured blackguard: always a popular part on the stage. The rest is mere 'support' for him. This simplifies the play and secures an Elephant and Castle success thanks to Donat's popularity (he does it very well); but it would not make a Pascal success; and there is no proof in it that Donat can give us the real Devil's Disciple.

I left the theatre without saying a word in praise of the performance; and I have written to Donat about it in terms which make my opinion of it quite clear. I have no objection to his being present at the screening: in fact I should like to meet him. Probably he is right about an American actor being desirable for Richard; but the part is on the plane on which there is no nationality. The sergeant and the two British officers would have to be English. With Trouncer as Anderson and either Thesiger or Arliss as Burgoyne I could make a production that would astonish the simpletons who think the show at the Piccadilly a good one.

I dont think Madame Charlotte will venture to make a day of it at

Denham; but if we could drive there for an hour or so at half-past four or five I daresay I could persuade her to come. But when I am in London I can always run down by train.

G. Bernard Shaw

The **Elephant and Castle** Theatre, London, which became a cinema theatre in 1928, used to be associated with melodramas. Ernest **Thesiger** (1879–1961) played the Dauphin in the first London production of *Saint Joan* (1924) and other Shavian roles. George **Arliss** (né George Augustus Andrews, 1868–1946), British stage actor, was a film star in England and the United States.

101 / To G. Bernard Shaw [Denham Film Studios
Denham. nr. Uxbridge. Middlesex]
23rd August 1940

[TL(c): Delacorte: U]

My dearest G.B.S.

Thank you for your letter of the 16th August. I have been very busy for several days past finishing the last scenes of the first act; and to-day I have started on the third act. So more than three-quarters of the picture is definitely finished; and what is even more important, I have come to a satisfactory arrangement with the bank, Woolf and Rank – without any outside help, on the contrary, with the elimination of Sidney Wright and Davenport – to secure the money to finish the picture in *my* way. It was a great help to me that Jock Whitney was ready to send me the money on bank interest, and that another friend of mine was also ready to put down the supplementary capital; so that with the material worries over, I think I will produce the most dynamic last part ever made in any picture.

Herewith the latest stills, which will show you the completion of the first act ...

I am very grateful that you refused to license any American Joan for the stage until our film is established, which it will be very soon.

About the Piccadilly production of 'Devil's Disciple' I agree a hundred per cent that it is a provincial concept. I think Donat makes it very easy for himself by playing Richard as the mere 'bonhomme adventurer,' and it certainly takes away all the great tragical shadows behind him, with[out] which spiritual background the dualistic character of

Richard – who was certainly a 'Gemini' – is lost. I never for a second really contemplated casting Bob for Dudgeon. I always wanted him for Dubedat in 'Doctor's Dilemma,' but I am afraid he is now too old for it. The best Richard Dudgeon is, as I have always said, Gary Cooper. I also have always thought that the part should in any case be played by an American actor; but I shall certainly cast English actors for the two British officers and the sergeant. Thank you for your excellent suggestion of Arliss for Burgoyne. I will write at once to his Hollywood manager ...

[Gabriel Pascal]

102 / To Gabriel Pascal [4 Whitehall Court. London SW1]
29th August 1940

[APCS: Barbara]

... The stills are first rate. It is an immense step from the stage, where however you may disguise it, the characters have to be in a row facing the audience the same way all the time, to the screen as you handle it.

[GBS]

103 / To G. Bernard Shaw [Denham Film Studios
Denham. nr. Uxbridge. Middlesex]
6th September 1940

[TL(tr): Delacorte: U]

... These last weeks since I saw you it has been very hard to work, because there have been three, four or five air raids every day. Just when I had finally reorganized myself, and everything was going according to schedule, the fat pig Goering upset the apple-cart with his air-armada; and certainly I am doubly grateful to our heroic pilots, because it is only thanks to them that I shall be able to finish this picture. Otherwise, Denham would be a heap of ashes, and our negative[s] so much dust in the air. But I feel now that if I can do only three or four hours daily, I shall still finish everything in a few weeks ...

G.P.

Hermann **Goering** (1893–1946) was Hitler's air minister.

104 / To G. Bernard Shaw

[Denham Film Studios
Denham. nr. Uxbridge. Middlesex]
6th September 1940

[TL(c): Delacorte: U]

My dearest G.B.S.

As I wrote to you on the 23rd August, I have made a new deal with G.F.D. and Mr Woolf, who have given a guarantee to the Bank to advance me an additional £50,000 to finish this picture.

When I made the deal three weeks ago, the 5th October was established as the final shooting date; but through these air-raids I have again lost six or seven days, so that it should be around the 12th October. But I am afraid it may be the 15th before I can actually dismiss the unit.

Accordingly a supplementary letter has been appended to the original financing and distributing contract. I will send you a copy of this letter as soon as the lawyers hand it to me. My first condition, as I told you at our last meeting, was the protection of your 10% royalty, which is automatically included in the supplementary agreement; and my big fight with the distributors and the bank has been to protect the money which you so kindly put at my disposal from your 'PYGMALION' income, which will amount, at the end of this year, to about £20,000. The distributors have now consented to allow £5,000 of the money the Company owes you to rank as a charge *pari passu* [at an equal rate] with the distributors' charge on the American receipts; the distributors' charge, as you may remember, counting second to that of the Bank.

When the Bank agreed to finance MAJOR BARBARA, I was obliged to sign a letter stating that I mortgaged to the Bank not only the 'MAJOR BARBARA' income (always excluding your 10% royalties), but also the entire 'PYGMALION' income; so when I made the new deal with C.M. Woolf my condition was that the money the Company owes you on 'PYGMALION' should rank *pari passu* with this additional £50,000; but as always, when the deal came into the hands of the respective lawyers everything looked differently, and they agreed only to the above-mentioned £5,000.

Finally, as a compromise, Mr New of the National Provincial Bank has agreed that all the future income of 'PYGMALION,' which is not inconsiderable, shall be free from any mortgage; and I arranged with the Board of Directors that the whole of this should be paid to you as soon as the

Company receives it, in monthly payments starting from the 1st October. So I think you should be able to calculate on receiving a considerable part of your 'PYGMALION' income by the end of the year; and I hope I did my best for you.

Now that I know with a good conscience that your interests are protected, I don't regret that I have not forced the issue in fighting for my own material interests any further than I did. After this picture I am convinced I shall never need any capitalists in my life. Then the distributors will distribute our pictures on a smaller percentage basis than the present rate. So I look very optimistically towards the future, and close this unpleasant business letter with my most affectionate greetings.

[Gabriel Pascal]

105 / To Gabriel Pascal Denham
12th September 1940

[ANU: Delacorte: U(e)]

On this date, Shaw went to Denham studios and, before he left, sent Pascal nine small pages, the first of which he dated and titled 'SHAW'S REHEARSAL NOTES.' It is unclear which scenes he saw while they were filmed and which he saw in rushes.

Cusins thinks that when an actor is unfortunate enough to have to speak old fashioned verse, he should be as colloquial as possible so as to make it sound like cup and saucer small talk. This of course only throws the verse away. When I write verse it must be deliberately declaimed as such.

Morrison's part does not come off. Miles plays the conventional self-possessed butler. He should be older, mortally afraid of Lady B., and knocked all to pieces by the amazing reappearance of Undershaft. This is all the more important as Aylmer now introduces the self-possessed valet.

Snobby has not thought about his part. He makes him a smart cockney from beginning to end without the least variety.

The acting value of the part lies in the contrast between the smart cockney talking honestly to Rummy, and the snivelling canting mock-pious hypocrite when the others are present. Emlyn ought to be ashamed of himself.

Nobody seems to have been brought up religiously. Such passages as the two ways to salvation (from the Church Catechism) and 'the peace that passeth all understanding' are slurred over because nobody recognizes nor understands them. The two ways – baptism and the Supper of Our Lord – in their contrast to money and gunpowder go for nothing.

Lomax, like Snobby, is on one note all through: a stage 'silly ass.' But he should be portentously slow and solemn when he pontificates about 'a certain amount of tosh.' The point is that though he is a foolish figure he always says something sensible. He should 'take the stage' every time he pontificates. And his laugh is all wrong in the first act. It should burst out like the neigh of a horse, loud enough to scandalize Lady B, and provoke her explosion. She needs the cue.

When Lady B. calls them all names in the last act the whole effect is lost by her moving about from one to the other. She should stand like Jove hurling thunderbolts, only her eyes flashing in all directions – a close-up – and then turn her back and march away. A glimpse of the expressions of her victims may follow if you like. Lady B's explosions should be helped out by solo pictures close up as much as possible.

I doubt whether Wendy understands Barbara. As Eliza, whom she *did* understand, her face changed marvellously with every wave of feeling. In Barbara her face never changes at all. But to tell her so would only discourage her. If she is a heathen, like all these young people, you cannot convert her at rehearsal.

Bill Walker misses the full effect of his repeated 'Leave me alone's to Barbara. They are merely petulant and brusque. They should be agonized. He should be writhing, not bullying.

This is the only fault, almost, in his performance. He is very good. He is quite new to me: I never heard of him before.

[GBS]

'**Cup and saucer**' refers to mid-nineteenth-century realistic dramas in which characters drank tea while discussing their problems. Felix (later Sir Felix) **Aylmer** (né Felix Edward Aylmer-Jones, 1889–1979), British film actor, played Undershaft's valet, a role Shaw created for the film. The quotation in paragraph five is from Philippians 4:7.

106 / To G. Bernard Shaw [Denham Film Studios
Denham. nr. Uxbridge. Middlesex]
14th September 1940

[TL(c): Delacorte: U(e)]

Shaw returned to Denham on the 13th to film a preface for American audiences, observing that as they are sending Britain their old destroyers for use against Nazi Germany, he is sending them his old plays. Shaw's address is published in his Collected Plays with Their Prefaces, *vol. 3.*

My dearest G.B.S.

Let me thank you for all your kindness to me yesterday, and for your wonderful speech. I believe this great message will help our country more than all the diplomatic speeches of boring old gagas which we listen to on the radio. I shall send this speech over on the next Clipper – unfortunately the laboratory cannot have it ready for the Clipper today; and the second speech I shall use only a few weeks before the premier.

I will make the few corrections you suggested, and I think we shall have a decent film-translation of your play. The only thing that is worrying me day and night, as I tried to express to you yesterday a few minutes before your departure, is the opening of the picture. Marie Lohr, in the first scene with Stephen, is a disaster, in spite of the fact that I have retaken it three times. The simple truth is that she has not the personality. Her lips are not following the reflections of her brain, because the poor old girl has none; so she is acting on my direction like a puppet in the most horrid materialistic way, and killing the wonderful points in this first scene one after the other. I hope, however, to be able to save the scene by clever cutting and editing; but we need something similar to the prologue you wrote for me in 'PYGMALION,' a short introductory sequence of two or three scenes between Barbara and Cusins. So I have dictated a suggested series of scenes, which I am sending you herewith. The whole thing sounds long on paper, but it would take at the outside two minutes on the screen.

For Wendy Hiller's speech, which I propose should be the closing speech of a short meeting, I remembered a speech I heard last year in New York, when I went to see Katharine Cornell in her last play, and walked outside the theatre during the interval onto the corner of Forty-

Fourth Street and Broadway. I asked Major Sowton, the head of the Intelligence Department of the Salvation Army in London, to trace the young Major who was speaking there on the 16th June of last year; and she cabled her speech back to him. Here it is:

Amid all the noise and hurry of this street it is still true that God is in this place. We do not need a temple, built by the hands of men, in which to worship Him. Here on this street corner, beneath God's open sky, we can draw near to Him. Some of you feel Him near you, even now, and feel, too, how much you need Him. Won't you let Him come into your life to-night? You want His guidance, His strength, His comfort – you need His forgiveness and friendship. Is there anyone who has courage enough to raise his hand as a sign that he would like us to pray for him? Make the decision now – in your need and loneliness God can meet with you. (She pauses and looks round the audience.) Someone feels that he should raise his hand, but it isn't easy. You feel too shy, perhaps? Never mind. I can feel who wants to raise his hand. Shall we bow our heads in prayer, and pray specially for him who should decide to-night?

You would certainly need to rewrite this in your own way; but believe me, my dearest maestro, I have an unfailing instinct for pictures as you have for the stage, and I believe that a prologue of this kind is needed very badly, to introduce the relationship between Barbara and Cusins in short flashes, with a musical background by William Walton. After such a prologue the audience would follow the opening scene of the play with more concentration, and be willing to swallow Marie Lohr's slow acting.

The sets which I need for these scenes would be here at my disposal, taken from the Shelter sets, so it would not cost me a penny of supplementary money; and it would mean no more than one-and-a-half days' work, which I could fit in very well next Tuesday and Wednesday, because the Administration Building and Terrace, with the big Woolwich gun, set will not be ready before Thursday, and I am paying the artists on a weekly basis without doing anything.

So I ask you, as Undershaft asks Cusins: 'Be reasonable,' and revise my suggested prologue scenes. I will send my driver for them on Monday morning ...

[Gabriel Pascal]

In 1939, the Pan-American Dixie **Clipper** began the first regular transatlantic flights to Lisbon. In 1940, the Clipper was making weekly flights between New York and London. The Cornell **play** was *No Time for Comedy* (1939) by S(amuel) N(athaniel) Behrman (1893–1973). Major George **Sowton** (1902–49), born in the United States, was in the Salvation Army's Publicity Department. Shaw rewrote Barbara's opening speech along the lines Pascal proposed.

107 / To G. Bernard Shaw

[*no address*]
20th September 1940

[TL(c): Delacorte: U]

My dearest G.B.S.

For days I have been trying to write to you, and every day I have had to postpone thanking you for the wonderful prologue you have written. I am convinced we shall now have the best start a picture ever had. Strangely enough these stupid Pagliacci, Rex Harrison and Wendy Hiller, are grumbling about the scenes being too long etc; but actors are the silliest children in the world. In their conceit they believe they have the right to criticise a scene which they ought to be grateful and happy to play.

I am particularly disappointed in Wendy Hiller, whose grumbling over your heavenly lines has estranged me from her completely; and I think we should very seriously consider the proposition of Katharine Hepburn for 'ST JOAN.' I have again received news that she is mad to play it, whereas I have the impression that Wendy is anxious to do a non-Shaw picture next, and I am not interested in producing anything besides your plays. You see, dear G.B.S., the actress who plays St Joan should adore each phase of her part religiously, should have a limitless love and adoration for your work, should be a girl without any exterior vanity, who would work in full harmony with me, the director; and I cannot, unfortunately, say this of Wendy Hiller. She wore the white blouse in the first act against my express wish; and she is always grumbling against your river scene with the night watchman, where she throws her bonnet into the river, which I find most moving, but she has the courage to ridicule it. So I believe the poor girl's too great success as Eliza went to her head, and she thinks that with one picture she can have the allure of a world star. She will have an even greater success as Major Barbara, and it will be impossible to work harmoniously with her in the future. Don't believe I have anything against her, but I am afraid we must put her out of our minds for St Joan. If you agree with me, I will take immediate steps to negotiate with Katharine Hepburn, or else to find a new actress; because while I am editing and dubbing the picture, I would like to start on the preparations for 'SAINT JOAN.'

I have one more set to do. This is on the Terrace of Undershaft's Administration Building. After that there are some little unimportant bits, close-ups etc; so if this set is ready next week, I hope that in eight days I can finish all the Terrace scenes, which are: the foundling confession scene, the whole argument between Undershaft and Barbara, the earthquake speech, the 'Scrap it!' speech, and the final scene of the picture ...

P.S. After I had dictated this letter (incidentally, your scenario posted last Monday afternoon arrived only yesterday!) I received your rehearsal notes of the 12th September. When I had finished dictating the letter I asked Marjorie if she thought I should give Wendy another chance, because I was so in despair about her lack of feeling after the second act. Marjorie advised me: 'No, send the letter. You must tell G.B.S. how you feel.' And here we are, my dear great master! Practically, we don't need to write to each other, our spiritual contact is stronger than anything else.

Your last phrase about Wendy in the rehearsal notes: 'If she is a heathen, like all these young people, you cannot convert her at rehearsal,' judges her for our future plans for St Joan. I could convert, maybe, a naive heathen, but not such a heathen as Wendy Hiller, with the little intellectual support of her school-master husband. She never understood Major Barbara, she never loved the part, and she never will understand it, because she is a little materialistic speculating girl, and nothing else. The freshness she had in 'PYGMALION' is lost. Nevertheless, I hope to push her through the last scene of the picture to a certain spiritual height which will save the finish; so I am not in despair about 'MAJOR BARBARA.'

How completely she lacks any religious feeling is shown by a little episode with the sweet man from the Salvation Army, Major Sowton, who was present one day at the shooting of the scene: 'I want to convert people, not to be always begging for the Army in a way I'd rather die than beg for myself.' I had a difficult argument with Wendy, trying to emphasise Barbara's religious feelings and her love for the poor; and Major

Sowton naturally assisted me in my efforts to explain how much your lines are really in the spirit of the Salvation Army. I asked Wendy very kindly to lunch with Major Sowton, who would like to explain to her several things about the religious feelings of a Salvation Army major; but she refused in her brusque way, saying that she was not interested in Major Sowton, and that she disliked him. I don't like to bore you with plenty of similar episodes, which proved to me that this girl lacks real devotion to art in our sense.

Lady Britomart: I agree completely about her outburst, and will shoot it in the way you suggest.

Snobby: I could not agree more about Emlyn Williams' performance. He behaved himself like a self-conceited narcissist in his part.

Bill Walker: I am glad you like Newton. I have another take for the line 'Leave me alone!' which is more in the sense you indicate.

Morrison: I agree with you, and I think I have a better take where he is more scared of Lady Britomart, which I will use instead of the one you saw.

Lomax: I agree with your conception of Lomax, but as I explained to you Marie Lohr is so slow that I was obliged to change Lomax's speed; and you will see that David Tree will do his part credit.

[Gabriel Pascal]

The **non-Shaw** film Hiller wanted to do was *Love on the Dole*, which was made in 1941, starring Deborah Kerr (née Deborah Kerr-Trimmer, b. 1921), who played Jenny Hill in *Major Barbara*, her film début.

108 / To Gabriel Pascal 4 Whitehall Court. London SW1
25th September 1940

[TLS(tr): Delacorte: U(e)]

The day before, Marjorie Deans wrote to Shaw that Pascal had cut Cusins's 'You really are an infernal old rascal' (she gave no reason, but 'infernal' was a word banned by the Production Code Administration) and needed a line to follow Undershaft's 'No; but I can buy the Salvation Army.'

My dear Gabriel

You must cut out the entrance of Shirley, who can reappear without any explanation when he is wanted later. The sequence will then read

UNDERSHAFT. No; but I can buy the Salvation Army.
CUSINS. Tell that to Barbara if you dare. Here she is.
BARBARA. We have just had a splendid experience meeting etc etc.

The alternative is to restore the omitted 18 speeches between the two
men ending with

UNDERSHAFT. And not on Trade Unionism and Socialism. Excellent.
CUSINS. Bah! You are only a profiteer after all.
UNDERSHAFT. And this is an honest man.

This retains Shirley's entrance; but I recommend the first version, as
it will be much easier, and the omitted altercation, though effective as a
climax, is much more stagey than screeny and not worth the trouble.

In haste
G. Bernard Shaw

109 / To G. Bernard Shaw   [*no address*]
                                                     5th October 1940
[TL(c): Delacorte: U]

Thank you for your additional line for Cusins in the chapel. I prefer the
first suggestion: 'Tell that to Barbara if you dare. Here she comes.' So I
have retaken the scene using this line.

I saw the finished version of your prologue yesterday, and I must congratulate you again. It is a masterly introduction to the play. I made a little change in the setting, and I think you will like it very much. I played
Barbara's speech in the open air, in front of the entrance to the Shelter;
and she and Cusins go inside after her line: 'Friends: you will now sing
"How sweet the name of Jesus sounds."' The reason for this was that if I
had played her scene inside the Shelter I should have had to rebuild the
whole Chapel set, instead of using only a small portion of it, which was
still standing. As it is, I have saved money by using different corners of
the same East End street-market set for both Cusins' and Barbara's
speeches. Their scene inside the Shelter is played in the little office.

I have covered the time-lapse by arranging that before Barbara and

Cusins go to Wilton Crescent for the scene beginning: 'I ring the servants' bell, I suppose?' the preceding scene: 'Have we far to go? What
about a taxi?' is played on a broad East-end street beside a bus-stop. It is
a clear, sunny Sunday afternoon. From Wilton Crescent I dissolve to a
silent scene of Barbara coming out through the doors of the Shelter, followed by Cusins, struggling with the big drum, and children laughing at
him. Then another dissolve to the same bus-stop, with Cusins and Barbara coming down a flight of steps as they did on the first Sunday, this
time in heavy rain; and from there I bring them to their Act I entrance
to Wilton Crescent, which you have seen in the entrance-hall stills. So I
think the motivation for the time-lapse is ingenious enough.

As you will see from the stills I am sending with this letter, I am now
shooting on the last big set, the Terrace in front of the Factory Administration Building. I am also erecting a kind of round vestibule inside the
Building, with the portraits of Undershaft's predecessors on the walls,
where we shall play the Armourer's Faith scene.

I shall have finished the main work by the end of next week. After that
there will be a few bits and pieces, and then I start on my job of editing,
musical recording, and dubbing in two weeks' time; and I hope that in
six weeks the last station of the Calvary will be passed! It was an adventure making your picture during the air-raids; but I confess to you that I
would not like to do it again in these circumstances.

110 / To Gabriel Pascal   Ayot St Lawrence. Welwyn. Herts.
                                      8th October 1940

[APCS(p): Delacorte: U(e)]

*The previous year, Pascal received a proposal to build film studios in Nassau, in
Britain's Bahama Islands (part of the West Indies). Largely because of filming in
Britain during wartime conditions, the proposal was attractive. He and Shaw
referred to the location by all three names.*

Have you the scenario of St Joan I made for Czinner-Bergner? If not, it is
in London and I must get it for you. The snag in the West Indian project
is that I shall not be within reach as I have been for Barbara; so we must
settle the text beforehand.

I am not sure that I did not spoil the play for C-B. I had not then seen what you could do with the stage version or what Elizabeth couldnt; and I broke up the tent scene, and made other changes with her in mind which I should probably not have made with you and G.G. in mind.

We have never discussed Cauchon, the fanatic churchman, nor Stogumber (a terrific acting part never half touched yet), nor Warwick. I suppose Aubrey is now too old: he was always a fine figure of a man – a possible Archbishop anyhow.

GBS

G.G. may be Greta Garbo or Greer Garson. Considering Shaw's attitude towards Garbo, the initials are more likely Garson's.

111 / To Gabriel Pascal   [Ayot St Lawrence. Welwyn. Herts.]
                                           11th October 1940

[TL(tr): Delacorte: U(e)]

All but these two paragraphs of this transcription of Shaw's letter are blacked out.

My dear Gabriel

A letter from New York this morning informs me that K.H. is very very keen on Joan. Wendy did not make much impression in it in Malvern. I thought this was the fault of the producer, who made the fatal mistake of slowing down her last speech, which ought to be a blaze of fury from beginning to end; but after Barbara, and your confirmation of my suspicion that she does not feel religious parts and dislikes them, I am doubtful about her being right for Joan. I have not seen Hepburn act, even on the screen; but the stills of her are very appropriate.

Elizabeth Bergner persists in wanting to play the part on the stage, assuring me that you cannot possibly release the Joan film before 1945. She wants me to make a Pitoëff success by leaving out everything except the crying. I have told her finally that I dread nothing more than a success on these lines, and that she must lasciar ogni speranza [abandon all hope (ye who enter)]. I hope Hepburn is not a cry-baby. She does not look like one; but you never can tell.

[GBS]

Hiller played Joan at Malvern with only six rehearsals. Georges **Pitoëff** (1886–1939),

French director and actor, produced *Saint Joan* in 1925, starring his wife Ludmilla (1895–1951), which was Shaw's first major success in France; but it was an unauthorized revised version of the translation by the Hamons. When Shaw saw it in London in 1930, he disliked it and the star. The phrase '**lasciar** ogni speranza' is the inscription on the entrance to Hell in *The Divine Comedy* (c. 1310–20), *Inferno* III.9, by Dante Alighieri (1265–1321).

112 / To Gabriel Pascal   [Ayot St Lawrence. Welwyn. Herts.]
                                                    15th October 1940
[APCS(p): Delacorte: U]

My dear Gabriel

I still think more and more that the intrusion of Bill at the end of Barbara is a mistake.

But if you are bent on it, try it this way.

As the lorries pass, Bill, in the last of them, waves his hat to Barbara. She looks at him, astonished. Then cries 'Bill!!!' (not to him, but in surprise) and kisses Undershaft for having done this for her.

But nothing will prevent a cast back to Bill from spoiling the end.

The lorries should be simply a cue for Undershaft to point at them and say 'Six o'clock &c &c.' I tell you, drop Bill.

                                                    In haste
                                                    GBS

113 / To Gabriel Pascal   Ayot St Lawrence. Welwyn. Herts.
                                                    7th November 1940
[TLS(p): Delacorte: U(e)]

My dear Gabriel

I approve altogether of the Nassau scheme, and will send you the formal agreements when I get the necessary printed forms from my flat in London.

Meanwhile it is understood and agreed between us that three plays, Saint Joan, Candida and The Devil's Disciple, will be at your disposal on the same original terms, mutatis mutandis [with due alteration of details], *as Major Barbara.*

The experiment of founding a big British industry in the Bahamas is thrillingly interesting. The climate and the proximity to America mark them out for film work, which is much more remunerative than sponges and ambergris and precarious pearls. Their real industry is the tourist business, which is a reed that may be broken at any moment. The development of Nassau into a second Los Angeles would be a tremendous score for the Treasury. It gives new zest to our job; and you are unquestionably the man to carry it through with my plays to begin with.

Conditionally on the Bahama scheme going through you may hold this letter as your security if anything should prevent us from executing a full length agreement as usual. With that in view I sign across a stamp. Witness my hand this 7th day of November nineteen hundred and forty.

G. Bernard Shaw

114 / To Gabriel Pascal   Ayot St Lawrence. Welwyn. Herts.
11th November 1940

[ANS(p): Delacorte: U]

Shaw alludes to the following letter, accompanying this note. Jarka, which probably attracted Pascal as a possibility to make a movie before he found backing for his next Shaw film, has not been located.

Cecil Lewis could do a script for this but to direct it would be a criminal waste of your time and talent.

GBS

115 / To Gabriel Pascal   [*no address*]
11th November 1940

[TLS(p): Delacorte: U]

I cannot recommend Jarka as a war film. It is, in one word, *discouraging*.

The public likes horrors if they are horrible enough; but they do not enjoy having the mere unpleasantness of war rubbed into them when they go to the pictures to forget them. In the Jarka story there is no comfort, no fun, no bucking-up; and the horror at the end is not thrilling: it is revolting. A good boy actor could interest the audience in Jarka; but that sort of interest would not be satisfied by his murdering a sleeping man with a knife, especially after the victim has been presented as a pleasant and popular athlete all through.

The children are very prominent in the story but not in the way that children are attractive. Silent sulky children are not attractive.

The old soldier is a good acting character; but his execution calls the attention of the audience to the weakness in the business of the window bars. A very very small boy could comfortably wriggle between the bars; but he could hardly do it with a suit case. That is a trifle; but it is one of the trifles that pass in a narrative but not in an acted play.

The main objection, however, is that the story is unrelievedly depressing; and the children are very unEnglish and unAmerican.

GBS

116 / To G. Bernard Shaw
[Mumford's Farm
Chalfont St Peter. Bucks.]
12th November 1940

[TL(c): Delacorte: U]

My dearest G.B.S.

... Now about our West Indian project: I have a meeting next Thursday with the Treasury officials. Oscar Deutsch, who is participating in the scheme as exhibitor, is very grateful for your letter, and I think it will influence the Treasury to recognise the British Quota right of all of the pictures I produce there. Once this is established, no further obstacles stand in the way of the quickest realisation of our plans.

It is very strange how our thoughts run parallel. When I received your letter last Saturday, giving me the rights of Joan, Candida, etc, and approving the Nassau scheme, my first thought was that it would all be wonderful but for one thing – how can I work far away from you, and how much I shall miss you during production, humanly and artistically. Our co-operation has worked out so wonderfully on 'Barbara,' and it could be developed even more wonderfully on 'Joan' and our other films because the only way to create a great piece of film art is through this complete co-operation between author and producer. Such a harmony of collaboration can create miracles, and I can serve your ideas and translate them to the masses only if your guiding spirit is near to me. So the only way out will be to follow Madame Charlotte's suggestion and pack up your pigeon-nest next spring onto a nice Clipper, and I will fly over with you to the island of eternal spring, and to the new Renaissance of art which you and I will create there. You are feeling much younger than you did five years ago, when you and I started our strange adventure; so think it over and talk it over at your ease with Madame Charlotte.

Meantime, I agree with you, dear G.B.S., that we must arrange the text beforehand for 'Joan,' 'Devil's Disciple,' and 'Candida.' So I am waiting very anxiously for the script of 'Joan' you speak about, and I could come over every second day from next week onwards, so that we could work together for an hour a day without tiring you. I feel like a new-born Pegasus, with enough force to gallop over all obstacles, and wings to fly out through the stratosphere, and carry your message of truth to the farthest and least-discovered corners of the earth ...

[Gabriel Pascal]

117 / To Gabriel Pascal   Ayot St Lawrence. Welwyn. Herts.
16th November 1940

[APC(p): Delacorte: U(e)]

Shaw enclosed a copy of the Saint Joan *screenplay he had written for Paul Czinner and Elisabeth Bergner. A photocopy of the verso side of this card has not been located.*

My dear Gabriel

This thing is obsolete: it was written when Czinner was dreaming of locations and afraid of too much talk and too little change of scene, and of Elizabeth in the part &c &c &c. Now you have done away with all that Hollywood rubbish and can do better with the play as it stands.

But you had better have it by you, as some bits might be useful.

The idea was to do the Loire and Rouen scenes on location in France, regardless of expense. All nonsense. The original play was designed to be cheap; and your genius is independent of ten pictures a minute.

To change the subject – The Government have made new regulations by which I must pay Income Tax & Surtax on American credits *whether the money is actually remitted or not.* Out of the £25,000 paid me for Pygmalion I shall get about £3000, which, invested at 2½% would mean (less tax) an addition of about £6 a year to my income!!!

[GBS]

Either Shaw's arithmetic or my own is in error. With a total tax of 17 shillings per pound, which is 85% (see Letter 119), his net income from £25,000 would be £3750, not £3000; assuming the £3000 is accurate, 2½% interest would be £75, which after taxation would leave him 11 pounds and 5 shillings. Either way, Shaw's point is the same: his net earnings are a pittance.

118 / To G. Bernard Shaw   [Mumford's Farm
                                      Chalfont St Peter. Bucks.]
                                       20th November 1940
[TL(c): Delacorte: U]

My dearest G.B.S.

I received your note of the 16th November. Thank you for your kind words in the first part of this. I will read the script carefully, and I shall certainly stick to the play. I never intended to depart from it.

My idea for the production of 'SAINT JOAN' is to use as few sets as possible, and have a kind of stylised background. The effects will come – outside of your living words – from colour and lighting; colour as I intend to use it, in half-tones, real pastel shades, without the horrid blues and reds of the Hollywood colour pictures.

We can discuss the casting of Cauchon on my next visit, which I hope will be very soon. Also that of Stogumber and Warwick.

Herewith I am sending you a few stills of the factory scenes, which have been more successful than I expected. I hope you will like them also.

I am horrified by the last paragraph of your letter, and at a meeting which I had to-day with the Treasury I showed them this part of your letter, and declared that it is a bl— shame that the greatest living author

118

should be cheated out of his profits in this awful way. I think our West Indian scheme will protect you from such treatment in future. It is simply the result of governmental incapacity and nothing else.

I am a little worried about the cutting of the Mog and Todger Fairmile scene, because somehow Wendy's big speech in your new opening sequence is endangered in places by this speech of Mog's. There are two similar lines:

> BARBARA: The poor have only to reach out their hands for God's happiness and take it.
> MOG: I want to share my happiness with you. It is within your reach; you have only to stretch out your hands and take it.

The only possible way to get over this difficulty is either that I should cut both Mog's and Todger's speeches much shorter, or that I should cut out Mog's speech altogether. I leave this to your wise judgment, so please give me an answer when you have thought it over. The driver who brings this letter to you will wait for it.

Herewith I send you also a cheque which I received today from G.F.D. This month it is only a small one, for the month of September; but I shall receive a higher cheque at the end of this month, for October, which I will at once send on to you.

I am really worried about your tax situation. We must do something about it. As it is, it is a ridiculous state of affairs.

About the credit titles: I should like to call 'MAJOR BARBARA' 'a modern "Divina Comedia."' Maybe you have a better suggestion? Willie Walton, who is present while I am dictating this note, smilingly approves of it. Incidentally he is writing heavenly music for us, and says, with his youthful choir-boy arrogance, that it is much too good to go in our picture.

As for the other titles, I have decided that it is much better for you to write only the final title: 'This play of mine, Major Barbara, is, I hope, both true and inspired; but whoever says that it all happened, and that faith in it and understanding of it consist in believing that it is a record of an actual occurrence, is, to speak according to Scripture, a fool and a liar, and is hereby solemnly denounced and cursed as such by me, the author, to all posterity,' followed by your signature. I will send you the form for it by the next mail.

[Gabriel Pascal]

Mog's speech was cut. In the film, all of Shaw's lines were already handwritten and the camera showed Shaw signing his name.

119 / To Gabriel Pascal   4 Whitehall Court. London SW1
                                        22nd November 1940

[TLS(p): Delacorte: U]

My dear Gabriel

I return the cheque for your endorsement. It is payable, not to me, but to Pascal Film Productions Limited, therefore you must write on the back "Pay G. Bernard Shaw on order" and sign for P.F.P. Ltd. I put my own endorsement without noticing that I was not the payee.

It is quite useless to remonstrate with the Treasury about my taxes. They have no power to alter my assessment. I received during the financial year £25,000 pounds, and this put me into the most highly taxed category, taxed at 8s 6d income tax and 8s 6d surtax on the *gross*: that is every 11s 6d is counted as £1 for surtax purposes. Add to this that all the rest of my income and that of my wife is raised into the 17s in the £ category by this unlucky £25,000. Only by living abroad in a neutral country could I escape this; and as they are all preparing for war I should as likely as not be bombed out of the frying pan into the fire. The Treasury, I repeat, can do nothing to relieve me even if it wanted to – and why should it want to?

I should give up my percentages and sell my licence for a bond obliging you to pay me or my executors a terminable annuity for so many years. I am making enquiries as to this. Meanwhile it is the business of the Treasury to get as much money as possible out of me, and out of you. We are both in the soup; so keep your income low and your expenses high or you will share my ruin.

I await the form for the handwriting.

    sempre a te,
      caro Gabriello

                      G. Bernard Shaw

120 / To Gabriel Pascal 4 Whitehall Court. London SW1

5th December 1940

[TLS(tr): Delacorte: U]

Pascal was devious, sometimes to his own detriment. With Major Barbara behind schedule and over budget, he decided to eliminate the scene in which Barbara faints by the river and is taken home in an ambulance. To persuade Shaw to cut it, he reported that Wendy Hiller disliked it so much that she refused to play it. After shooting stopped, he recognized that the scene was necessary as a transition and he wanted to film it. To Hiller's mystification, since she had said nothing against the scene, Shaw wrote to her, explaining its need but giving her the option of refusing to do it. Although Pascal himself paid to shoot it, he had little money, so he filmed only an abridged version of it.

My dear Gabriel

I have written Wendy a letter that will bring her to the river scene with a run, if anything will.

As to the taxation question I have had counsel's opinion on it; and I am quite sure that any money lodged to our credit in an American bank or any other bank must be returned as income. The law is decisive on that point. The Treasury may wink at an evasion if it wants to; but the Special Commissioners of income tax will not. In England government departments do not work together; they delight in bowling one another out. But a joint stock company can lodge its reserves in its bank; and in the film business such large reserves are needed that no criticism of their amount is likely to be made.

Now a company can employ us in our professional capacity. I may agree to accept, say £1000 down (or £100 or £10) plus a first charge on the profits limited to 10% of the money paid by the exhibitors to the distributors, payable on demand. All I need demand is enough cash to go on with for the duration. The rest will not come into my possession. It will remain in the hands of the company. It will not form part of my income until I draw it.

You can do the same.

This, which is only a rough idea at present, gets rid of all the bother about our citizenship. For the moment it is the best method I can think of.

You should make clear that our special case as professional men depending for provision for our retirement on windfalls (aubaines) that occur at intervals of ten years or more was formerly made by assessing us for income tax on the average of three years income. Galsworthy, who did not understand this and thought it an injustice, complained of it; and it was abolished and not replaced by any new concession. Consequently, because I received £25000 within the financial year, I have to pay the same tax as people who have a settled income of £25000 a year. This is obviously unfair; so unfair that unless we can get round it in some way we shall have to go out of business. We are therefore not common tax dodgers.

Always yours
GBS

John **Galsworthy** (1867–1933), major and enormously popular British novelist and dramatist, was less financially astute than Shaw but was more influential.

121 / To Gabriel Pascal　　　　　　4 Whitehall Court. London SW1

22nd December 1940

[TLS(p): Delacorte: U]

Dear Gabriel Pascal

The film rights of The Apple Cart, The Millionairess, and Man and Superman, are unencumbered and at my sole disposal. They have never been filmed. I am quite willing to add them to the list of plays which you already command.

I may say at once generally that if the West Indian project materializes I am prepared to give it the refusal of all or any of my film rights on the usual terms if the payment of my fees can be arranged in such a way as to prevent their ruining me, and to make the enterprise independent of commercial finance.

I see nothing impossible in this, but can say no more until I know exactly what form the enterprise is to take.

Meanwhile I am entirely in favor of it, and shall be greatly disappointed if it does not come off without a hitch.

Faithfully
G. Bernard Shaw

122 / To Gabriel Pascal   Ayot St Lawrence. Welwyn. Herts.

31st December 1940

[APCS (tr) (p): Hampden: U(e)]

My dear Gabriel

Many thanks for the stills, which make a magnificent volume. Charlotte is convinced that the film will leave Pygmalion nowhere.

But the happy ending for the tragic Bill destroys the *depth* of the story at the last moment. I know it is tempting; but I absolutely object to it. Cut it out.

Did the try-out at Reading come off?

I can hardly believe that the West Indian project is far enough advanced for you to leave England by this week's clipper; but if you are really going you take with you all our best wishes. Why did I not discover you ten years ago?

GBS

P.S. I have just heard that the clipper is off until the 6th.

The **try-out** (theatre parlance, to which Shaw was accustomed, for one or more out-of-town test performances of a play before it opened in a major city) was a sneak preview of the *Major Barbara* film, which was cancelled.

123 / To G. Bernard Shaw   [*no address*]

3rd January 1941

[TL(c): Delacorte: U]

My dearest G.B.S.

Your card of the 31st December made me very happy, and Madame Charlotte's high opinion made me very proud, because she has a surer instinct for the audience's reaction than both of us together.

Never mind, my dearest adored Master, that you discovered me ten years late. Certainly it would have been a paradisial miracle if we had started our co-operation ten years earlier. We should have prevented mankind, through our pictures, from killing one another in the most stupid, unconstructive, joyless way; and we should have created a spiritual renaissance by now through our work. But we must do it nevertheless. So there is nothing for it but for you to live ten years longer than you intended to live, and to keep your youthfulness and all your energy, because our real task is only just beginning. It is my greatest hope that the realisation of the West Indian project will give Charlotte and you a new youthful background, to keep up your health and energy better than it is possible for the duration, on this Nordic island.

The first try-out in a cinema in Marlow yesterday went very well, and I am sending over the cards I received from the audience for you to see their reactions ...

The Reading try-out is being held on Sunday night at the Odeon cinema there, and I will let you know how it is received ...

[Gabriel Pascal]

Audiences at sneak previews were asked to fill out **cards** to indicate their reactions to the film. Pascal may have let Shaw know the response in person, as he hoped to visit Shaw the following week.

124 / To Gabriel Pascal [Ayot St Lawrence. Welwyn. Herts.
received Palm Beach, Florida, 26 March 1941]
[TEL(p): Delacorte: U]

Since Pascal had sold so much of his potential profit from Major Barbara *before the picture was released in London on 7 April, Shaw tried to protect Pascal's financial interests in the distribution contract for America.*

AGREEMENT A BOOBY TRAP I WILL NOT SIGN YOU MUST DEMAND 2000 DOLLARS ON ACCOUNT YOUR SHARE ELSE YOU DROP BARBARA AND TAKE HOLLYWOODS BIGGEST OFFER FOR ANOTHER JOB HOLLYWOOD THINKS HAYS CONTROLS TWENTY MILLION CATHOLICS HIS VETO WOULD KEEP AWAY PERHAPS TWO HUNDRED DEVOTEES DISREGARD HIM ABSOLUTELY DO NOT REDUB STAND FIRM   SHAW

The draft **agreement**, which is unlocated, apparently permitted the American distributor to cut the film as the censor might require. From 1922 to 1945, Will H. **Hays** (1879–1954) was head of the Motion Picture Producers and Distributors of America, Inc., usually called 'the Hays Office.'

125 / To G. Bernard Shaw Rivera Country Club
Pacific Palisades. Los Angeles
31st March 1941

[TL(c): Delacorte: U]

The Hays Office accurately discerned the intent of the General's (Mrs Baines in the play) speech at the great meeting in the Albert Hall. While the American print dropped her statement that Bodger, in effect, bought the Salvation Army, Pascal believed that the point, while lost on the character, is not necessarily lost on the audience. Perhaps because they were inessential and perhaps because he did not want to ignite another outburst from Shaw, he did not mention such substitutions as 'chucked out' for 'jerked-off' and 'Cor!' for 'Gawd!' Major Barbara opened on 13 May in New York.

My dear GBS

I received your cable at Palm Beach about the Hays office: at once I flew to Hollywood to make a last appeal and you know the results of my demarches [manoeuvres] by the Hays Office – the picture passed and the only change I agreed upon is that the word '*maggot*' will be deleted from Bill's line 'palsy maggot.'

This is A.

B. – in the General's speech: '*We will pray for him and rejoice in his salvation.*' I must record a new sound-track to substitute the line suggested by the Hays office, which reads: 'We will pray for him and hope for his salvation.'

C. – They request alteration of the following lines in the General's speech in the Albert Hall:

My friends, you may not know him on this side of the grave, but when we cross the river – over there – he will be there with us still. And we shall know him by the seal of God on his brow.

I compromised, after a terrific fight, in the following way – I substitute the end lines by the following:

My friends, you may not know him on this side of the grave, but when we cross the river, let us hope and pray that he will be there with us still. Then we shall know him even as we ourselves are known.

Or, if the recording of these lines, which I cabled to Marjorie Deans to have done with Sybil, will not match and synchronize with the picture then I shall cut out only the last words:

and we shall know him by the seal of God on his brow

So, I have in my hands the letter signed by the Hays office and ending so:

Upon the understanding that all prints which are publicly exhibited conform thereto, we take pleasure in sending you the *Association's Certificate of Approval #03074.*

It is very easy, dear GBS, to say 'ignore the Hays office' but unfortunately no picture in America can be exhibited without the Hays Office censorship's certificate, and I consider what I have done, namely from 22 cuts[,] suggestions which Marjorie knows about[,] to compromise on the changing of one word and the cut of a short line, as the best that could be done and I think you must realize that I faithfully fought for our cause.

The state Censorship of New York and six other states in which censorship exists in America passed the picture without any criticism or any cuts suggestions, and certainly it influenced the Hays Office to bow before this unanimous reaction of the states.

Now let me report to you about Nassau ... I don't see any possibility to build studios there during the war. I was however looking to buy some land while I was studying the whole production project: the advantage of having land there would be that no taxes are to be paid in the Bahamas at all if you have a property there and I thought we could establish our 'siège social' [head office] there, this means prepare our story and our script and then shoot the picture – according to possibilities – either in England or in New York or in Hollywood.

I was invited by one of the most amazing women in the modern world: Miss Betty Carstairs – her real name is Marion Barbara Carstairs. She has an island of her own where she is a kind of modern queen, with her own soldiers; she has her plantations, her own Anglican Church and hospital, and every modern comfort imaginable, but she has educated and disciplined her coloured slaves like human beings and they are happy and respectable citizens of the island.

She has two more islands: one is called the Bird's Cay (Cay means in Bahamian 'island') and the other Devil's Cay. I have taken an option of these two islands, if you select the Bird's Cay I will take – as the Devil's Disciple – the Devil's Cay; if you prefer the Devil's Cay I will take the Bird's Cay. She is ready to be our contractor and build anything we like – until then she has guest houses on her island: they are very agreeable with all modern comfort and she would be glad to have you and Charlotte, with Blanche and your own cook and gardener, as her guests. If this is agreeable to you I would fly home soon after the premiere and arrange, as we agreed with Madame Charlotte, to take you over. I don't think you would need the gardener and the cook because you could have the most wonderful servants there.

If you like to go I would – before I start 'St Joan' and 'The Devil's Disciple' – make quickly in London 'Doctor's Dilemma' with Larry Olivier as Dubedat, and do only the shooting there, and edit the picture, record the music and put everything together in Nassau or in New York, and then start 'St Joan' or 'Devil's Disciple.'

I have spoken with Garbo and Katharine Hepburn, and I have the impression that Garbo is too aged for St Joan, and Katharine Hepburn would be the ideal person for it. You saw a too bad picture of her, I will send you all of her new stills – she is really predestined for the part, but I will leave it open until you see her ...

The preview I held a few days ago at Santa Barbara, about 110 miles from Hollywood in the same theatre where I had the preview of 'Pygmalion' – all cards have been like the English cards, giving the picture '*excellent*' which means the 4 stars mark, and raving about you and giving me good credit as Director. The best performance they gave to Robert Newton, then Wendy, but also Morley and Harrison got their share.

Meanwhile I received a cable from England telling that the press-show went bigger than 'Pygmalion,' the only adverse critic is the Times ...

[Gabriel Pascal]

Sybil (later Dame Sybil) **Thorndike** (1882–1976), who starred in the first London production of *Saint Joan*, played the General.

126 / To G. Bernard Shaw   [*no address*]

26th April 1941

[TD TEL(c): Delacorte: U]

To Shaw's consternation, as well as his own, Pascal frequently changed his mind
about where he would make his next movie. Filming Major Barbara *during the*
Battle of Britain demoralized him, but the prospects of shooting a film in the
Bahamas, Canada, or Hollywood seemed – depending on fresh problems that
either arose or appeared to be solved, and on financial backing or governmental
approval that seemed suddenly to disappear or miraculously to become imminent
– less or more desirable.

... THE SITUATION IS NOT SATISFACTORY AND I CAME TO THE CON-
CLUSION THAT I CANNOT LIVE AND WORK WITHOUT BEING NEAR TO
YOU SO I DECIDED COME HOME AS SOON AS POSSIBLE AFTER NEW-
YORK PREMIERE STOP ALL LETTERS ARE USELESS I MUST TALK OVER
EVERYTHING WITH YOU ABOUT THE FUTURE WORK AS IT IS IMPOSSI-
BLE EXPLAIN BY MAIL REAL SITUATION ABOUT BAHAMAS PROJECT
OR CANADIAN PROJECT OR ABOUT PROPOSALS FROM HERE STOP ...
GABRIEL PASCAL

127 / To G. Bernard Shaw   Sherry-Netherland Hotel. New York, NY

21st May 1941

[TL(c): Delacorte: U]

Although Pascal misled Shaw as to the extent of Major Barbara's *success and lied*
that it was better received than Pygmalion *was, the American press and public*
admired it more than the British did. In the long run, it did not lose money, but
its earnings relative to those of Pygmalion *made it seem a financial failure.*

My Dearest G.B.S.

My calvary of 'Major Barbara' is finished. I have done the job. The New
York premiere is over. It is a terrific hit. All the parasites and my financiers, distributors, exhibitors will again make big money. The picture is
a so-called much greater hit than 'Pygmalion' and I have kept my promise to you faithfully. I enclose the few write-ups which will make you
laugh and maybe happy.

Against the hypocrisy of all the picture pariahs I fought it through, after three and a half months of fighting, that your message to the American people must be shown in all the cinemas where 'Major Barbara' is running. I am proud of this victory because I believe that your speech is the greatest thing ever to have appeared on the screen.

I am flying to Canada to-morrow morning to see the Prime Minister there and I am establishing my production activities in Canada. As soon as I have arranged everything I shall send you a long report from Canada.

I must then go back to New York to arrange the financial side of the business. As soon as I have organized the studio in Canada I must go back there. If I can I shall fly from there to England for a few days to speak to you. Then I start in about eight week's [sic] time my first picture in Canada.

Katharine Cornell is willing to play the lead in 'Doctor's Dilemma.' I shall make a test with her for her photographic possibilities as soon as I am back from Canada ...

[Gabriel Pascal]

128 / To G. Bernard Shaw N.Y. Athletic Club
59th Street & 7th Avenue. New York City
4th June 1941

[TD TEL(c): Delacorte: U]

DEAREST GBS ARRIVING END OF THIS MONTH BY CLIPPER STOP KATHERINE HEPBURN VERY ANXIOUS COME WITH ME TO SPEAK WITH YOU ABOUT SAINT JOAN WHICH I PLAN TO PRODUCE WITH HER NEXT YEAR BECAUSE GARBO ALL TIRED OUT AND LOOKS LIKE A SHADOW OF HERSELF AND WE BOTH AGREED THAT WENDY HILLER HAS NOT ENOUGH SINCERITY TO DO IT STOP IF YOU WOULD AGREE THAT I MAKE WITH HEPBURN THIS YEAR THE APPLE CART OR MILLIONAIRESS THEN I WOULD CONVINCE MY CANADIAN GROUP TO POSTPONE THE CANADIAN PICTURE STOP I WOULD PRODUCE IN LONDON IF I CAN FINANCE IT THERE EITHER APPLE CART OR MILLIONAIRESS HAVE ALL THE NECESSARY FINANCES ASSURED HERE FOR MY CANADIAN PRODUCTION STOP WOULD BE VERY GRATEFUL IF YOU WOULD CABLE ME YOUR REACTION ABOUT THE CANADIAN STORY MARJORIE

SENT TO YOU COUNTING THE DAYS UNTIL I CAN EMBRACE YOU AND
CHARLOTTE LOVE TO YOU BOTH AND BLANCHE AFFECTIONATELY
(SIGNED) GABRIEL PASCAL

The **Canadian story** was *The Snow Goose* (1941), a novel by the American Paul Gallico
(1897–1976).

129 / To Gabriel Pascal   [Ayot St Lawrence. Welwyn. Herts.
                                          Received 7th June 1941]

[TEL(p): Delacorte: U]

*On 6 June, Shaw wrote to Marjorie Deans that, as he cabled Pascal, he needed
more information before he could advise, but his letter to her indicated that he
agreed to the transfer of his film ventures to Canada if it were done piecemeal
rather than as part of a huge scheme.*

CANNOT ADVISE ON GENERAL PLANS WITHOUT MORE INFORMATION
FILMS MUST BE EMPHATICALLY BRITISH SO RECONSIDER WENDY FOR
JOAN OTHER LADY TOO INTENSELY AMERICAN AWAITING YOUR
RETURN IMPATIENTLY   SHAW

130 / To G. Bernard Shaw   [*no address*]
                                          19th June 1941
[TD TEL(c): Delacorte: U]

*Although he cabled Shaw three days earlier that he was reconsidering Wendy
Hiller for Saint Joan, Pascal preferred an alternative to working with her again.
With German submarines making the seas unsafe, he was experiencing difficulties in obtaining a reservation on a ship that would go directly to England and
not stop at Lisbon first.*

DEAR GBS: AFTER LONG REFLECTION FEEL OUR NEXT PICTURE
SHOULD BE CANDIDA WITH KATHERINE CORNELL WHO IS VERY ANX-
IOUS TO PLAY IT AS SHE IS AFRAID OF DOCTORS DILEMMA STOP HER
MANAGER IS ALSO AGAINST DOCTORS DILEMMA STOP YOU YOURSELF
DOUBTED THAT DILEMMA WOULD BE THE RIGHT FOLLOWER STOP I
WOULD LIKE TO KNOW YOUR REACTION BY CABLE IF I SHOULD SIGN

CONTRACT WITH CORNELL FOR CANDIDA BEFORE COMING HOME
STOP ALSO AM IN ADVANCE NEGOTIATIONS WITH LYNN FONTANNE
AND ALFRED LUNT FOR EARLY SPRING 1942 THEY ARE ANXIOUS TO
DO CAPTAIN BRASSBOUNDS CONVERSION WITH ME AND RONALD
COLMAN ANXIOUS TO DO ARMS AND THE MAN STOP AS SOON AS MY
CANADIAN PROJECT IS APPROVED BY THE GOVERNMENT I WILL
UNITE THE BEST BRITISH PLAYERS FROM BOTH SIDES OF THE ATLAN-
TIC BUT I NEED SIX MONTHS OF HARD WORK WITH YOU TO GO OVER
THE PLAYS WE SELECTED TOGETHER FOR MY THREE YEAR PRODUC-
TION PLAN STOP THIS PROBLEM SHOULD BE RESOLVED ALSO
BEFORE I START THE NEW YORK VENTURE HOME SOON.   GABRIEL
PASCAL

Ronald **Colman** (1891–1958) was a star in English and American silent and sound films.

131 / To Gabriel Pascal   [Ayot St Lawrence. Welwyn. Herts.]
                                                    22nd July 1941
[TLS(p): Delacorte: U(e)]

Dear Gabriel

I find that the suggestion of changing the location of Arms and the
Man from Bulgaria to Canada will not bear examination. The British
population of Canada is only 5 millions. A population of the British
isles plus the U.S.A. is about 200 millions. Not one of these 200 millions
think a Canadian soldier in the least interesting. But they are all psy-
chologically prepared to accept a Swiss as a typical matter of fact anti-
romantic comedian, and the Bulgarian as the hyperbolical Captain
Matamore.

The population of Bulgaria is 6 millions, the theatre going proportion of which is negligible. Their feelings may be disregarded.

Arms and the Man is so well known in Canada and all the English
speaking countries that the change would be detected at once, and
would be laughed at.

A change to Ruritania would be equally obvious and would weaken
the play instead of strengthening it.

I cannot think of any change that would not be for the worse. The

Canadians must be content with your Donald Duck film, if you find it practicable. Leave Arms just as it is.

sempre

G. Bernard Shaw

Pascal, who by this time had returned to England and was at Mumford's Farm, tried to get around Shaw's refusal to commit himself to a two-picture deal by proposing to film *Arms and the Man* and *The Snow Goose*, which Shaw meant by 'your **Donald Duck** film.' Captain **Matamore** is one of the names of the braggart warrior, derived from the *Commedia dell'arte.*

132 / To Gabriel Pascal

[Ayot St Lawrence. Welwyn. Herts.]

29th July 1941

[APCS(p): Delacorte: U]

I think I shall have to arrange that I am to receive *no* payments during the war, because my settled income from investments, plus my wife's, probably exceeds the optimum figure. I am asking Smee about this.

Unless you also have settled resources, you must make a different arrangement.

Do not give Candida a percentage of the profits; for though the profits are less than the receipts yet it may cost a lawsuit to determine what the profits are, whereas the receipts are absolutely ascertainable. But 15% on the profits would mean, say 2½% on the receipts at most. I doubt whether it is advisable to give a percentage at all instead of a bigger salary.

GBS

C. Walter **Smee** (b. 1890) was an accountant with F. Rowland & Co., London. On 9 August, Shaw wrote to him for advice on deferring film income.

133 / To Gabriel Pascal

[Ayot St Lawrence. Welwyn. Herts.]

1st August 1941

[TLS(p): Delacorte: U(e)]

My dear Gabriel

If these four plays are filmed before the end of the war we shall both be ruined. If I could, I would cancel the agreements you already hold, as the war has completely upset the conditions under which they were executed. The success of the Pygmalion film has not paid my London rent, and has made my financial situation quite threatening. As far as I can see, the only way in which I can save myself is by refusing to allow any more films of my plays to be produced until either (a) the war ends and taxation returns to a reasonable level, or else (b) some arrangement is devised whereby payment of my royalties can be deferred until then.

Your situation is pretty much the same. The Canadian authorities must be told that the taxation is heavier than the business will bear, and that we must stop filming until the war is over unless we can continue without ruinous loss. If we go on producing and are ruined the Canadian Government will simply say 'What is that to us? See ye to that.' You must therefore say flatly that we cannot go on with my plays, and that you must live in the U.S.A. and get other jobs there until a resumption of your Shavian activities becomes again possible. Meanwhile I must live on my capital. I may be forced to emigrate. Not pleasant that, at 85. You, in your abounding energy and reckless disregard of costs, persist in making plans for me on the assumption that I am 35; but I am, actuarially speaking, a dead man; and the grasshopper is a burden.

G. Bernard Shaw

'[T]he **grasshopper** shall be a burden, and desire shall fail; because man goeth to his long home, and the mourners go about the streets' (Ecclesiastes 12:5).

134 / To Gabriel Pascal [Ayot St Lawrence. Welwyn. Herts.]
6th August 1941

[TPCS(p): Delacorte: U]

Dear Gabriel Pascal

It is fully understood between us that if arrangements can be made whereby we can continue our film operations during the war without sacrifices which we cannot afford, I am pledged to license the filming by you of the four plays entitled Arms and the Man, Captain Brassbound's Conversion, Saint Joan, and the Devil's Disciple.

Beyond this I must not commit myself unless and until further steps are made reasonably possible.

Faithfully

G. Bernard Shaw

135 / To G. Bernard Shaw   Ottawa

11th September 1941

[TL(c): Delacorte: U]

Dear G.B.S.

I am in Ottawa at the Parliament Buildings, and dictating these lines to the secretary of my best friend here, Leonard Brockington, of whom I have spoken to you on a number of occasions. It is the day of the premiere, the proceeds of which are for the Allied Merchant Seamen's Committee, and every seat is already sold.

Your lawyer showed me a cable you addressed to him, and I had a long talk also with the leading exhibitor in this country who is supposed to take a partnership in my Canadian company. While I was home in England, this exhibitor and my few friends here investigated the plan to produce here in Canada. I came to the following conclusion, with which Brockington (who helped Grierson, the Film Commissioner of Canada, to get the co-operation of the government) agrees. Canadian financing is impossible in wartime. But an even more serious difficulty arises in connection with studios. Owing to the national needs, steel and labour cannot be diverted from what the government considers the most essential war purposes. The regulations covering this matter are very strict, and cannot be varied. On my last day in London, I held a press luncheon to tell the newspaper boys and girls about my plan to continue my production with eight Bernard Shaw stories and the one picture with the Canadian background, The Snow Goose. All my actors and actresses were present. Rex Harrison declared to the press that he would not come to Canada, as he prefers the Air Force. Robert Newton, my most faithful actor, declared he would go back to the Navy, and the little girl Deborah Kerr, who played Jenny in Barbara, refused to cross the ocean.

I investigated in Hollywood and had a long conversation with Lunt and Fontanne and other British players in New York. They all prefer to stay in the United States, especially when their tax adviser proved to them that in Canada they would pay taxes twice as heavy as they would in the United States. My friend Brockington assures me that it would be quite impossible to make the Canadian government a party to my contract with you, or in fact in any film contract. Your lawyers will write to you, explaining that the new contract for the film rights of your plays will be with my new American Company, Gabriel Pascal Productions, incorporated under the laws of New Jersey. It will guarantee you a yearly income as you asked, and leave the balance on deposit in trust with my new distributors the R.K.O. Company. This company is financed half by the Rockefeller group and half by Floyd Odlum, President of the Atlas Corporation, who is a very dear friend of mine. In the new two year contract of distribution, I arranged that your ten per cent royalty will be left in a trust fund for the duration of the war. This means that no one can touch it except you and your successors, and what is equally important, it will not be subject to taxation.

With these arrangements, I will go back to Hollywood and start immediately with preparation for Arms and the Man. I agreed in principle with Ginger Rogers for Luka and I am writing to my casting director in London, David Hanley, to arrange with Edith Evans for the part of Kathleen. If Rex Harrison cannot come for Benchley, I will take Charles Boyer. Ernest Cossard, who played with Lunt and Fontanne, will play Petrov.

I will keep my very steady contract with Canada until the times are better and the labour and steel situation permits me to realize my plans. Then maybe I will do next summer the exterior shots for my Canadian picture, 'The Snow Goose.' In the meantime, before I go to Hollywood to start Arms and the Man, I will go to Quebec and try to find a girl suitable for Saint Joan. The Catholic Church will, I believe, give me every help. I will make tests with several girls, and send the tests to you for final selection.

These, then, are my definite plans: (1) Arms and the Man; (2) Captain Brassbound; (3) Saint Joan; and then, if the political situation is favourable, Devil's Disciple ...

[Gabriel Pascal]

Sir Leonard Walter **Brockington** (1888–1966), born in Wales, was chairman of the Canadian Broadcasting Corporation 1936–9 and special assistant to the prime minister of Canada, (William Lyon) Mackenzie King (1874–1950), 1939–42. Scottish-born John **Grierson** (1898–1972), a producer, director, and leading figure in documentary films, was founder (1939) of the National Film Board of Canada. American financier Floyd Patrick **Odlum** (1892–1976) was chairman of R.K.O. Radio Pictures.

Hollywood star of the thirties, forties, and fifties, Ginger **Rogers** (1911–95), best known as dancing partner of Fred Astaire (1899–1987), also acted in non-dancing roles. Perhaps Pascal employed a temporary secretary to whom he dictated this letter, who typed the spelling that her shorthand of his pronunciation suggested, and whose letter he did not examine carefully: **Luka** is an error for Louka, **Kathleen** for Catherine, **Benchley** for Bluntschli, and **Petrov** for Petkoff. In Hollywood, Charles **Boyer** (1897–1978), stage and screen actor in France and the United States, was known as 'the great lover'; his most memorable stage appearance was as Juan in *Don Juan in Hell* (Act 3 of *Man and Superman*) in 1952. Ernest **Cossard** is an error for British actor Ernest Cossart (1876–1951), whom Hollywood usually cast as a butler.

Although the United States did not enter the war until the Japanese attacked Pearl Harbor on 7 December, many people in Great Britain and elsewhere felt that to depict Americans fighting the English, as they do in *The Devil's Disciple*, which is set during the American Revolution, would aid Nazi propaganda.

136 / To Gabriel Pascal [Ayot St Lawrence. Welwyn. Herts.]
20th October 1941

[TLS(tr): Delacorte: U(e)]

A week earlier, Shaw had written to Marjorie Deans, emphatically refusing both to write anything more for the Arms and the Man *film (the new scenes he composed are published in* The Collected Screenplays of Bernard Shaw*) and to permit the filming of the 'anti-British'* Devil's Disciple *until after the war.*

My dear Gabriel

Marjorie has been pressing me to change Arms and the Man into The Chocolate Soldier, with Louka written up as the star part with a dance and plenty of laughs for Miss Rogers. That would suit Hollywood to perfection: they love The Chocolate Soldier there, and have not the faintest notion of serious comedy. Marjorie insists that this is what you want; and she evidently quite agrees with you, and thinks I am an obsolete old relic of days before cinemas were invented.

Now read attentively. Arms is a play for four comedians, two of front rank, Raina and Bluntschli, both juveniles, and two elderly ones with well worn parts suited to their age. These four make all the fun and get all the laughs. They must be real actors: their parts will not play themselves. On them the play depends.

As a background to throw them into comic relief and give dignity to the play there is a secondary group who are striking and tragic, never funny though they are in scenes which are funny, with parts that play themselves if they are properly cast and professionally competent. They are Sergius, Louka and Nicola. They function as a dark background; and must not for a moment intrude on the function of the comic four. If Nicola were played by a low comedian; if Louka uttered a single joke or danced a single step; if Sergius ceased for a moment to be Byronically tragic and sardonic, the play would be ruined at once, and would drop to the level of The Chocolate Soldier, in which all the men are cads, cowards or *vieux marcheurs* [old rakes] and all the women amateur whores; and Gabriel Pascal would sink into the common ruck of Hollywood hack producers.

Tell Miss Rogers that Raina is the star part, and if she is to be the star she must play it. If not she goes out of the cast; for it would do her no good professionally to play a part secondary to that of the star. If she suggests that the part of Louka might be made the star part by giving her more to say and introducing a dance for her, do not argue with her: just throw her out of the window and tell her not to come back.

Do not change the scene in the last act. Once the play gets hold of the audience, it no longer wants changes and interruptions; the play must concentrate and accelerate towards the end. You can do fifty things in the first act that would be intolerable in the last. Petkoff's library has a big window shewing the landscape. Changes from that to the stove or opposite corner, or from the ottoman to the kitchen table will give you all the variety you need.

I have seen the first act played as a melodrama with Bluntschli as a sympathetic hero and Raina as a tender innocent heroine taking all her operatic affectations quite seriously: the effect was unbearable. Such a misunderstanding is possible; so look out for it and crush it at the start.

Take care to secure a serious actor for Nicola: a funny man would upset everything.

Bluntschli must speak crisply and matter-of-factly and never declaim: Sergius always declaims.

Marjorie says Olivier will play Sergius. Will Vivien play Louka? I should not advise her to; but if she does not object you need not. But Raina must be the leading part no matter who plays Louka, though Louka may play as strongly as she likes on the lines of the part. Wendy could play Louka; but so could lots of other actresses. The only question therefore is whether her previous association with our two successes is not worth keeping up. I think it is; but then I have not to deal with her personally; and you have.

Everyone in Hollywood will give you the wrong advice about this, because the technique of high comedy is quite beyond them. But you are in a supremely strong position at the moment and need not conciliate their folly in any way. You will never be in as strong a position again, though you may be a much richer man. There will be a rush of producers to imitate you by putting wellknown plays on the screen unaltered. Most of them will make a mess of it; but some of them will succeed; and when this happens you will have competitors. You have none at present, though one film magnate is pressing me hard and swearing that he always does what you do. So make the most of your supremacy while it lasts; and tell all the important people, whether they are stars or financiers, that you are the star this time, and that what you say goes. I took this line strongly with General Films here through the National Provincial Bank when they refused to settle your bills; and they immediately coughed up £3000. Nevertheless they are still frightened by the cost of Major Barbara; so be as economical as your nature permits. They are divided between their fear of losing their money, and their tendency to think you as great as the sums you cost them.

Stern's letter of the 27th Sept. has reached me. I was quite prepared for the breakdown of the Canadian plan; but I was surprised at being told that your United Artists contract was 'onerous,' and that I had complained of it as unfair. That is not my recollection of the affair. I understood that it was the Metro contract that was onerous, and that the U.A. one was a great improvement on it. However, if RKO is better and safer it doesnt matter. The letter is satisfactory as far as it goes or can go until the documents are agreed and executed. The celerity with which you find a new plan of campaign when the old one breaks down is very reassuring.

I take it that Brassbound is to follow Arms. I forgot to say that the part of Katharine in Arms does not need a star with a temperament and a huge salary. (It is a mistake to give a big noise a part not good enough for her merely to get her name into the bill. It inevitably produces a disappointment; and disappointments are the very devil: they spread over the whole performance. Much better give a good part to a nobody who can make a surprising success of it.) She would not only not be worth her cost in money but would upset the balance of the play, which is extremely delicate in comedy, though in big stuff like Major Barbara or Methuselah it would not matter.

Take care of yourself, and do not rush into too many sidetracks and burn the candle at both ends. RKO should insure your life heavily. That would replace their money if you started again in another world; but I could not replace you. So be good.

always yours

G. Bernard Shaw

The popular operetta *The Chocolate Soldier* (Der tapfere Soldat, 1908), music by Oscar Straus (1879–1954), libretto by Rudolf Bernauer (1880–1953) and Leopold Jacobson (b. 1878), was an unauthorized adaptation of *Arms and the Man*. Benjamin H. **Stern** (1874–1950), an authority on international copyright law, was a partner in the New York law firm Stern and Reubens, Shaw's American lawyers. His letter has not been located.

137 / To G. Bernard Shaw   [Santa Monica, California]
                                                            23rd November 1941

[TL(c): Delacorte: U]

On 24 November, Stern wrote to Shaw, explaining that financiers such as Whitney and Odlum would try to reduce Pascal to a producing director on a small salary; that while the proposed contract was the best to be got in Shaw's interests, the situation was problematic; and that if Pascal could not conclude a contract with RKO, he was unlikely to continue in Hollywood.

My dear GBS

My friend, Leonard Brockington, who has been until now, the Canadian Prime Minister's personal advisor, has been invited by the English Government to lecture for a few weeks in England. He is not only one of my few personal friends whom I trust implicitly, but he is also my Canadian Counsel, and he is a member of the board of my newly founded American Company, Gabriel Pascal Productions, Inc. in New York City. As a

Director of this Company he is taking over with him the contract Mr Stern prepared for you ...

I hope Charlotte, you and Blanche are well. I am floating between heaven and earth like a restless spirit until our Author Rights Contract is clear. I knew all the time that this trouble would come but I didn't want to insist on its clearance because I felt, as you said many times, that between us contracts are not necessary but American lawyers of banking have another opinion about this point.

I hope to see you as soon as I have finished 'Arms and the Man.' The preparation work for it is shaping very well indeed.

My private address is 602 Ocean Drive, Santa Monica, California. It is better that you send letters and cables there because I don't trust RKO's Studio Mail Department. I think they automatically have knowledge of all cables.

[Gabriel Pascal]

138 / To Gabriel Pascal   [Ayot St Lawrence. Welwyn. Herts.
                                              c. 23 January 1942]

[HD TEL(p): Deans: U]

Having received financial statements on the income from Major Barbara, Shaw realized at least three weeks earlier, as he wrote to Marjorie Deans on 2 January, that Pascal had deceived him about its success and that Pascal's own profits from the film were practically nothing. Since Pascal had not cabled him since Christmas eve, Shaw told her, he inferred that Pascal was broke. Shaw cabled Pascal, he wrote to her on the 23rd, in order to 'restore his equilibrium' by giving him a comedy that would enable him to make a two-picture deal with Hollywood.

United Artists cannot bind us to two plays without binding themselves most unwisely also. I consent to Millionairess with Hepburn not Fields on Brockington terms as your next job but one but will not go a step farther. If Mill shares Barbaras fate Shaw films come off the screen for years. You knew about the flop in September. I have only just heard of it from Chenhalls. Can I ever believe you again.

SHAW

Fields may be Gracie (later Dame Gracie) Fields (née Grace Stansfield, 1898–1979), popular actress and singer who moved to the United States in 1940. A(lfred) T. **Chenhalls** & Co., Ltd., was a firm of chartered accountants in London.

139 / To Gabriel Pascal

[TEL(tr): Colgate: U(e)]

Do not worry about me as I am all right. It is I who have to take care of you. Marjorie wants Cleopatra here because she wants you back in England but to boil the pot you had better close with United for non-Shaw and Millionairess. Barbara is a triumph flop or no flop and will finally justify itself so let nothing discourage you.

[GBS]

140 / To G. Bernard Shaw

[*no address*]
17th February 1942

[TL(c): Delacorte: U]

Probably still in the Hollywood area, Pascal did not conclude a contract for The Millionairess. *As he continued his efforts to wheel and deal, a film of* Saint Joan *seemed, at this time, more likely to materialize.*

My dear G.B.S.

So all these tribulations and all this searching have had a deeper reason and I am happy that we have arrived at the solution that the only worthwhile production to do now is 'SAINT JOAN.' The price of one year of suffering, humiliation and self negation is not too highly paid for this result.

I am starting work at once and hope in two weeks time I can send you further news that the business angle is settled, and that I have my cast together. I have a strange destiny. I made 'MAJOR BARBARA' under the German blitz and I have a premonition that I will make 'SAINT JOAN' under the Japanese blitz. But I don't care if everything will burn around and over me, I am like a steel arrow and I will finish my job and deliver to you and to the world the screen version of your masterpiece of spiritual integrity – which is the only thing that counts in building up a new world on the ashes of the old one, which value was doubtful anyway. I don't like to use big words. I am not interested anymore what happens around us. I will work like Savonarola worked – and I think under similar circumstances. If my work is done and the picture is finished and you love it, and the people of the world love it, I don't mind if I am put in jail or they kill me or if I perish with the rest of the old world if I am not young enough and good enough for a coming new and better one.

At the end of this week I shall go to Canada and try to find the girl. You remember you approved my plan to look for the right girl in a French Canadian convent. I am inspired and I feel that – through the magnetic forces latent in me – the right girl will be found. If not it is a sign of destiny that the real Joan is Katherine Hepburn.

I sent you a message through Marjorie that you should not think of Wendy Hiller. You yourself wrote me twice that she is a materialistic pagan. She has as much inner contact to St Joan as you or myself to the ghost of Chamberlain. Since we both decided on 'ST JOAN' practically all my troubles are over because I don't consider them anymore. All the dirt of parasites, lawyers and accountants cannot come near me – and he who dares to come near me I kick so that he lands in Jerusalem or somewhere in a Japanese prison camp. I will be pitiless against anybody who disturbs my work – but will be sweet as an angel to him who helps me in it.

Take care of yourself, my dear Master. You must see, on the living screen, your 'SAINT JOAN' before you go on your great pilgrimage, and you must show to the British and American people that there is only one way out from all this mess and that is to follow the spirit of St Joan. If we reach the broad masses and awaken them to a new way of thinking then it was worthwhile that we met. So please give me your blessing and your limitless faith for my work. It is more valuable to me than the approval and blessing of the Holy Father we received two years ago when with your permission I visited Cardinal Gonfalonieri, who was the private secretary of the old Pope, and who transmitted to me the approval of the Pope that I should go on with the picture. Much higher forces are guiding me to surmount all obstacles and do the picture in your spirit, and I am convinced that doing it so the holy spirit and the great cosmical universal spirit will cover it.

Embracing you and Charlotta,

> Always faithful,
> [Gabriel Pascal]

Girolamo **Savonarola** (1452–98), an Italian Dominican priest inveighed against artistic
licentiousness and social corruption. Excommunicated for trying to depose the pope, he
was executed as a heretic.

141 / To G. Bernard Shaw   [New York City]
                                                                6th May 1942

[TL(tr): Delacorte: U(e)]

... After the Canadian plan collapsed – my friend Brockington explained
the reason for this to you – I decided to go on as you know with ARMS
AND THE MAN; but before signing a definite contract with R.K.O. your
lawyer Stern reminded me that your option letters would not be satisfactory to the Legal Derpartment of R.K.O. and he insisted that I send you
a contract which he worked out and I sent it to you through Brockington. I was against this contract because I believed that any distributing
company would respect your original formula, but I gave in to Stern's
desire to send you the contract. I think his wish to simplify matters was
genuine, but unfortunately, he only complicated the situation. So then
after weeks of waiting, the news came from Brockington that he did not
bring the contracts; therefore, I had no other choice but play the mad-
man at the R.K.O. studio, because I could not very well put the fault that
I stopped production on you due to Stern's advice that I could not sign
without having your supplementary contract, so I ran away from the
Hollywood battle field and found myself with you, my dear Maestro, in
our strategy against the Hollywood generals exactly like the United
Nations in their cooperation against Hirohito and Herr Hitler, only you
have been playing the United States and I was playing England. I wanted
to go on and fight, but I needed the tools, and I needed your war declaration, but you said, 'let him battle alone and I will step in, in the last
moment when he is losing everything,' so exactly like America lost two
years of preparation with playing around in the world struggle, we lost
nearly eighteen months not creating anything.

My good peasant instinct was right, when I told Blanche many times
to let me go to Whitehall and I will bring your printed contract formulas, so that all the plays you entrusted me with would be on your original
contract and not in the different option letters.

I could have made since I left England, at least two pictures of your plays if Blanche had only listened to me procuring from your Whitehall apartment your printed contract formulas. With them signed by you, the bank would have given me all the money necessary to go into production and I would not have been at the mercy of the stupid distributing companies, but I believe now, we are both recompensed for our errings; otherwise, if everything went smoothly, I would have already finished ARMS AND THE MAN and after the United States war declaration, this picture would have been banned by the Hays Office, so in the end we have been lucky with all the physical difficulties to be forced to stop this production. Then arrived your cable that I should make St Joan and in the first ecstasy I wrote you a letter which I include hereby.

I went to Montreal and Quebec to find a French Canadian girl for Joan because in my opinion she should be a girl who has never been before the camera and who should never face it again after St Joan, and for this reason I was looking for her in French Canadian convents, but by strange coincidence Cardinal Villeneuve, to whom I went in order to secure a letter to the different Mother Superiors to allow me to select a novice who had not yet taken the veil to play the part of Joan, had already written a letter to all Mother Superiors two years ago that the cinema in its 'actual form is immoral' and any direct or indirect contact with it would be a sin. All the advisers of this gallant cardinal have been very embarrassed because the cardinal liked my idea, but he had not the greatness of a Pacelli to admit his own mistake; therefore, I left the perplexed Jesuits. I will, however, certainly find the girl in some California-Spanish convent when the time is ripe for it ...

I am very glad that from this chaos of misunderstandings and errings, the Madonna-appearance of Candida came out like a vision and I feel that superior forces worked in our behalf, most likely inspired by your guiding spirit so that I could produce the most perfect and most sincere picture ever made, from your play Candida. Also, Cornell believes that mystical powers worked together to enable us to make this picture.

I do not need to describe to you how wonderful Katharine Cornell is, you know it much better than me, and also Raymond Massey was astonishingly good as Morell. However, I believe that Spencer Tracy would be even better; in fact, I had already discussed this part two years ago with him very intensely. Burgess Meredith, a very intelligent young actor, is

the best Marchbanks I ever saw. He is about thirty-eight years old, however, he gives a perfect illusion of youth on the stage, but I must make
tests of him before I can decide casting him in the picture. Mildred
Natwick is a better Prossy than Athena Seiler, which really means something.

For the Burgess part, I have Edmund Gwenn or Charles Laughton in
mind. Old C. Aubrey Smith likes very much to be in my next picture,
but I am afraid he will be too old for Burgess and also play the part too
straight, which also may be the trouble with Gwenn ...

I had a long conference yesterday with Cornell and we both feel that
between the second and third act, you should write for us two short
scenes. One, Morell's meeting; and the second after the meeting, Burgess' invitation to Prossy and Bell. I am afraid this will involve a new figure, the introduction of the chairman of the Works Committee of the
County Council. The use of this persona, I leave to your wise judgment.
All the rest of the play I put in picture sequence without the slightest
alteration and if somebody in Hollywood dares to come near to me and
discuss anything about it, from the dark rays of the fury of my eyes, he
will fall dead at once. So you can imagine what a cemetery will be built
near the studio where I shoot the picture ...

[9 May 1942]

P.S. I dictated the letter on the sixth of May, but waited to send it away
because my friend Brockington promised me daily that he would come
to New York and send it for me by bomber from Canada. Since then I
had many talks with Cornell and her husband, Guthrie McClintic, who
is a very sympathetic honest man, and he became a part of my deal with
Cornell as a dialogue supervisor during the shooting. I accepted this
proposition, so this way, he will not be jealous and besides, I prefer to
have him on the set rather than back stage influencing Kit, like a certain
husband of a certain ex-star of ours. We will therefore start to prepare
everything in great harmony and Papa Stern is working out a formal
contract which will be signed next week ...

After careful reflection about the scenario, I would like to suggest to
you for the beginning two short scenes. One, the first meeting between
Morell and Marchbanks, and the other sequence with Marchbanks and
Candida on the seashore with the children, and then both of them com-

ing back to London by train. This would give me possibility for shooting some exteriors and bring visually some fresh air in the picture.

Cornell asked me to please send you the message that she would be very grateful for such a scene. Principally, if she could wear a period bathing costume. (This last is Kit's personal suggestion!?)

I would also need a few lines in the kitchen which I would inter-cut in the Second Act, Page #46 after Candida's line:

CANDIDA. Yes, onions. Not even Spanish ones – nasty little red onions. You shall help me to slice them. Come along.

Your stage direction: She catches him by the wrist and runs out, pulling him after her. Here I need a short comedy scene to show how the desperate Marchbanks is completely helpless with his onion slicing. I need some teasing line from Candida to Marchbanks saying that Marchbanks should get used in time to dominate his tears.

I went again to the theatre with a stop watch and the play plays actually one hour twenty seven minutes and the picture should run (so not to be endangered of being put with a double feature program) for one hour fifty five minutes, or possibly two hours, so I need from you in these different scenes about thirty minutes supplementary dialogue. I count from five to eight minutes for silent action for the whole picture.

The speech of Morell at the meeting should not be longer than the speech in the Albert Hall you wrote for Sybil Thorndike in our MAJOR BARBARA, with the reaction of some ecstatic old spinsters in the audience.

I should also like, and please don't scold me for my immodesty, a short scene which would take place before the beginning of the second act. This scene should be in the dining room as they are sitting at the table, when the lunch is nearly finished and Candida brings in the coffee and she was called out by the young stitcher girl to whom Burgess refers in the second act Page #39. A short dialogue sequence should be between Morell and Burgess after Marchbanks quietly sneaked out from the dining room. Maybe they are talking about Marchbanks, then I need time lapse. We then come to the beginning of the second act with Marchbanks playing with the typewriter. How would it be for the time lapse that Marchbanks before he enters into the sitting room is walking in the park dreamingly whispering Candida, Candida, Candida, Candida ...

Having from you these supplementary short scenes, I can cut the continuity in order in four weeks and by the second half of July start rehearsing with make-up tests for Cornell and the very latest the tenth of August start shooting so that by the end of September finish the shooting and hope also to finish within four weeks cutting, dubbing, scoring, editing and be able to fly back end of October with the completed negative and the master print, thereby having the premiere in the best part of the season in November in London, and then start with either DOCTOR'S DILEMMA or CAESAR AND CLEOPATRA with Viven Leigh immediately after Christmas and then go on to ST JOAN. This is how the program stands now, and I am like a horse with blinkers, nothing can hold me back in my race.

[Gabriel Pascal]

Hirohito (1901–89) was Emperor of Japan. Through classrooms, speeches, articles, brochures, and books, Canadian Cardinal Jean-Marie-Rodrigue **Villeneuve** (1883–1947) spread his view that movies were immoral. Raymond **Massey** (1896–1983), Canadian-born, was a stage and screen star in the United States. Spencer **Tracy** (1900–67) was a perennial major American movie star. Burgess **Meredith** (b. 1908), American, has been a versatile stage and screen star for decades. Mildred **Natwick** (1908–94) was an American stage and screen actress. Athene **Seyler** (1889–1990) was a British stage and screen actress. None of these actors played in a Shaw film. **Bell** is an error for Mill.

Guthrie **McClintic** (1893–1961) was a Broadway director whose work included *The Doctor's Dilemma* and *Candida*, with his wife Katharine Cornell. The '**certain husband**' and 'certain ex-star' are Ronald Gow and Wendy Hiller.

142 / To G. Bernard Shaw　　　　New York Athletic Club
180 Central Park South. New York City
26th May 1942

[TL(c): Delacorte: U]

My dear G.B.S.

... Now that I heard that Guthrie McClintic, maybe involuntarily, allowed the press to make an issue out of the fact that he has improved Bernard Shaw, it is of utmost importance that these write ups are put on the very next bomber and you read them carefully and [are] kept informed about these children's mumblings. Just because a few critics are impressed by the success of the actor Marchbanks, they forget in their naivety that Burgess Meredith has the success with your *own* lines, and nothing changed with his conception of Marchbanks, only that instead of being eighteen or twenty-four as played the first time, he is now about thirty-four.

I argued with many of the critics about your stage instructions regarding Marchbanks. You write as follows: 'He is a strange, shy youth of eighteen, slight, effeminate, with a delicate childish voice, etc.' My argument being that by the word effeminate, you did not mean a sissy-like young man, the way the Americans understand it, but that you meant the neo-romantic type of the aristocratic bohemian of the late nineties, which was typical of that period. In my opinion nevertheless, the brilliant acting performance of Burgess Meredith's Marchbanks is not exactly in your spirit, but I believe, in spite of this, I could use this actor for the picture and put him back on the right track.

If you think it useful, you can send me an official letter on how to interpret Marchbanks which eventually I can give to the press.

I had a long talk yesterday again with Miss Cornell because they recasted Prossy with a young actress Helen Forbes who is very good, but in her speech not as good as Mildred Natwick, and if I cannot get Natwick out of her Noël Coward play 'Blithe Spirit,' I will use this young actress Forbes. They had also Ernest Cossart for the part of the father. They like him very much because he looks real as the possible father of Cornell but I prefer to use Dudley Digges who has the right tempo and dialect for the part. I think Charles Laughton would disturb the harmony of the ensemble. As for Cossart, he is for me like the old fashioned Ibsen player, but they like him; also, they came yesterday again with this awful proposition that I should take for Morell, Raymond Massey. For me, my dear G.B.S., it is a physical pain how he is killing all your lines and in the picture audience's mind, he is definitely associated with playing the villain's part, so my choice is Spencer Tracy or Walter Pidgeon, and I will send you photographs of this last one.

Out of faithfulness to you, I am going through great trouble with Cornell since six weeks and your lawyer Stern is witnessing it, but not approving and is admiring my patience in this uncreative situation because now that Cornell and her husband said several times that they liked and agreed to make the picture, the new version is that after she finishes next week in Washington, she likes to go with me to Hollywood and make a test and she will not make up her mind before she has seen herself on the screen to see whether she looks young and beautiful enough.

I also made arrangements with Burgess Meredith who will take two weeks leave for this test because first Miss Cornell likes very much to have him with her in these tests and then too, I want to know if he looks young enough on the screen ...

[Gabriel Pascal]

Noël (later Sir Noël) **Coward** (1899–1973) was an English actor, director, and writer. One of Natwick's best roles was Madame Arcati in his *Blithe Spirit* (1941). Dudley **Digges** (1879–1947), Irish character actor, performed on the American stage and screen. Neither he nor Walter **Pidgeon** (1897–1984), Canadian-born American film star, acted in a Shaw movie.

143 / To G. Bernard Shaw   New York Athletic Club
180 Central Park South. New York City
16th June 1942

[TL(c): Delacorte: U(e)]

On 3 June 1942, Cornell sent Pascal a letter, listing her terms for making a screen test. They included using Guthrie McClintic as co-director or supervisor, having S.N. Behrman write the script, and being under no obligation to do the film if she were dissatisfied with the test, in which case the test film would be destroyed or given to her. Behrman was then writing The Pirate *for the Lunts; it would open on Broadway on 25 November.*

My dear G.B.S.

... I am forwarding you herewith copy of Miss Cornell's terms under which she agrees to make the film test.

Yesterday Metro definitely refused acceptance of these conditions to finance not only the picture but also the expenses of the test under her terms. They do not want Miss Cornell pushing her husband as co-director on me because he does not understand about pictures at all. I forced him through as dialogue supervisor only to please Cornell. I don't need him as I have more sense for the beauty of the English language and for the right rhythm of your dialogue than all the American stage producers together. Secondly, they criticised also Miss Cornell's insistence that her playwright, Mr Sam Behrman be at hand for the test as he is a very expensive man and besides he is doing now a new play with Lunt and Fontanne and it is not certain whether he can arrange to be there.

Regarding Burgess Meredith, I made arrangements personally with him and it is not certain yet whether the War Office will grant him a furlough in time.

The most important point in Miss Cornell's letter is that the entire proposition is one sided, stating that she accepts to play the part with the condition that it must be satisfactory to her regardless of whether Metro or myself should find out that she cannot be photographed since she may be too old for the part, because she must be well over fifty now.

With one word, I put myself again as so many times in life in 'cul de sac' with my loyalty.

My dear G.B.S., no major company is ready to accept the risk of an experiment as Miss Cornell wants because she believes that she is not only the star, but also the boss of the whole production and my past experience proved that if I am not the absolute master of my production things will go hay wire. It was for this reason that MAJOR BARBARA was so costly because too many people tried to interfere.

I am the least expensive producer in the world if I have clear artistic and financial situation. If you tell me, go on Gabriel, make the picture according to your conscience and to the best of your knowledge and ability and if my backer or distributing company gives me fifty, seventy, one hundred or only five thousand pounds and I must make the picture with any kind of budget, and nobody interferes with me while in the process of making it, I will make the picture like the soldier keeps a fortress within budget and time, and better than any human being, but if I am disturbed during production and if I feel I do not have the blind faith of those whom I believe to be my friends, I become the most uncertain amateur and am worse and more useless than the most ordinary director in the world ...

You tell me for example that I should use only the one set in the picture, then the easiest thing would be that I go to the theatre where Miss Cornell is playing and turn the camera and in one hour, thirty seven minutes the picture will be ready and the job costing only five thousand dollars; certainly such a kind of picture would be a picture, but we both agree that the picture medium is the most modern art for popular consumption and requirements, and this art has its iron laws just like any other form of artistic expression, but I did not think you seriously meant it that I should let play the whole picture in one room. (I explained this to Dicky Norton, so if he repeated it to you in his own inimitable way, maybe you laughed about it, but you should reflect seriously about it now.) But, my dear maestro, I promise you though, that not one word, not even a comma, will be changed in your dialogue, but the rest you must leave to me.

The only way I could make the picture on Miss Cornell's terms would be as independent production through my own American company, but I know you have very little respect for this company or for my business ability and I think you are wrong. If I have my wings free and I am the master of my own decisions, I am a very good and clever business man, but not when I am hanging between heaven and earth and depending on the mood and whims of so many people ...

I lost again many months of time with inactivity and I don't know where I really am now. I have a proposition from another major company to do after Candida with Miss Mae West MRS WARREN'S PROFESSION. I would like to have your opinion about it because this picture I could do very quickly in a few weeks, before coming back definitely to England.

I have refused every kind of offer to do pictures, not of your plays, but kept to my last healthy drop of blood my faith in you. It is now your turn to say something ...

[Gabriel Pascal]

Richard Henry Brinsley **Norton**, Baron Grantley (1892–1954) was chairman of the British Film Producers Association 1938–40 and became chairman of Pascal Film Productions in 1941.

144 / To G. Bernard Shaw   [New York City]
                                                27th July 1942
[TL(c): Delacorte: U]

Later this year, RKO filmed Katharine Hepburn in a colour scene of Saint Joan, designed by Robert Edmond Jones (1887–1954), an outstanding American stage designer whose sets were very influential, which may be what Pascal means by 'made school.'

My dear G.B.S.

... I started at once to work with Robert Edmond Jones on the sketches
for our picture St Joan. I believe you know about him as he is considered
one of the greatest art directors in America. He made school with his
sets for John Barrymore's HAMLET. The character and style of his work is
very similar to Laurence Irving's. Anyway, he understands my ideas
about color because I will not use the usual technicolor which scream-
ing heavy colors definitely distracts the audience's concentration from
the dramatist's action. I will use our own invented colors inspired from
French goblins and contemporary paintings in such a way that the audience will practically not be conscious that the picture is in technicolor ...

I met Granville Barker at a luncheon last week and spent a wonderful
hour with him. It was thrilling for me to speak about you, your plays etc.
with him. In the midst of our discourse, it suddenly dawned upon me
that he could be the best possible INQUISITOR among all our living
actors, and it also seems to me that he is about the only man who could
deliver your long speech in such a way that the picture audience would
not become nervous or impatient for a second.

When I approached him with this, he did not say no, and since he did
not refuse outright, I hope it is a silent acceptance. Nevertheless, before
I see him again, I would appreciate a cable from you regarding your
reaction about this casting possibility ...

[Gabriel Pascal]

The **French goblins** may be the typist's error for the Gobelins, a family of dyers that in 1601
lent their Paris factory to King Henri IV, who brought two hundred workers from Flanders
to make tapestries. An actor, director, and dramatist, Harley Granville **Barker** (1877–1946),
as a young man at the Court Theatre (1904–7), where Shaw's playwriting reputation was
established in England, formed a close personal and professional relationship with Shaw.

145 / To Gabriel Pascal   [Ayot St Lawrence. Welwyn. Herts.
                                          April or May 1943]

[APCS(p): Delacorte: U(e)]

*The top of the copy of the card, the first surviving piece of correspondence after a
gap of about nine months, is cut off. Shaw planned to revise his 1935 Saint Joan
screenplay, prepared for Czinner and Bergner, which deleted the soldier from the
Epilogue.*

Rex H. as the Dauphin would be a zweiter Liebhaber [second hero] instead of a gargoyle or a Gothic building. Rex must play Dunois.

I dont see Newton as Stogumber. I should cast him for the soldier in the epilogue if he can sing. It is an important part. A mere utility cannot pull it off.

Trouncer is first rate either as Baudricourt or the Inquisitor. Why do you underrate him?

GBS

146 / To Gabriel Pascal [Ayot St Lawrence. Welwyn. Herts.]

8th May 1943

[TLS with autograph postscript (p): Delacorte: U]

Understandably, Shaw seems to confuse P.F.L. (Pascal Films, Limited) with P.F.P. (Pascal Film Productions), which differs from G.P.P. (Gabriel Pascal Productions). As mentioned earlier, G.F.D. is General Film Distributors.

My dear Gabriel

We are grateful for the supplies you sent us from Mumford's; but you must not do it again. We are doing quite well on our rations and have no excuse for sponging on you for extra food. And the regulations are so complicated that we never know when we shall both be fined several hundred pounds for breaking them – perhaps imprisoned as well. You must consume all you produce on the farm or else sell it to the local authority to be distributed to those who really need it.

Now to business. As to the letter you have drafted for me to sign about Pygmalion I will not sign it. I will have nothing to do with Pascal Films Limited, which ought to have been wound up and abolished. I understood Chenhalls to agree with me on this point. I was horrified to find that you had been promising actors engagements for Joan on percentage terms, which would leave them all with a hold on the receipts and no way of settling the question of priority except by lawsuits. Nobody except we two should have a percentage, with priority to you up to a certain figure if your remuneration depends to any extent on a royalty. My agreement will not be with you or with P.F.L., but with G.F.D. only. It will contain a clause that the direction shall be in your hands; and on the strength of this you can make your own agreement with G.F.D. The players contracts also should be with G.F.D. and not with you.

As to the capital it must be sufficient to cover the cost of the film and something to spare. What ruined you over Pygmalion and Barbara was that in your eagerness to get to work you began with enough capital to start with, and not enough to finish. When you came to the end of it and had to raise more capital at any cost you were at the mercy of the capitalists and made nothing out of two jobs that should have made you a rich man. Therefore it is no use telling me that Mr Rank will finance you. Is he ready to put down a sum sufficient to cover the utmost cost you can reasonably expect to incur? It is stated in the press that he is prepared to spend £250,000. That should be enough even for Gabriel Pascal, especially as film material is rationed and endless retakes impossible. But is it true?

You must consider all this attentively before we meet again. I shall be glad to make Anderson's acquaintance, but not until my wife is a little better able to receive visitors. For the moment she is badly crippled, but improving.

As to Pygmalion I will sign nothing but an extension of the original agreement with G.F.D. to the end of the year 1946. That agreement covers the case of legal censorships; and I object to any others being submitted to or even consulted in any way.

Now you have something hard to bite on.

Newton is quite out of the question for Stogumber and right for the soldier. Do not give him his choice. Donat wants to play Dunois; and if Rex Harrison fails you he is a good alternative. He wants Deborah Kerr to have Joan: they are all in love with her. I should say she is not yet thick enough for it. How far are you committed to Garbo; and is her engagement a condition of the Rank finance?

hardheartedly

G. Bernard Shaw

Stogumber is not a young man's part. He should be round about 50 in the play, and between 70 and 80 in the epilogue.

Anderson may be American dramatist Maxwell **Anderson** (1888–1959), whose play *Joan of Lorraine* would be published in 1944 but not produced on Broadway until 1946.

147 / To Gabriel Pascal   [Ayot St Lawrence. Welwyn. Herts.]

13th May 1943

[APCS(p): Delacorte: U(e)]

Three companies and one superfluous director to share the plunder!
'Where the carcass is, there will the eagles be gathered.'
Oh, if only you were a schoolboy! Unfortunately you are a genius, and
the whole gang of film speculators is out to pick your bones.
They shant pick mine.
Tell them I have other views, and that St Joan is off.

GBS

148 / To Gabriel Pascal   [Ayot St Lawrence. Welwyn. Herts.]

16th May 1943

[ANS: Delacorte: U]

*Written on Pascal's draft letter to Pascal Film Productions for Shaw's signature,
consenting to agreements with Loew's and with Gabriel Pascal Productions, and
to royalties from the latter.*

This makes nonsense of the letter, which should be addressed to Loews.
But it does not matter, as it will not be signed in any case.
Obviously I cannot sign this. I have not seen the agreement, which is
with a not-yet-existent firm whose formation I deprecate, and to which I
shall certainly not shift the responsibility for my royalties.
The effect of the letter would be to relieve Loews of all obligation to
me and by the same stroke make me guarantee the solvency and services
of G.P.P.
In vain is the net spread in sight of the bird. Tell them it is useless trying to get me to cancel my agreement by letters.

GBS

The first sentence of the last paragraph is from Proverbs 1:17.

149 / To G. Bernard Shaw   [*no address*]

8th June 1943

[TL(c)(tr): Delacorte: U]

Dear G.B.S.

I am working now on the preparation of 'SAINT JOAN' and find that in the second scene of the script (corresponding with the first scene of the play) at Vaucouleurs, the presence of Poulengey is needed at a certain point to motivate the change in Robert de Baudricourt's attitude towards Joan, which is too abrupt in the script as it now stands.

So after Joan's line: 'The blessed saints, Catherine and Margaret, who speak to me every day, will intercede for you. You will go to Paradise: and your name will be remembered for ever as my first helper,' I propose having Robert call Poulengey in from the courtyard without sending Joan away. He can then take Poulengey aside, out of Joan's hearing, in order to re-establish these few lines:

> ROBERT: Look here, Polly. If you were in my place would you let a girl like that do you out of sixteen francs for a horse?
> POULENGEY: I will pay for the horse.
> ROBERT: You will!
> POULENGEY: Yes, I will back my opinion.
> ROBERT: You will really gamble on a forlorn hope to the tune of sixteen francs?
> POULENGEY: It is not a gamble.
> ROBERT: What else is it?
> POULENGEY: It is a certainty. Her words and her ardent faith in God have put fire into me.
> ROBERT: (Giving him up) Whew! You are as mad as she is.
> POULENGEY: (Obstinately) We want a few mad people now. See where the sane ones have landed us!

After this last line Robert stares uncertainly at Poulengey for a moment, obviously shaken in his scepticism by the other man's conviction. He then goes back to Joan and resumes the dialogue with the words: 'What did you mean when you said that St Catherine and St Margaret talked to you every day?'

I feel that this short interruption of the scene between Joan and Robert will be a great relief and will help the climax of the second half of the scene. And what is more important, I would not like to miss your line which puts into the mouth of Poulengey 'We want a few mad people now. See where the sane ones have landed us!' for anything in the world. So please do not rob me of these two lines. I hope that you agree with me.

I will not disturb you very often, because the script is very sound and I shall need very few weeks work on it to put the technical shooting script in shape.

I followed up your suggestion about Vaughan Williams and I shall see him at the beginning of next week, and I hope everything will go well.

The studio space is fixed from October for four months, and I hope I can make the few exteriors in September when the sun is the most reliable friend of the camera man in this country.

I hope Charlotte is not suffering too much. I will include her in my prayers, as I always do.

[Gabriel Pascal]

Ralph Vaughan **Williams** (1872–1958) was a British composer.

150 / To Gabriel Pascal   [Ayot St Lawrence. Welwyn. Herts.]
                                              11th June 1943

[APCS(p): Delacorte: U]

On 29 May, Shaw wrote to Loew's, giving what he thought was the termination date of his Major Barbara *agreement. Upon discovering that he erroneously gave the dates of his original* Pygmalion *agreement and the new termination agreement, he cabled a correction to Loew's and General Film Distributors.*

Immediately on discovering my mistake I cabled Loew and wrote G.F.D. to correct it. The £1500 credit now vanishes, as G.F.D. owes me nothing on Pygmalion; but if its accounts are correct you have overpaid me on Pygmalion. I cannot find the Barbara agreement. Was that with G.F.D.? Whoever it was with owes me £20,000 or thereabouts.

I was much taken aback on learning that A.R. [(J.) Arthur Rank] is a novice in films instead of an old hand. They will skin him alive if we let them. That is what I[ndependent] P[roductions] Limited is for. As far as I can see it is neither a producing nor a distributing company, but a purely parasitic one trying to cash in on A.R.'s money for nothing. One company, G.F.D., is enough.

Under the Loew contract you can be charged with expenses that will leave you nothing.

All right about Poulengey. I will work him in for you presently.

GBS

151 / To G. Bernard Shaw [*no address* after 11 June 1943]

[TL(c): Delacorte: U]

The agreements and contract to which Pascal alludes are for Pygmalion.

Dear G.B.S.

I received your card of the 11th June, and I think I must insist on the situation with G.F.D. being clarified. You are making a great mistake in believing that G.F.D. has overpaid you. If anybody has overpaid you, it is me or my Company, Pascal Film Productions Ltd., as Chenhalls proved to G.F.D. with Weinstein that they owed us money from the Continent for all kind of accountancy differences. It was established that they paid us £5,000 under the Termination Agreement for the difference on the old Distribution Contract and £10,000 for the Reissue Agreement, so the £1,500 is from these two sums. If you refuse it, it is automatically due to my Company, which needs the money very badly to pay taxes.

When I came back, as you know, I corrected the Agreement so that in all the countries where the picture could not be screened, such as Germany, Austria, Russia, Lithuania, Greece and Italy, the old Agreement should hold good on the percentage basis.

As Chenhalls is now better occupied than being part of the British picture industry, and the Directors of the Company are now myself and Capt. Richard Norton, I have a great interest in putting my old Company in shape, for the income of 'Major Barbara' from the Continent will prove it to be an even greater financial success than 'Pygmalion.' So I am sure that your £20,000 in 'Major Barbara' is safeguarded.

I repeat again that I am a much better business man than you believe, but unfortunately I had not one faithful man around me since making pictures in this country. Like Lazarus at the rich man's wedding, I was only sitting at the gate while parasites and third-rate talents made fantastic money in this business, because at the moment when I needed your co-operation you let me down, as you know, for reasons which I accepted blindly. When we signed our first deal I promised you real classics of your plays; I fulfilled my promise and am ready to fulfil it further without any egotistical ulterior motive; but your pride is that I should not be poor and should not be called a 'sucker' (I hope you know this American expression?) by this crooked trade, so I need your co-operation this time more than ever, but in a sense that is really helping me and not leaving me in a vacuum. We have a terrific chance to get back the artistic leadership of the British cinema if we play our cards well. I am offended and hurt when second-rate writers like Noel Coward are hailed as the Saviours of the industry and are heard to boast that you do not count any more. However, I have always followed your counsel, even if it is sometimes against my common sense and I am determined to follow it again, because I believe in your wisdom and foresight; so I told Mr Rank that I am ready to make 'St Joan' under a personal contract with G.F.D. because this is your advice to me.

You are right when you say about Rank that 'they will skin him alive if we let them,' but it is our duty; – certainly my duty – to prevent this. I have limitless faith in his honesty and integrity, so I am sure that everything will work out all right now. Certainly many people try to cash in on his money for nothing; that is not my business. I cannot control all the parasites who constitute at least 90% of the British film industry. I must protect the interests of the other 10% who are the creative ones, including ourselves, and I will do so ...

[Gabriel Pascal]

The **Lazarus** reference is to Luke 16:19–23. **Coward**'s patriotic film, *In Which We Serve* (1942), which salutes the Royal Navy, was so **hailed** and become enormously successful on both sides of the Atlantic.

152 / To Gabriel Pascal Ayot St Lawrence [Welwyn. Herts.]
20th June 1943
[ANS: Delacorte: U]

G.F.D. owes me nothing on Pyg. Pascal Films has overpaid me on Pyg. if G.F.D. accounts are correct. The £1500 figure falls through with the discovery that I have no contract with G.F.D.

On Barbara I am owed upward of £15,000, whether by P.F. or G.F.D. I dont know, as the contract must be in London: I cannot find it here.

Bring Mr Rank with you on Tuesday if you can.

GBS

153 / To Gabriel Pascal [Ayot St Lawrence. Welwyn. Herts.]
24th June 1943
[TLS: Letters]

My dear Gabriel

Wash out everything I said to you last Saturday. A.R. is not an innocent novice: he has been in the game for 15 years, and is chairman of ten companies engaged in it. He is a director of nearly 60 companies. I am more anxious than ever to have a look at him; but what I have learnt since we met entirely changes my view of the situation. Do not let yourself be entangled in his companies by becoming a shareholder. Have a separate agreement for each production, your remuneration to be a royalty on the gross and not a share of profits, with advances, nonreturnable, for you to live on, and a deposit of capital by the shareholders sufficient to cover the utmost cost of the whole production. Do not bind your future activities in any way.

You will notice that Korda, in becoming a film speculator, has ceased to be an artist, just as so many good engineers, in becoming mining speculators, have ceased to be engineers: a miserable deterioration ending sometimes in their ruin.

On reflection I am against putting C and C, or any other production, in front of St Joan. I cannot afford to have two films running at the same time; and I think the distraction of public expectation by starting a new and less popular hare would be an error of artistic judgment. There is

plenty to do on St Joan beside the Loire scene, which you will not be
ready to do before the spring.

I have a set of flashlights of the Dublin production of C and C for your
inspection, as the Egyptian scenery is so good that you might find the
designer useful. I can easily find out who he is ...

We are expecting you on Saturday the 3rd July, with or without A.R.

always yours

G. Bernard Shaw

Dorothy (Dolly) Travers-Smith (1901–77), a Dubliner who for many years was the Abbey
Theatre's leading scene **designer**, created scenery and costumes for its 24 October 1927
production of *Caesar and Cleopatra*. As Dorothea, she exhibited paintings in London. In
1931 she married Irish dramatist Lennox Robinson (1886–1951).

154 / To G. Bernard Shaw

[*no address*]

7th July 1943

[TL(c): Delacorte: U(e)]

*As Pascal's letter of 25 March 1947 reveals, he was not candid with Shaw about
Rank's promise to protect Pascal's financial interests. Rank told him he had no
intention of giving him 10% of the gross receipts. Shaw could only try to persuade Rank and Pascal on the terms of their agreement, which the two arranged
together, as Shaw and Rank arranged their own terms together.*

My dear G.B.S.

I am most grateful to you for your kind and valuable help in discussing
my financial status with Arthur Rank on Saturday. I am also very anxious
to know your impression of him from the meeting. He himself seemed
to be very happy when we left you, and he certainly went away inspired,
and promised me that he will take care to protect my financial interests
in the spirit you wish it to be done. I think that man is really sincere to
me and he will always respect his given word to you. So if we do a picture
before St Joan, he will not exhibit it until after St Joan, and you can rely
on his keeping his promise.

I am very grateful to you for agreeing to my doing Doctor's Dilemma
first ...

In your own interests, my dear G.B.S., the contract questions should
be cleared up as soon as possible ...

If you like I can come next Monday afternoon. I need to have another talk with you regarding Rank; I realise again, after our last meeting, how clear your vision is, and what a fool I was not to appreciate sufficiently your financial genius ...

[Gabriel Pascal]

155 / To Gabriel Pascal   [Ayot St Lawrence. Welwyn. Herts.]
                                                    10th July 1943

[APCS(p): Delacorte: U(e)].

We shall expect you on Monday round about 4.

I am as anxious as you are to get the agreements settled; but I do not yet see your safe way. When Charlotte and I die, as we may any day and must pretty soon, you will be in the hands of the Public Trustee, who will at once come down on you for the royalty on Barbara. That points to making you a company. But then you would have to share the booty with the other shareholders, who contribute nothing, A.R. contributing everything.

We must talk it over ...

GBS

156 / To Gabriel Pascal   [Ayot St Lawrence. Welwyn. Herts.]
                                                    18th July 1943

[APCS(p): Delacorte: U]

Contract negotiations continued for two more months.

I have written to J.A.R., both about our affair, and his own political position. Until I hear from him I cannot draft the agreement or do anything more.

I have said that in your place I should demand for each film a director's fee of £2600 (fifty a week) for a year, and *in addition*, a royalty of 10% on the receipts, without any share in the profits. Any expenditure on production exceeding an agreed figure is to be deducted from your royalty, leaving your fee – the £2600 – untouched.

I still think that your agreement and mine should be separate ones with Rank or his company and not with one another. Where is the Barbara money? I am not sure that in your interest and against my own I should not call it in at once if it is really available, to guard against the possibility of bankruptcy and forfeiture at the hands of the Public Trustee, or raising the money at the price of utter enslavement.

GBS

157 / To Gabriel Pascal   [Ayot St Lawrence. Welwyn. Herts.]
16th January 1944

[APCS(p): Delacorte: U(e)]

You have broken the Caesar agreement the very first thing. The Cinema says that you have announced that Brian Desmond Hurst is to be your co-director. I put the clause expressly forbidding this into the agreement to enable you to say non posso [I am not able] when you were pestered for a share in the publicity. You had better tell Mr Hurst that you had not read the agreement when you made the announcement, and that you are sorry his name cannot appear as having any share in the artistic direction.

In haste

GBS

Brian Desmond **Hurst** (1900–86), Irish-born film director, was uncredited for a few scenes he directed in *Caesar and Cleopatra*.

158 / To Gabriel Pascal   [Ayot St Lawrence. Welwyn. Herts.]
24th January 1944

[TLS(p): Delacorte: U]

Dear Gabriel

I will send you a copy of the agreement when I get it back from Woodham Smith. Your publicity girl broke it in two places. She advertized me as GEORGE Bernard though there is a clause expressly stipulating that I am to be Bernard Shaw in all announcements. And she announced your Irish assistant as Co-Director in the teeth of the agreement that it was never to be suggested that your supreme artistic direction was to be shared with anyone.

This last condition is very important, and also very convenient for all parties. It is convenient because when your assistants want to be billed as Cos, you can without offence declare that nothing would please you better, but that unfortunately the agreement forbids it.

It is important because without it you could sublet your job by paying the Irishman, or any other ambitious beginner, £500 to do it, and then going to bed until the film was finished, giving us nothing but your name in the bill without a stroke of your work. There is a parallel clause, equally stringent, to prevent G.C.F.C. from subletting the contract to another and poorer company, who could sublet it again, and so on until you would be left to work for a company which in desperation had paid its last penny to get the contract and had nothing left for the production except what it could borrow on ruinous terms.

All good bargains are good for both parties; but the snag in this is that, if they are transferable, subletting will be possible. Hence I give good terms, but not for sale. If you or Rank sell out bang goes the contract.

As to your health troubles I expect they will vanish when you get down to your proper work in the studio and are well rid of your old Company and the business entanglements that you should never have undertaken. Also you need a foyer of your own instead of a hotel. Cigars wont help, but neither will carrots. Get your mind easy and the rest will follow. Knitting is useful only because it makes idling possible just as cigarettes do. To occupy your mind try mathematics. They are very interesting as long as you dont try to do sums. I cannot do sums; but I like finding out how they are done. And physics, especially astro-physics, are enthralling. Buy Hogben's Mathematics for the Million, and see whether you can stand it ...

If I do not hear from you to the contrary I shall expect you next Thursday, the 27th, after three. But the place is pretty dismal in this weather, and I am empty of any helpful suggestions; so do not come if the day is not fine and you fit and inclined.

GBS

George Ivor **Woodham-Smith** (1895–1968), a solicitor, had a long business association with J. Arthur Rank. **G.C.F.C.** was one of J. Arthur Rank's companies, General Cinema Finance

Corporation. English scientist and educator Lancelot Thomas **Hogben** (1895–1975) wrote *Mathematics for the Million* (1936).

159 / To Gabriel Pascal   [Ayot St Lawrence. Welwyn. Herts.]
15th February 1944
[APCS (tr): Delacorte: U (e)]

Choose Bliss without hesitation: Walton has had his turn; and the more leading composers you give a chance to, the better for your prestige.

No need to shew them to me: I cannot tell what a man's music will be like by looking at him.

Bliss's competence – distinguished competence – is beyond question. So that is settled.

I shall expect you after 15 (3) on Thursday next unless you phone to the contrary.

You say the Sphinx picture is in America. If it is in intelligent hands, why not cable to them to have it photographed and send you six prints reduced to 10" × 8"?

GBS

Arthur (later Sir Arthur) **Bliss** (1891–1975), British composer and director of music for the BBC, found Pascal uncongenial. Georges Auric (1899–1983), French composer and member of the group called Les Six, would compose the music for *Caesar and Cleopatra*. The **Sphinx picture**, *Répos en Egypte* (1879) by French painter Luc Olivier Merson (1846–1920), is the source of the tableau that opens Act I, Cleopatra asleep in the Sphinx's lap.

160 / To G. Bernard Shaw   [The Raven Hotel. Droitwich. Worc.]
24th February 1944
[TLS(p): Delacorte: U]

My dear G.B.S.

I enjoyed our last meeting and your morality speech to my secretary about the farewell kiss.

I have now definitely decided to take Bliss as the composer for the picture.

I am delighted that you are writing Cleopatra's bedroom scene for the picture. I think it would be very good, as you planned, to start the scene with Cleopatra and Ftatateeta, but instead of Ftatateeta saying that Caesar has gone, which is not strong enough, she should tell Cleopatra that she heard in the town that Caesar is already defeated and 'What fools we have been to trust Caesar and rely on him. He is encircled and lost.' Cleopatra is raging with anger, slapping Ftatateeta's face, and then a sudden change comes over her mind: 'I will go and see him.' The girls arrive to make her morning toilet, with all the wonderful flacons (I think about seventeen she had) of the different perfumes from which she should choose the right one to perfume her bath for the old hook-nose Caesar. She dashes the flacons to the ground, and walks from the bedroom in her neglige towards the bathroom, and descends from the marble steps into her bath of pure water. She is thinking of Caesar's line 'He will know Cleopatra by her pride, her courage, her majesty and her beauty.' The girls, shivering with horror: 'What happened to the Queen; she is taking a bath of pure water.' Fade out.

This should be only a small inspiration for the length of the scene, which should be about 2½ to 3 minutes dialogue reading, and can occupy a composite set on the small stage from the bedroom, the alcove between the bedroom and the very pompous marble bathroom in Pompeian style.

I arrived here last Saturday. Your French chateau in Impney has been taken over by the military, but I have a nice room at the Raven Hotel, and already, after three baths, my shoulder is much better. The doctor tells me that in ten days I will be in perfect health again. My sickness is called fibrocitis.

I have given my Art Department all your instructions and suggestions about the sets, and passed on to Oliver Messel your ideas about Cleopatra's costumes. They are all working very hard in the right spirit, and the whole picture seems to be progressing under good spiritual auspices.

I am no longer grumbling in my heart about the loss of your speech of God Ra, because however 'ghostly' you may consider you look, after much reflection I realised that you would steal away the first two reels of the picture from our stars, Claude Rains and Vivien Leigh. But as soon as we start shooting, I would like to have you on the set one day before my colour camera; or, if you prefer, I could come to see you at your place with my camera man as soon as there is some spring sunshine.

I would be very grateful if you would send me the scene you are writing to Droitwich, so that I can incorporate it in my script and give instructions for the sets.

> Sempre tuo fedele [Always your faithful]
> Gabriele

Oliver **Messel** (1905–78), English stage and screen designer, created costumes and settings for *Caesar and Cleopatra*. Pascal wanted Shaw to play the Egyptian god **Ra** in the prologue. Claude **Rains** (1899–1967), British stage actor, became a Hollywood character actor and star in 1933.

161 / To Gabriel Pascal [Ayot St Lawrence. Welwyn. Herts.]
27th February 1944

[TLS(p): Delacorte: U]

Shaw typed this at the foot of Pascal's 24 February letter.

The new scene, if I can write it, will not be exactly like that, because you have changed the child Cleopatra into the wily woman of forty with all her flacons and fripperies; and this does not even begin to occur in the play until after the lighthouse scene, which is the first breach in unity of time. As to her caring about the war news, or dragging in resemblances to the present war, of which everyone is now heartily sick, it is out of the question. The Cleopatra of the new scene must still be a child ...

> GBS

162 / To Gabriel Pascal [Ayot St Lawrence. Welwyn. Herts.]
15th March 1944

[APCS: HRC: U(e)]

Note that this greatly strengthens the part of Ftatateeta. Has she the figure for it?

Has Caesar got the smile?

Your idea of a following scene in which Cleopatra's feet only are seen needs no words.

It is extremely important that Cleopatra's charm shall be that of a beautiful child, *not of sex*. The whole play would be disgusting if Caesar were an old man seducing a child. Ftata must be the sexual attraction.

Shew the script to Bliss; and ask him whether he can do something with it.

GBS

Ftatateeta was played by Flora (later Dame Flora) Robson (1902–84), British stage and screen character actress, who was not the **sexual attraction**.

163 / To Gabriel Pascal [Ayot St Lawrence. Welwyn. Herts.]
27th April 1944

[TLS(p): Delacorte: U(e)]

On 26 April 1944, The Star *reported that Rains had talked for hours with Shaw about his plays, but not* Caesar and Cleopatra.

My dear Gabriel

This press foolishness must stop absolutely. You and I, Rank and Rains, have a first class publicity which cannot be improved on; but it can be spoilt and made offensive by such silly rubbish as appears in the papers today, the work evidently of the press agent whom you so wickedly planted on me on Tuesday.

In future unless our proceedings are treated as sacredly private I will take no part in them. A report of what passes at rehearsal or production is worse than a betrayal of a confession. The Americans do not know this: they have no sense of privacy; but you must not Americanize the British studios. Get rid of all your press people: they damage you every time, and offend everyone else.

If Rains really thought I took no notice of him for 15 minutes he was very much mistaken. I remembered him and was perfectly satisfied in the first split second.

Do take this about the press to heart.

G. Bernard Shaw

164 / To G. Bernard Shaw   Mumford's Farm
                                        Chalfont St Peter. Bucks.
                                            4th May 1944

[TPCS: HRC: U]

Dear G.B.S.

Don't you think 'You are old and rather wrinkly' is what we need instead
of 'Rather thin and stringy' in the Sphinx scene?

We are also anxious to know about the intonation of the name Cleopatra. Should it be pronounced with a long 'a' (ah) or a flat 'a' ?

                                            Gabriel

Rains was not **thin**.

165 / To Gabriel Pascal   [Ayot St Lawrence. Welwyn. Herts.]
                                            7th [May] 1944

[ANS: HRC: U]

*Written on Pascal's postal card, the first sentence is after the first paragraph, the
rest after the second.*

I have settled this.

The Italian long ah of course. To call her Cleopaytra would stamp the
film as American. In America they call a tomato a tomayter.

I am expecting you tomorrow (Monday) without a publicity retinue.

                                            GBS

166 / To G. Bernard Shaw   [*no address*]
                                            22nd June 1944

[TL: Sphinx]

*D-Day occurred six days before Pascal began shooting. On 16 June the Nazis
began their V-2 rocket attacks on London, which made filming conditions even
more difficult than they had been for Major Barbara.*

My dear G.B.S.

I started shooting on the 12th of this month. During the first week I struggled with great technical difficulties; but I hope to finish the Sphinx scene next week.

Last Saturday I had a narrow escape on the Pharos set, which is built out of doors on the studio lot, when a flying bomb exploded about 150 yards away in a nearby field. Last night the french windows in my sitting-room on the farm were blown in and the ceiling in my bedroom was cracked completely, so I am having the same gay start on the picture as I had with Major Barbara during the blitz. I hope these pilotless planes are not reaching your district.

I enclose herewith the first batch of stills. I hope you like them.

[Gabriel Pascal]

167 / To Gabriel Pascal   Ayot St Lawrence. Welwyn. Herts.

1st July 1944

[TLS: Letters]

Shaw visited the Denham studios on 29 June.

My dear Gabriel

You have surpassed yourself in this production already in one scene. When it is finished it will lick creation.

There is one thing wrong with the desert sky. The stars and planets are all the same size and brightness. You should have engaged an astronomer to correct this. It is the only thing that gives away the artificiality of the scene.

Britannus is so hopelessly wrong that he will hold up all the scenes in which he appears until he is redressed. I enclose a suggestion of what he should look like. At present he is a handsome young military man instead of an elderly academic literary secretary, very unlike all the others. He must have an academic gown.

But I pity poor Rank. The film will cost a million. On Thursday there were hundreds of men in the studio; and only twelve at most had anything to do but take snapshots and pick up scraps of my conversation for sale to the papers. Most of them did not do even that much. Were they all on the payroll?

And the retakes! with Vivien gabbling tonelessly such sounds as cummineechoo [come and eat you] and oaljentlmin [old gentleman]! Does she always go on like that or should I have had her here to drill her in the diction of the part?

However, I am beginning to complain, which is monstrously ungrateful; for the film promises to be a wonder.

sempre a te
GBS

Cecil Parker (né Cecil Schwabe, 1897–1971), British character actor of stage and screen, played **Britannus**.

168 / To G. Bernard Shaw

[no address]
8th July 1944

[TL: Sphinx]

Portions of this letter, on three separated pages, are in their probable sequence.

My dearest G.B.S.

Your letter of the 1st July made me very happy, because it gave me hope and assurance that I am on the right road with this production.

Your criticisms are not complaints, but the most creative and helpful suggestions, which I have immediately realised in action.

Regarding the desert sky: you have not seen this in the right light. I not only consulted an astronomical expert, but he designed for us the whole possible sky formation of that period in summertime, which we copied as well as we could. When you see the real sky on the screen, you will be astonished to see how differently it looks from the half-lit sky you saw in the studio, without the reflected clouds which give the sense of distance between the stars. There are about six different sizes.

Britannus: since I received your sketch, I have discarded his original costume, which I never liked very much, and have had a long gown made for him; and he will have a kind of shepherd's plaid, which I hope to get next week. I am sending you herewith a photograph of the gown, with a completely different belt, which I hope you will like very much. His wig I have had remade with red hair, as you suggest, and a new moustache, turning down. It is not yet completely to my satisfaction, but they are making a new one which will be nearer to your design.

Don't worry about poor Rank. Most of the people you saw at the Studio had nothing to do with my unit. They sneaked in from all the other stages to be silent witnesses of the historic moment of your arrival at Denham.

I had a long argument with Claude Rains, who wanted to play the Pharos scene wearing his wreath. My logical argument is that from the moment when Cleopatra puts his helmet on in the Council Chamber, saying 'How nice! You look only about fifty in it,' he cannot wear anything except the helmet on his head; and the only thing he can do on the Pharos is to take it off and put it down beside him on the faggots, to mop the sweat of African heat from his forehead, so that he can play the carpet scene bareheaded. Then when the tumult is heard in the distance and Caesar turns to Rufio saying: 'Come, Rufio,' he puts his helmet on again ready for the battle; and only after Apollodorus has made his dive, and he sees there is no other way to escape, he gives his helmet to Britannus, like a gentleman in evening dress handing a *chapeau claque* [opera hat] to his valet, jumps onto the parapet, and dives in himself, bareheaded.

Again, my dearest G.B.S., accept my most affectionate thanks for your visit, and your so helpful suggestions, and your encouraging note, which will be for the whole picture a continuous inspiration, especially in the moments when I am weakened in face of the endless technical difficulties which I must overcome. I realise more than ever during the making of this picture that filming your plays has become my life work, and that you are the greatest inspiration to me in this or any other life.

[Gabriel Pascal]

Basil Sydney (1894–1968), British actor of English and American stage and screen, played **Rufio**.

169 / To Gabriel Pascal Ayot [St Lawrence. Welwyn. Herts.]
9th July 1944
[APCS(p): Delacorte: U(e)]

Caesar may be so excited by Apollodorus's dive that he snatches off his

172

helmet and hurls it at Britannus like a ball at cricket; and Britannus fields it like a first class wicket keeper.

But I am not sure that he should not dive with his helmet on, to save his head, as Rufio must. It was a point of honor to swim the Tiber in full armor.

Was Apollodorus's wonderful head of hair a wig? If so, he can change it for a fair one, modelled on the Apollo Belvedere or the Hermes of Praxiteles.

Britannus must be mainly in blue: the shepherd's plaid is only for the tunic. That is why the blue overall should be an academic gown, opening all down the front. They have plenty of such things in Oxford still.

GBS

Apollodorus was played by Stewart Granger (né James Stewart, 1913–93), British and American film star who, at the 1936 Malvern Festival, had acted Warwick in *Saint Joan* under his real name, and in 1937 played King Magnus in *The Apple Cart* there under his new name. His hair was his own.

170 / To Gabriel Pascal

Ayot St Lawrence. Welwyn. Herts.

9th July 1944

[ALS(p): Delacorte: U(e)]

Caesar couldnt possibly have his wreath in the Pharos scene. He wont want to when he gets into the spirit of the scene, the main bit of acting in which is the change from the old baldheaded discouraged futile disillusioning superannuated dug-out before lunch to the ebullient impetuous steel nerved Caesar after it. That will play out Claude's whole gamut as an actor!

Putting on the helmet is good business.

Vivien's shyness doesnt matter. I can knock all that out of her and get her really going in half a jiffy.

As to the costumes, read what I have written on the proofs.

In haste – the chauffeur is in a hurry.

GBS

171 / To Gabriel Pascal   [*no address*

July 1944]

[APC: Sphinx]

Caesar never succeeds in pronouncing this name: he always calls it
either Totateeta or Teetatota. But Cleopatra and Ftata herself must
speak it clearly and perfectly. To do this they must practise it as
Aftatateeta, and when they have got this quite glibly, drop the A.

It will then be as easy as saying 'left a message' or 'laughed to scorn'
or 'lift a suitcase' or any other phrase with an ft in it.

[GBS]

The phrase '**laugh to scorn**,' used in *As You Like It* 4.2 and *Macbeth* 4.1, derives from 'Laugh
no man to scorn' (Ecclesiasticus 7:11).

172 / To G. Bernard Shaw   [*no address*]

23rd July 1944

[TL: Sphinx]

*Portions of this letter, on three separated pages, are in their probable sequence. For
weeks, the sun did not shine, eventually forcing Pascal to move to Egypt, where
sunshine continued to elude the director.*

My dearest G.B.S.

Please forgive me for answering your inspired costume notes only today;
but I have had such a hard time fighting against St. Petrus who – coward
as he is – has not favoured me with sunshine on the Pharos set. But I am
over the worst of it, and at the end of next week I shall start on the Mem-
phis Palace set.

I made a new costume, a new wig, and a new moustache for Britannus, and am sending you herewith photos of his costume and make-up.
The costume is now a lovely cornflower blue, and the shepherd's plaid
hood is checked in pinkish-white and a natural brown, woven in Scotland.

Incidentally, when I come to the Music Room sequence, reading from
the play and the script, I always have the feeling that a very short new
scene would be useful to bridge the time gap of six months since the

foregoing scene on the Pharos. You start Act IV with the following statement: 'Cleopatra's sousing in the east harbour of Alexandria was in
October 48 B.C. In March 47 she is passing the afternoon in her bou-
doir in the palace.' It is this interval that I want to cover smoothly on the
screen, instead of leaving the audience in ignorance of the time-situa-
tion until Cleopatra tells Pothinus: 'These six months we have been
besieged in the palace by my subjects.'

[Gabriel Pascal]

St Petrus may be Peter, bishop and patriarch of Alexandria, martyred in 311.

173 / To Gabriel Pascal Ayot St Lawrence. Welwyn. Herts.
26th July 1944

[APCS: clipping from German magazine]

Dear Gabriel

Britannus's costume is all right now; but the moustache is hopeless. He
must have Dundreary whiskers – yellow whiskers.

In great haste

GBS

Dundreary whiskers are long-flowing side whiskers named after Lord Dundreary, a character in *Our American Cousin* (1858) by Tom Taylor (1817–80), English dramatist. Accompanying the postal card was a watercolour sketch of Britannus's head.

174 / To Gabriel Pascal Ayot St. Lawrence Welwyn. Herts.
28th July 1944

[TLS: Letters]

My dear Gabriel

In the sketch of Britannus I rushed off to you I painted his eyebrows
black. They should of course be yellow. The wig, moustache, and whiskers can all be made on a frame which he can put on like a helmet: it
cannot be stuck on with spirit gum. The color should be auburn or
downright yellow.

As to the music I can make nothing of the orchestral score you have sent me. I advised Bliss to compose a complete C. & C. suite for use at orchestral concerts, and to let you use such parts of it as you may require to accompany the film. You are quite right in ruling that when my music begins his must stop. Thus we need a nocturne for the opening of the Sphinx scene; but it must die away into silence when Caesar arrives at the Sphinx and contemplates it before he speaks. And there must be no more until the scene is over. Any 'melodrame' during the dialogue you must cut out ruthlessly: it is detestably inartistic: neither drama nor opera. The BBC has reduced it to absurdity. I urged Bliss not to be oriental but just Blissful to his heart's content. As a taste for his music, like all new music, has to be acquired, we must not lightly turn it down. Have you recorded any of it? It is impossible for me to say anything until I have heard more of it than I can finger out from the very unreadable score.

Try to impress on C.R. that unless the other characters are made the very most of – they are all minor figures who are there only to build him up – he will lose heavily. A star who is jealous of his support throws away half his lustre.

I am not sorry that there is a time limit for both C. and Cleo: time limits are badly needed in the studio, as the temptation to retake is so strong when the director is a real artist: in short, when he is Gabriel Pascal.

Hitler celebrated my birthday by smashing my bedroom window with a bomb; and in the afternoon I had to do a newsreel about it.

I think there must be a definite break in the continuity after the lighthouse scene; but I will study it and see what can be done with the help of your suggestions.

come sempre

GBS

In the nineteenth century, **mélodrame**, originally a pantomimic action play with accompanying music, meant a thriller with emotional or suspenseful music buttressing the dialogue.

Rains's contract called for a huge salary increase, with Pascal paying his income tax, if he worked more than six months. Pascal's arrangement with David O. Selznick, who held Vivien Leigh under an exclusive contract, was also for a fixed term.

175 / To G. Bernard Shaw   [*no address*]

24th September 1944

[TL(c): Delacorte: U]

*Six weeks after shooting began, Pascal changed the schedule because Vivien Leigh
was pregnant. When she miscarried, he rearranged it.*

My dearest G.B.S.

I am sadly disappointed to have to cancel my coming this afternoon, as I
have too bad a cold and am shivering so that I am scared both of going
out and perhaps of infecting you. I tried to reach you on the telephone
several times today, but your line is out of order; so, as I don't like to let
you wait, I am sending the chauffeur with a few stills. The rest of the
stills of Acts IV and V I will bring next week.

Vivien Leigh has been ill ever since I saw you last. It looks as though
she will return next week to the studio, and I can finish the interrupted
Act IV. After that I shall have nothing to do except the Council Chamber and the Music Room and Bedroom, for which the sets will be ready
in about three weeks' time.

There are all kinds of strikes and labour troubles at the studio, which
are not helping the smooth progress of the picture. Yesterday the head
of the extras' union came and tried to blackmail us, and Rank told me
on the phone that the Ministry of Labour will go into the question next
week and settle it. He sends his kindest regards to you, and is always
begging me to ask you to reduce the length of the Council Chamber,
because he cannot make money on the picture if it runs over two
hours. Actually it looks more like two hours and twenty minutes, if not
two-and-a-half hours; but we can discuss this next week-end when I am
with you ...

[Gabriel Pascal]

Shaw's reply comments on the **length**. In the event, the British print of *Caesar and Cleopatra*
ran two hours and fourteen minutes; the American print, seven minutes less.

176 / To Gabriel Pascal 4 Whitehall Court. London SW1
25th September 1944

[TLS(p): Delacorte: U(e)]

My dear Gabriel

Take care of yourself; for if you go I know not whither to turn for your successor.

Now to business. First, as to the dispute with the trade unions. If Independent Producers, instead of sticking to its business of producing is going to engage in the class war with its extras, and make friction when it should be making films, then I shall rule it out of my future arrangements. I prefer oil to sand in my bearings. Extras who do not belong to a union and will not join it, are, in the lump, stupid, disloyal, selfish undisciplined vagabonds. Those who belong to a union are sensible, provident, steady, punctual, and can be disciplined by their union if they behave unreasonably. The war between employers and trade unionists is a hundred years out of date. Urge Arthur to make it a rule at once that no extras shall be employed by him unless they belong to their union. Let him make another rule that if there are any grievances he must not be troubled with *ex parte* [one-sided] individual complaints; but they must be brought before him by the union secretary. This will at once put an end to the present friction, delay, expense, and distraction, and improve the quality of the personnel at Denham.

An employer who is not a member of an employers' federation is a fool. So is an employee who is not a member of a trade union.

Second, there must be an end of this funk about the length of the film. If films are to be restricted to two hours to please the one horse cinemas who must have two features and a slap-stick comic to make up their programs then we must at once scrap Caesar and rule out St Joan with all my major works which run for three hours, and fall back on Arms and the Man, Androcles, and the like. Caesar is hardly long enough for a one-feature program; and the first condition we must impose on the exhibitors is that Caesar-plus-a-news-reel must be the whole and sole program, and the occasion marked as a very special one, possibly even by doubling the charge for admission. Any other policy will only confirm Hollywood in its conviction that Shaw is a detrimental author. That was what made United Artists sabotage Barbara.

So much for business: now for art. Septimus is terribly wrong. He is so like Rains in feature and figure that on my first glance at the stills I mistook him for Caesar. He looks ten years older than Caesar instead of at least ten years younger. He is dressed like a civilian, fat and overfed. Such a creature could no more cut off Pompey's head than he could win a hundred yards sprint. Septimus must be under forty, in Roman military uniform, an athlete and a swordsman without an ounce of fat on him, swift and disciplined in movement, crisp and hard in speech, as unlike Caesar as possible, and as like Hitler (barring the moustache).

Is it possible to remedy this – to recast and retake? The effect shewn in the stills is desperately bad.

The lighthouse scene is wonderful. A glance at it sweeps all the rubbish about two hours and twenty minutes into the dustbin. If the audience got nothing but this and the Sphinx they would go away feeling they had first rate value for their money, and come again the next night. If only Septimus were not such a let-down!

I must stop here, or this letter will kill you and send Arthur to bed for a fortnight.

G. Bernard Shaw

P.S. Was Olivier as good as Sergius as the papers say? It is the real acting part in Arms: Bluntschli is actor-proof. I should rank a really good Sergius high as a Shavian actor.

Raymond Lovell (1900–53), Canadian stage actor who performed in Britain, acted Lucius **Septimius** (not Septimus). On 5 September, *Arms and the Man* opened at the Old Vic. Among the stellar cast were Ralph Richardson as Bluntschli and Sybil Thorndike as Catherine.

177 / To Gabriel Pascal   Ayot St Lawrence. Welwyn. Herts.

5th November 1944

[APCS: Sphinx]

A crook in England means either a shepherd or a bishop.

Its presence or absence in the film will not affect the receipts by a single centesimo [hundredth of a penny].

Its introduction at so late a stage may involve retakes which will cost J.A.R. thousands of pounds for nothing.

There is no speech in my dialogue so bad that it needs a crook to give it its full value.

A crook is a hindrance to a speaker, and an asset only to a dumb figure in a processional pageant: z.b. [*zum Beispiel* (for example)] a bishop.

Your phoned message leaves me quite in the dark as to who is to wave the crook, or when or where or how or why. It is certainly not worth spending an extra twopence on.

GBS

178 / To G. Bernard Shaw [*no address*]
12th November 1944

[TL: Sphinx]

My dear G.B.S.

Don't worry about the crook. Certainly I will not use it through my actor to emphasise any of your lines. I know they don't need any emphasis, and the actor Britannus, Cecil Parker, is the finest understating actor we have, so there is no danger of that at all. Also I won't need any retakes because I only use the crook in the first half of the Council Chamber for his first scenes, and I lose it afterwards.

[Gabriel Pascal]

179 / To Gabriel Pascal Ayot St Lawrence. Welwyn. Herts.
16th November 1944

[APCS(p): Delacorte: U(e)]

After Caesar, which will be a great pictorial success, any modern indoors comedy will be a come-down for you. Androcles & the Lion is pictorial. Arms & the Man (screen version) is pictorial. St Joan is pictorial. The Doctor's Dilemma isnt; and it needs an outstanding comic actor for B.B. The Devil's Disciple is not sympathetic to the Anglo-American entente.

Arms & the Man will be just right for demobbed audiences: it proved so last time.

I cannot understand this new tack of Arthur's. Is he losing his nerve?

GBS

Since Pascal's letters to Shaw before and after this postal card have not surfaced, what Rank's new '**tack**' or course of action was, is unclear. However, Pascal's next letter, over a month later, suggests that Rank was having second thoughts about financing another Pascal film of a Shaw play and was equivocating about his promise to make studio space available to Pascal.

180 / To G. Bernard Shaw

Mumford's Farm
Chalfont St Peter. Bucks.
15th December 1944

[TLS: BL 50524 f 257: U]

In a letter of 14 December to J. Arthur Rank, Pascal reminded Rank that out of loyalty he did not sell his half interest in Deborah Kerr's contract to Hollywood to solve his financial problems, that Rank had rejected his proposals to film another Shaw play, that he had Hollywood offers, and that his contract with Kerr called for a starting date in mid-June. He asked for a decision by the end of 1944.

My dear G.B.S.

I was so happy about our meeting last Sunday, and as we agreed, I sent a letter to Mr Rank, asking him for the Studio space which he originally promised me next late Spring. As there is terrific jealousy about my privileged position which our current picture gives me, I cannot see any other way to get a decision about Studio space from Arthur. I hope he will have the commonsense to give me the space in time[;] otherwise I will make arrangements with another Studio here in England to shoot the picture.

Sempre
Gabriel

P.S. I enclose copy of my letter to Mr Rank.

181 / To Gabriel Pascal

Ayot St Lawrence. Welwyn. Herts.
16th December 1944

[TLS: Letters]

The music for the Caesar film should not be difficult if we can get the right composer. The only snag is that the right composer would be too good for a job of incidental theatre music of no use in the concert room. Therefore what we should do is to let the composer see the film, and ask him whether he finds in it the program for an orchestral suite: Overture, Desert Nocturne, Barcarolle, March, Egyptian Music Lesson, Banquet, Triumph ending in Calm Sea and Prosperous Voyage, with perhaps Til Eulenspiegelish character numbers labelled Ftatateeta and Britannus, making a complete independent work to be broadcast or performed at the Three Choirs and other Festivals. This would belong exclusively to the composer: all we should need would be his licence to have suitable parts of it fitted to the film, and his help in arranging it, and adding a few fanfares and scraps of '*melodrama.*' For this of course he would be paid; and he would be left in possession of a musical property as lucrative as Grieg's Peer Gynt suite. This would be well worth the best composer's while if he felt inspired by the subject.

The question remains, who is the best man? I was very much struck by a broadcast of a classical play (Greek) with music by Benjamin Britten. It had style and great refinement. He handled his trumpets beautifully; and his manner was not the lawless post-Wagnerianism that now sounds so tiresomely oldfashioned, but in the tradition of Gluck, Berlioz, and Chopin. It had the forgotten quality of elegance. And it was all original: he will not plant any ersatz Aida on us.

Do, pray, sound him on the subject. In the form which I suggest the proposition would be good business for him; and a view of the film may rouse his artistic interest. He need not complete the suite for publication in full score and concert performance until he has experimented with its themes in the studio and seen us through. This part of the work must be put through at once, or the release will be held up very seriously.

faithfully

G. Bernard Shaw

Calm Sea and Prosperous Voyage is the title of opus 112, a composition for chorus and orchestra (1814–15), by Ludwig van Beethoven (1770–1827) and of the much better-known opus 27, an orchestral overture (1828) by Felix Mendelssohn-Bartholdy (1809–47), both based on the same poem of that title ('*Meerestille und Glückliche Fahrt*') by Johann Wolfgang von Goethe (1749–1832). The **Three Choirs**, based in turn in the cathedrals of Gloucester, Worcester, and Hereford, is an annual event lasting six days, chiefly but not exclusively choral in nature, with programs of sacred and secular music, and regular per-

formances of Handel's oratorios. It began about 1715 and had its heydey in the late nineteenth century, when it was a focal point of new British music. Edvard **Grieg** (1843–1907),
Norwegian composer, composed the *Peer Gynt Suite* (1875) for Ibsen's play.

Benjamin **Britten** (1913–76), British composer, wrote music for the BBC's *Pericles*,
broadcast 21 February 1943, by the Irish poet (Frederick) Louis MacNeice (1907–63).
Composers Richard **Wagner** (1813–83) and Christoph Willibald **Gluck** (1714–87) were
German, Hector **Berlioz** (1803–69) French, and Frédéric **Chopin** (1810–49) Polish.
Giuseppe Verdi (1813–1901), Italian, wrote the opera *Aida* (1871).

182 / To Gabriel Pascal

[Ayot St Lawrence. Welwyn. Herts.]
29th December 1944

[TLS(tr): Delacorte and SHD(tr): BL 50560 ff 235, 1–4: U(e)]

*Conflation of a transcription of the letter and Barbara Smoker's transcription of
the shorthand, corrected by John Wardrop, which differ in a few minor ways.
Since Rank, who was a businessman, aimed to maximize his profits in the large
American market, he easily adjusted, more than Shaw hoped, to the desires of
American film exhibitors.*

My dear Gabriel

I am sorry the Americans have captured our friend Arthur Rank; for we
both like him personally; and I believe we could have landed him in the
House of Lords as the creator of a British film industry leading the
world in its quality, and actually made money for him at the same time.
As a matter of fact we have half done it already. But as he has decided
that Hollywood is better, and has been persuaded that American transcript writers hired for the job at five dollars a day, and quite unknown
to the public, know our job better than we, and that talkies are endur-
able only when they are made as like movies as possible, we must leave
him to go his own way, which is no longer ours.

It must, however, be a friendly parting. There is no reason why it
should leave the least ill feeling; for he has done very well by us; and we
have done very well by him. The British press campaign against him will
be triumphant; but he need not mind this, as his command of the cinemas and their furniture will enable him to make plenty of money out of
American (or Americanized) films; and he will have the satisfaction of
liking them better than ours.

As for us we must turn over a new leaf and take my plays elsewhere.

But we must play fair with Rank. We must not spend a penny of his money or involve him in any engagement outside the completion of the Caesar film. The Doctor's Dilemma scheme must be dropped at once. We go into the market with Arms and the Man and Saint Joan. Why Rank, having gone so far with us, has thrown away these two plays, which were just what was necessary to finish the Rank-Shaw-Pascal scheme, is beyond any possible explanation except that he has gone over completely to Hollywood, where they are still twenty years out of date in the illiterate movie period when there was no screen drama but only 'the pictures,' and really does now believe that not only American transcript writers, but he himself, know our business better than we do. Of course this may be only a well known sort of infantile paralysis from which he may recover; so you must break with him as kindly as possible; but we cannot bank on this, and must now rule him out of our operations as an Americanized anti-Shavian.

It is a pity; for he financed us very handsomely; and my personal contacts with him have been quite pleasant and friendly.

In our next venture we must try to secure an up-to-date studio reserved (perhaps built) for our use exclusively, and lettable only during your holidays. You must take a holiday when Caesar is finished and ready in the can.

G. Bernard Shaw

183 / To Gabriel Pascal Ayot St Lawrence. Welwyn. Herts.
30th December 1944

[APCS(p): Delacorte: U(e)]

The first act means the Syrian Palace 'alternative' prologue.

What!!!

Cut out the first act!!!

Throw Rains at the audience's head before it knows who he is or where they are!

Spoil a £300,000 ship for a ha'porth of tar!

This is not mere ignorance of the job. There are plenty of people who would like to see Arthur ruined and get rid of us. Some of them have got into the studio and are making suggestions with this in view. Shoot them out of it, since it would be unlawful to shoot them in it.

Put A.R. on his guard.

G. Bernard Shaw

184 / To Gabriel Pascal Ayot St Lawrence. Welwyn. Herts.

9th September 1945

[TLS(p): Delacorte: U]

Pascal did not complete the shooting of Caesar *and* Cleopatra *until this month, nine months after Shaw's last known correspondence on the film.*

My dear Gabriel

You must have taken away the list with you. I cannot find it here, nor the centurion photographs.

There was one serious omission from the top of the list. After you must come M U S I C B Y G E O R G E S A U R I C .

Mr Tom White must not be starred in any way or connected with the artistic work. He must be described as Manager for J. Arthur Rank, or, if he prefers it, Studios Manager or Business Manager.

Marjorie should be Literary Secretary or Director's Secretary. She can come first after the Big Three: Pascal, Shaw, Auric.

The term Continuity Girl should not be used. If it is, we may as well put in the Office Boy as well. She must be either quite simply Continuities or Continuity Clerk or Continuity Expert.

I cannot remember any of the other titles without the list.

As to the barber's shop you had better cut it out altogether. I saw from the photograph that it is not, as I supposed, an elaborate and expensive scene: in fact it is not a scene at all. I wrote it against my judgment only to account for what it cost.

GBS

Tom **White** (d. 1945, age 74), an important figure at Pinewood Studios, was credited as General Production Manager, Marjorie Deans as Script Editor. The **barber shop** scene, which is not in the film, is published in *The Collected Screenplays of Bernard Shaw.*

185 / To G. Bernard Shaw   [*no address*]
24th November 1945

[TL(c): Delacorte: U]

My dearest G.B.S.

... I enclose a copy of a little article I wrote for the book which Marjorie is editing, 'The Making of "Caesar and Cleopatra."' I hope you like it.

I was told yesterday by Technicolor that they are not satisfied yet with the grading of the colour and need another ten days to have a perfect colour print ready, so I postponed the day of the screening from Tuesday, 27th November, to Friday, 7th December ... The screening takes about two and a half hours and will be in the small theatre in Denham Studios at 10.30. We can have lunch afterwards at my Farm 1.15 ...

I had a great deal of trouble during the final dubbing of the dialogue and music because while they were editing it in the Laboratory to start printing, the sound negative was scratched. Their excuse was that they haven't the skilled labour during the war, but the most horrible thing was that the negative was not kept clean and dust sneaked into the negative cans and the whole of Caesar's long speech to the Sphinx was in danger because the smallest dirt and dust endangered the clearness of the sound. My sound engineer worked for two weeks on this one speech, painting out the dirty spots between the lines. I have really been through a terrific panic during these last three weeks, like a pregnant mother, but finally I feel satisfied with it.

The whole of next week I must devote to work with Technicolor and help them in grading the colours. The danger is that if I do not supervise every sequence myself, they will exaggerate the colours and take away the audience's attention from the dialogue which is essential in all pictures ...

[Gabriel Pascal]

Marjorie Deans's **book** was *Meeting at the Sphinx* (1946), which Shaw disliked. Pascal's **article** was a one-page 'Credo' glorifying art, cinema, and especially his indebtedness to the integrity and inspiration of Shaw.

186 / To Gabriel Pascal　　　　Ayot St Lawrence. Welwyn. Herts.

19th February 1946

[TLS(p): Delacorte: U]

Pascal's financial situation was dire. He had earned little money from Pygmalion, *less from* Major Barbara, *and still less from* Caesar and Cleopatra. *What with cost overruns, partly the result of the shooting going 50% over schedule and partly the result of Pascal's indifference to costs,* Caesar and Cleopatra *was enormously expensive. His inept management of schedules and his dealings with onscreen and offscreen personnel were disastrous. Several of his assistants resigned and technicians went on strike. The leading actors, Rains and Leigh, pleaded with the Rank Organisation to intervene. If the critical and box-office response had been highly favourable after the London première of 13 December 1945, the Rank Organisation would probably have considered none of these problems to be significant. As the response was not laudatory, these problems became vital. Some reviewers praised the film extravagantly and others denounced it vehemently. The critical consensus fell in between; and the verdict, shared by movie-goers, was that the film was ordinary. Its New York première was on 5 September 1946. As with Pascal's other Shaw films, Americans liked it better than the English did, but opinion was similarly divided. Whether the film made or lost money depends on what figures are used and who calculates them. High studio overhead costs attributed to* Caesar and Cleopatra *rather than dispersed among several films, for example, can demonstrate a loss. Estimates of the final cost range from £600,000 (Pascal's, according to a 2 July 1947 letter from Shaw to Arthur Cox) to £1,200,000 (on negative cost alone, according to* Variety *["Cleo" $3,000,000 Into the Red,' 30 October 1946]), and such other costs as salaries could raise it to £1,500,000. In a 13 June 1947 letter to Arthur Cox, Shaw pointed to his royalty statement to reveal that as of 31 December 1946 exhibitors paid £600,000 to the Rank Organisation. If Pascal's cost estimate is correct, then the film made its money back in a little more than a year. If the figure in Pascal's 7 January 1950 letter is correct, the film earned a million or more pounds either by the end of 1949 or between Shaw's last royalty cheque and the end of 1949.*

Shaw tried to help Pascal by extending the agreement to Pygmalion *through 31 May 1948 and by adding rights to include distribution in other countries, including Russia and China. He also examined Pascal's contracts and gave advice.*

My dear Gabriel

This is a straightforward agreement; but the omission of the schedule containing a list of your debts makes it impossible for me to judge whether the bargain is a good one or a bad one for you.

Its effect is that G.F.D. is to take all your income and pay all your debts. You on your part acknowledge that they are lending you £50,000 at interest; and you undertake to repay that sum within five years. Deborah Kerr is included with all your film securities.

What you are to live on during the five years if your debts amount to £50,000 does not appear.

In your place I should hand over all my securities to my bank, and live and pay my debts on overdraft as far as it would let me.

Under the agreement you will be the slave of G.F.D. alias Arthur Rank.

G. Bernard Shaw

187 / To G. Bernard Shaw   [Mumford's Farm
                                            Chalfont St Peter. Bucks.]
                                            13th March 1946
[TL(c): Delacorte: U]

Since Shaw and Pascal were still corresponding about the trip at the end of May, it is unlikely that Pascal went to New York in three or four weeks to arrange, not to attend, the première of Caesar and Cleopatra, *as his words imply.*

Dear G.B.S.

... Thank you for sending me the David Selznick Company's announcement about Joan of Arc. I don't see anything alarming in it, because he has been talking about it for ten years, and nothing has happened yet. I was telephoned from Hollywood last week by another group of very important producers who have Ingrid Bergman under contract, to ask if I intended to do 'St Joan.' I said I will do it definitely, but I would not like to join their association. From that call I see that they don't consider the David Selznick announcement definite ...

As I must go to New York in three or four weeks for the premiere of 'C & C,' I think the best thing will be that I see Greer Garson and make a deal with her, if you agree on that; because she is ready to come next year to England and play St Joan for us. So, if I announce in all the leading papers that Metro allowed me to have Greer Garson for our picture, and that I will do 'St Joan' after 'Devil's Disciple,' I am certain that all the American companies will stop playing around with the idea of Joan of Arc. Anyhow that little girl, Jennifer Jones, is a joke for Joan. Marjorie is also of that opinion.

I am afraid that the whole thing was again the usual power politics between Rank and Selznick, and now I see the whole thing clearly: why Rank received that telephone call from Hollywood the day of the premiere, and why, after being so eager to have your approval on Ingrid Bergman or Greer Garson, he then suddenly, following various telephone calls between the Rank Group and Hollywood, withdrew his interest altogether, and apparently left the camp to Selznick (whose pictures he is distributing in this country!). All this is kindergarten stuff, however: because, as soon as I arrive with your letter saying that you approve Greer Garson, in forty-eight hours the power politics of Metro Goldwyn would be behind me, supporting their interest in the distributing of the picture (without having anything to do with its production): and then all the little vassals of the Hollywood Babylon would be silenced by our joint atomic energy! ...

[Gabriel Pascal]

On 18 November, Ingrid **Bergman** (1913–82), international stage and screen star born in Sweden, would open on Broadway in Maxwell Anderson's *Joan of Lorraine.* By Hollywood's reckoning, Jennifer **Jones** (née Phyllis Isley, b. 1919), who won an American Academy Award for playing the title role in *The Song of Bernadette* (1943), was a natural to play another saint, however dissimilar Shaw's Joan was to Bernadette.

188 / To G. Bernard Shaw   [*no address*]
27th March 1946

[TL(c): Delacorte: U]

Dear G.B.S.

... Arthur Rank seems upset that you should refuse to change the line of the Persian 'He has made short work of [them].' Nobody has any doubt that you are and have always been a philosemite and did not write the line with the intention that it should bear an anti-Semitic meaning, but the advisers of Rank are worried about the American re-action so I leave it to your judgement whether to change the line or not.

I know the whole thing is childish but in case the Americans grumble it might be advisable to have an alternative version as you promised to send it to me.

[Gabriel Pascal]

The **line**, in Act V, follows a response to a question when Caesar might arrive: 'He was settling the Jewish question when I left.' The American print omits the entire exchange.

189 / To Gabriel Pascal   Ayot St Lawrence. Welwyn. Herts.
27th May 1946

[TLS(tr)(p): Delacorte: U(e)]

The end of the penultimate paragraph and the last paragraph are from the original letter.

My dear Gabriel

You have gone quite mad. You ask me to take this illustrated prospectus of my goods round to celebrated people whom I do not know and try to interest them in them, as if I were a commercial traveller selling vacuum cleaners. And I am to bribe the press with my autograph to boost my sausages. You have really made me ill and given me a bad night. I loathe those books, and have with great difficulty refrained from tearing them to pieces.

My plays do not need nursing. Our financial situation does not need it. We have only to sit tight and when the time comes hold up our finger. If you go begging and bargaining and piling up expenses for a publicity which we have already got you will end by getting deeper into debt instead of making thousands out of your monopoly, and forcing me to break up our partnership by refusing to endorse your entanglements.

I see no need for your trip to America, where you can only make mischief. Cancel it and throw that bag of advertizing trash into the dustbin.

You may present the copies for Vivian, Rains, and Grantley as from me. Also of course that volume for Ingrid Bergman. But as to the four which I signed under the frontispiece before my disgust overcame me you can present them to whom you please as from yourself, but not as from me.

190

And now, no matter what arrangements you may make or how many, the last word is with me, and Ich liege und besitze.

GBS

The **prospectus** is *Meeting at the Sphinx*. The names of four **celebrated people** are on a page appended to the letter. They are Henry Agard Wallace (1888–1965), vice-president of the United States 1941–5; (Anna) Eleanor Roosevelt (née Roosevelt, 1884–1962), widow of President Franklin Delano Roosevelt (1882–1945); Toscanini; and Charlie (later Sir Charles Spencer) Chaplin (1889–1977), actor, director, screenwriter, and composer, whom Shaw, like most of the world, considered a comic genius of the cinema. On that page, beside their names, Shaw wrote, 'These four I have signed, as I dont know the recipients personally except Chaplin. Gabriel must present these as from himself. I hate the book.' The page was probably for Marjorie Deans, the book's author.

The last sentence is a pun whose meaning is lost in translation: I lie and sit down / am in possession (of the rights).

190 / To G. Bernard Shaw [*no address*]
29th May 1946

[TL(c): Delacorte: U]

Dearest G.B.S.

I am heartbroken that you should have had a sleepless night over this stupid question of signing the books; but it is very difficult for me when the Rank organisation have been pressing me for weeks for something which they believe – in their commercial minds – is important for them, to refuse it out of hand without first approaching you with their request. I personally think the book is very badly printed and in bad taste, but I think the writing in it helped many people to understand how the picture was made, so I don't see why you should 'loathe' the poor bastard of a book, which is not doing you any harm!

But let's forget the episode and look into the future. It is too late to cancel my trip to New York, because I must clear my financial situation, and there are several questions with the Treasury about my tax position which I can only clear by going over there. Then I must listen to Leland Hayward's proposition from the American Music Corporation. I must speak to Ingrid Bergman. I must speak to Cary Grant and his company about Arms and the Man.

I certainly have not the slightest intention of staying one hour longer than necessary, and I shall be back, at the latest, in three weeks' time. So there cannot be any mistake in my going there. I will refuse to have anything to do with the advertising of our picture, and will give no interviews. I will respect your desire to give the signed copies as a present from me and not from you; and I agree with you that we have only to sit (not lie!) tight, and hold up our finger when the time comes.

I don't intend to beg or bargain – I never did it in my life – and I don't intend to get deeper into debt. My whole intention is to clear all the debts once and for all. And I will prove to you that I will make not thousands but hundreds of thousands for us both through the monopoly with which you entrusted me; so you will sit up from your lying position when I report to you on the whole set-up for your ultimate approval.

So, my dear G.B.S., let me say *auf wiedersehen*, leaving you *sitzend und besitzend* in all your great Llama magnificence until I return.

[Gabriel Pascal]

Leland **Hayward** (1902–71) was an American film and stage producer. London-born Cary **Grant** (né Archibald Alexander Leach, 1904–86), a Hollywood star for decades, did not act in any Shaw film.

191 / To G. Bernard Shaw
[Mumford's Farm
Chalfont St Peter. Bucks.]
12th August 1946

[TL(c): Delacorte: U]

Dear GBS

After reflection I think you are right that in our future production programme Devil's Disciple and The Showing-Up of Blanco Posnet should follow one another in succession; so Androcles and the Lion should be made in Italy in 1949 after Blanco Posnet is completed.

Then we have forgotten one of your most important works for which I have an arrangement that whenever we make the picture all the exteriors in Spain shall be financed with the approval of the Spanish Government by a Spanish Film Bank headed by an Englishman, Montagu Marks, so I suggest that in the contract you are contemplating sending me you should incorporate for the second half of 1949 and the first half of 1950 Man and Superman.

Candida and Mrs Warren's Profession, as we have always discussed, should be two in-between pictures in case I have some hold-up in the preparation of our major productions. Also, we should not forget that we agreed that the first Indian picture we make in Ceylon will be The Simpleton of the Unexpected Isles, so perhaps you would include this too somewhere in the programme? ...

[Gabriel Pascal]

Montagu **Marks** was connected with Fairbanks International.

192 / To Gabriel Pascal　　　　　　　Ayot St Lawrence. Welwyn. Herts.

13th August 1946

[ALS(p): Delacorte: U]

My dear Gabriel

I enclose Korda's letter and a couple of clauses omitted through haste from the draft agreement.

No further engagement or complication must be entered into at present.

The agreement makes you master of the situation; but I cannot protect you against yourself. You will probably spend £500,000 on the film and when you are [at] the end of the £275,000, have to raise the money yourself at any cost.

GBS

193 / To G. Bernard Shaw　　　　　　　　[Mumford's Farm

Chalfont St Peter. Bucks.]

17th August 1946

[TL(tr): Delacorte: U(e)]

Wheeling and dealing on a global scale, Pascal juggled several possibilities in the hope that one would come to fruition. His chief options were The Doctor's Dilemma *in America,* Saint Joan *in Ireland, and* The Simpleton of the Unex-

*pected Isles in Ceylon or India. Since the photocopy of the transcript is not cen-
tred, some words or parts of words on the right side are lost.*

My dearest G.B.S.

We have come to a crucial point and we must act accordingly.

As I told you at our last meeting, unless I could present to Korda last Monday, or at the latest Tuesday, a contract from you giving me a new license for DOCTOR'S DILEMMA, signed and sealed, he would be obliged to dispose of his studio space for another production, and I would not be able to start building the sets on the 15th, nor should I be able to use Deborah Kerr for the picture, and it would be doubtful if I could find any studio space in the whole country before next spring.

I received your kind notes of the 13th August, for my contract with Korda, and I think you have been perfectly right in discovering the weaknesses of the Korda proposition, and have done a remarkable work as my legal adviser and manager!! A contract for a producer should look as you drafted it; but because I had not a contract signed from you to me, Korda found an excuse for not signing the whole deal, telling me that I should explain to you that he cannot give me the organisation which you put down as essential for my making the picture. I think he was even very sincere in his statement because however keen he was to distribute our picture, his studio is not ready yet, it is badly organised, many items of equipment are missing, and many stages must be rebuilt. I went very deeply into all these questions with his brother Vincent, the art director, and Vincent told me that he could not conscientiously advise me to go into all the difficulties and problems arising from not having a fully equipped and organised studio. Indeed I am only glad that when we had the plan to buy these Sound City Studios, I did not follow it up, because nowadays it is easier to build new studios than to reconstruct a badly-built one.

In one word, dear G.B.S., as the facts stand, I have no studio space any longer at my disposal this year in England.

I immediately contacted Leland Hayward of the Music Corporation of America, and they are ready to arrange studio space for me at Warner Brothers on the same basis as the projected deal for DEVIL'S DISCIPLE and BLANCO POSNET. Also Arthur Rank called me up to ask me why I am not doing the picture in America, for his distributing organisation, and he instructed Colonel Lawrence to call up his American associates to ask if they would give me studio space. A great advantage for making DOC-TOR'S DILEMMA in the United States would be that practically the whole cast, as follows: Herbert Marshall (Ridgeon), Aubrey Smith (Sir Patrick), Roland Young (B.B.), Cedric Hardwicke (Walpole), and the young Broadway actor, Montgomery Clift (Dubedat), are American residents, and I was already having great difficulty with the Ministry of Labour in arranging to bring them over here. Arthur was very humble on the phone, and everything happened as you predicted to me. He told me he would like to talk to me. He had received cables and telephone calls from America that our picture, in Cincinnati, Chicago, San Francisco, and other cities where they started to show it before it opens at the New York Astor Theatre, has broken all-time records in the cinemas. Also in the various English provincial towns where it has been shown – Brighton, Weston-Super-Mare, Blackpool, etc. – the picture has broken every box office record since 'Gone with the Wind'; while the Gallup Poll, which as you know is the greatest organisation to estimate public reaction on books, pictures and political events, cabled Colonel Lawrence that they must correct their original estimate of the income of the picture by 200%. Certainly Rank will try, influenced by his American partners, to lure me into a new deal; but I was very reserved, and told him that I must talk over the statement with you before I made up my mind.

Besides all this, I have an audience with De Valera in Dublin on Saturday morning next. Several groups have suggested to me that I should set up my production headquarters in Dublin and that they would build studios for me there. I discussed also with the Maharajah's minister, the Financial Secretary Ceylon, Sir Oliver Goonetilleke, and told him that before I [enter] into any big plans in Ceylon maybe I should establish my headquarters in Ireland. Because as long as this studio mono[poly] exists here, I don't see how I can make our pictures smooth[ly in] England; and I realised through these weeks of negotiation [with] Korda and British Lion, that a producer of my rank is not without his own studio.

So I would like that before I arrive on Monday you consider the whole position and decide that [it is] time to establish our programme in a legally–written form. [We] cannot go on in such ventures without a new contract since the old ones are, according to your own views, ou[t]. And with whatever group I would sign a distribution [contract, as] you yourself pointed out in your note to me, we must al[ter] the licensed contract signed between yourself and myself [and we] cannot confuse or intermingle this contract with my s[igned] production or distribution contract.

I shall, in a few days' time, be able to liquidate all my tax debts and other debts. The Bank of England has finally granted me permission to settle all my American debts out of the 200,000 dollars I shall receive from selling the Deborah Kerr contract; so I have a clear-cut financial situation with which to start in a new, solid, simple and sensible way to carry out the programme we discussed at our last meeting. And maybe it is a wonderful stroke of luck that everything has happened as it has happened; and however sad it is that I must miss our weekly meetings, it is perhaps better that I should make the next three pictures in America, and come to see you in between pictures every four months or so.

The suggestion is that I should fly over from Dublin to New York and establish dates for DOCTOR'S DILEMMA, DEVIL'S DISCIPLE and BLANCO POSNET. I would then do these pictures in America, and would come back when my studios are ready, and start with SAINT JOAN, ARMS AND THE MAN, ANDROCLES AND THE LION, and so on.

I will be in New York only for a few days to put everything in train for DOCTOR'S DILEMMA. Then I will fly back and take Deborah Kerr over with me to play the part of Jennifer. This has all been thought out in the last three days after tiresome nightly long distance telephone calls. The whole cast is waiting for definite confirmation. So I hope that you realise our problems, and that when I come to see you on Monday we can make decisions for the immediate future ...

[Gabriel Pascal]

Justus Baldwin (Jock) **Lawrence** (d. 1987, age 83), American film publicist and executive, was deputy press representative for the American Army in Europe in the Second World War with the rank of Colonel, a title he kept afterwards. Herbert **Marshall** (1890–1966), born in Britain, was a leading man and character actor in British and American theatre and cinema. With the 1948 releases of *The Search* and *Red River*, (Edward) Montgomery **Clift** (1920–66), American stage actor, became a major film star.

Éamon de **Valéra** (1882–1975), American-born Irish activist involved in the Easter 1916 uprising, was prime minister of Eire (and later president of the Republic of Ireland). Sir Oliver (Ernest) **Goonetilleke** (1892–1978) held numerous governmental positions in Ceylon, including financial secretary (1945–47) and governor-general (1954–62). On 4 February 1976, four years after Ceylon became the Republic of Sri Lanka, the Sri Lankan high court found Sir Oliver, who was living in London, guilty of illegally buying and selling foreign currency, and sentenced him, *in absentia*, to four years' imprisonment in Sri Lanka.

194 / To G. Bernard Shaw

[Mumford's Farm
Chalfont St Peter. Bucks.]
1st September 1946

[TL(c): Delacorte: U(e)]

On 29 August 1946, at Pascal's suggestion, Taoiseach or Taoisigh (Prime Minister) de Valéra wrote to Shaw of his enthusiasm for Caesar and Cleopatra.

My dearest G.B.S.

I arrived yesterday evening from Dublin and I am hurrying to report to you about one of the most instructive weeks I've experienced in a long time.

I saw the Taoiseach three times the week I was there, but, before meeting him I had a long talk with one of his ministers, Patrick J. Little, who is the minister of the post-telegraph and broadcast. I also met his finance minister Aikens, who was as a finance minister should be, at first very reserved towards me. Patrick Little told me that I was expected the following day by the T. who was anxious to hear my views regarding the eventual foundation of an Irish picture industry. I was also informed that he had already refused not only Rank and Korda, but all other attempts made to create an Irish film industry, but that if he liked me, this would be the opportune time to go into action.

Not only because of my respect in meeting such a wise and certainly great man, but, due to this warning that everything depended on whether he took a liking to me or not, put me in a kind of inferiority complex, but this was for the best because in meeting him I forgot all that I had planned to say and instead of trying to impress him with my ideas, I discussed freely and casually all the problems he put to me. Apparently, he was very pleased with our first meeting, because at the end of our audience, he asked me to prepare a memorandum for him outlining how to create a film industry in Ireland with the most modern studios in which I could produce my Bernard Shaw pictures.

The day before meeting with the T. Mr Little invited me to a chamber music concert and after the concert, I was introduced to the President of Eire. He asked about your health and expressed his sadness that there is not sufficient artistic activity in Ireland. I told him that maybe, I will be helpful to his premier, de Valera, in doing something about it.

When I met the T. he also inquired very affectionately about your health and was much impressed with the letter you sent him lately. He said the wonderful twist you gave it on the end, he would like to discuss with you personally and hoped if our project materializes, he will be able to greet you some day in your native Dublin.

Also before I met de Valera, General O'Neill took me about fifteen miles away from Dublin to Carton where there is an estate of nine hundred acres with an old Georgian building that belonged to the Duke of Leinster. This building would make ideal headquarters not only for the new Irish picture company, but for a dramatic school, which is an essential thing in order to feed the company with new talents and it offers also wonderful accommodations for all kinds of offices, studios for designers and architects and ample space for projection and cutting rooms and there is a big hall which could be used for the orchestra to record the music and for dubbing purposes, etc. Near to the building is a very large field, about forty acres, where stages for studios, carpenters and painters shops could be erected. I explained all this to the T. and he seemed very pleased about it and declared that Carton would make an ideal art centre for Ireland.

It was very exciting when de Valera saw C.C. Also, all the ministers and their wives were present. I was sitting with the T. in the projection room at the censor's table and when we came to the scene where the Roman troops entered with Rufio in the market place of Alexandria, I whispered to him 'poor Musso, how happy he would have been had he seen this scene' and de Valera whispered back 'exactly this second I was thinking of him.' I believe he had a great sympathy for the 'old Caligula' and after the screening we sat for about a half hour in the projection room forgetting all formalities and discussed many things which I prefer to report to you in a few weeks as soon as I am back in London.

He has a very clever secretary, who is from the west of Ireland; her Christian name is Kathleen, but he calls her his angel and I think that without this woman he could never have done the work which he is doing. His wife was not at the screening; she doesn't like pictures at all and I warned him that I will convert her from her prejudice to which he smilingly expressed his hope that I would be successful also in this task.

He was very excited about the idea that when the studios are ready, our first Irish picture should be ST JOAN and I told him that until then, I will wherever I can best find studio space and return to Ireland every four months to supervise the building and organization of the studio.

The day I was leaving I saw the T. again and he gave me a letter for you, which I am enclosing here. Also, I am enclosing a copy of my letter to him which enables you to see in what spirit the great venture started. He agreed also that as soon as I am back I should sit down with Mr Lamaze, his minister of industry and commerce, my Irish solicitor Arthur Cox (who looks like Dr Miracle in Offenbach's 'Tales of Hoffman') and Mr Little and work out a detailed memorandum. Meanwhile, Mr Cox worked out some rough headlines of the project in agreement with Mr Little which I approved hurriedly before taking off and which was sent over with my letter to the T.

Before leaving I agreed with his ministers that I will go to Washington and get from my friend, Henry Wallace, who is now head of the Board of Trade, all the priorities for the studio equipment, cutting tables and everything that is needed to be independent of both American and English studio slavery.

Somehow, I feel that all the cowardice of the English technicians towards me had a superior meaning because of the organical development for my work and my artistic predestination may be that I should settle down in Ireland. The Irish race suits my temperament. I like them and they like me and I can laugh and enjoy myself with them which I cannot do with the English.

Also, before leaving Dublin, Patrick J. Little told me that the T. was pleased with me and that now I have everything at my disposal there, but that much depends on my successful trip to America in getting the necessary equipment.

The studio will be an independent government backed company and will be called the G.B.S.–Pascal Studios and through a long term contract, one-half of the studio will be at the exclusive use of our productions and the other half will be rented to others and serve for documentary and educational films and short pictures in the Gaelic language.

I will be absolute boss in all artistic questions and the government will put in a kind of Board of Directors to advise me in financial matters. Incidentally, the finance minister after my meeting with the T. and after the screening of C.C. he was an entirely different man and became less reserved and opened his heart to me (he will have to open many coffers of the Bank of Ireland).

I am quite convinced that these studios could be operated with about a 5% overhead (Rank's are operated with a 38% overhead). Wages of the Irish workers are certainly lower and I told the experts after speaking to their leaders of the unions, that we should establish better wages in order to create a good family spirit so that everyone would have the feeling of working more or less for himself and for a service with a great goal.

I told the T. that when I mentioned to you the possibility that I would work in Ireland that your eyes became veiled with joy and you certainly as their greatest son have been inflamed by the idea that I will create a real Irish production founded and based upon the picturization of your plays.

I could write you pages and pages about the emotional experiences I had that week, but now find that the ecstasy is over, I must return to the battlefield and go on with the job but while I am preparing this great scheme, I cannot stop and stay idle.

C.C. in the states is an 'unprecedented record-breaking success' quoting the American papers, and the most important thing now is that I get the equipment for the Irish studios and I hope I have all the contracts ready in about two weeks and I can fly back to Dublin and see the T. again and I will then stay there only two or three days and fly back to London and upon the hour of my arrival report to you my dear G.B.S. and embrace you with joy.

I feel my wings are open again after three years slavery at Denham; the idea alone that I can very soon work in Ireland inspires and fills me with the greatest creative powers.

Do not feel that I am unjust to our English friends or ungrateful to Dickie ([Richard Norton,] Lord Grantley) and don't believe that I am deserting them. Had they left me in the Pinewood Studios, I could have created a renaissance in picture making, but when they pushed me over to the corrupted Denham place, I knew then that there was no future for me there because I could not do justice to our pictures.

On the other hand, Arthur Rank fooled us for nearly a year with SAINT JOAN preventing me from signing with anybody else and using Lord Grantley as a go between to justify his delaying game, but the game is now over, Rank and his technicians must realize that new times command new methods and our Irish friends captured the importance of our situation unhesitatedly; so, destiny helped to put me on the right path to have finally our own studios which has always been your wish and my fondest dream ...

[Gabriel Pascal]

Patrick J. **Little** was minister of the Department of Posts and Telegraphs. A former IRA leader, Frank Aiken (1898–1983), not **Aikens**, minister of Finance, served in the Irish parliament for fifty years. Sean Thomas O'Kelly (1882–1966) was **president** of Eire 1945–59. **O'Neill** is an error for Major General Hugo MacNeill (c. 1900–c. 1963); the **Carton** Estate was headquarters of the Second Division of the Irish Army. **Kathleen** O'Connell was personal secretary to the prime minister. **Lamaze** is an error for Sean Francis Lemass (1899–1971), minister of Industry and Commerce, who in 1959 would succeed de Valéra as prime minister. Arthur **Cox** (1891–1965), head of a firm of Dublin solicitors, drew the contract between Shaw and Irish Productions Ltd (later called Irish Screen Art Ltd), formed to film Shaw's plays in his native country, and was one of its directors. *Tales of Hoffmann* (1881), with music by Jacques **Offenbach** (1819–80), derives from three stories by E(rnest) T(heodor) A(madeus) Hoffmann (1776–1822).

195 / To G. Bernard Shaw

[Mumford's Farm
Chalfont St Peter. Bucks.]
10th November 1946

[TL(c): Delacorte: U(e)]

My dear GBS

I am back from Paris, where I had various talks with General Corniglion Molinier, who is the new President of the French Gaumont Company; and he urged me to make, after I finish the two or three pictures in the Mary Pickford combination, Saint Joan in France, in both English and French versions. For the French version I found the greatest French actor – maybe the greatest living actor of our time – Jean Louis Barrault of the Comedie Francaise, who is very anxious to play the Dauphin. Practically the whole cast there is at my disposal, with the cream of the Comedie Francaise and the independent theatres.

I also had a very important talk with Scalera, the owner of the biggest Italian studios, with whom I was negotiating when I was last in Rome, to make 'Androcles and the Lion' there, after I finish 'Saint Joan.' This would be in the English version only. There too the whole finances are at my disposal.

I have telephoned yesterday and today with Arthur Cox, and I am enclosing herewith a letter from him, in which he tells me that the Government are in favour of the intermediary studio which Mr O'Farrell, the owner of the Capitol Theatre, proposes to build. I mentioned this to you at our last meeting, and you were very happy about this solution, whereby we need not wait for one-and-a-half to two years before establishing our own studios somewhere in an English-speaking country ...

I must remind you, my dear GBS, that you have several times made written and verbal statements that whatever happened I should have all the picture rights of your plays. Since I finished 'Cleopatra' I have refused to make two pictures for Arthur Rank – 'Uncle Silas' and the Gallico story – each of which would have given me £25,000 salary. I refused two or three other propositions from America for other stories, because I thought it would be a bad thing for you and for me if I did not follow upon our programme; and in spite of all the technical difficulties with the Korda studio, if I had had a clear contract for 'Doctor's Dilemma,' I should have fought these difficulties and overcome them.

... Meanwhile, I have today received a cable from Mary Pickford telling me that her business manager, Margulies, and her business partner, Lester Cowan, are preparing the draft contract between her group and myself. According to my telephone conversation with Margulies yesterday, this should be here in about ten days' time.

Before this contract arrives, it would be wise for you to find the way to let me know how you intend to protect yourself and myself in a legal form, licensing the pictures I have to do in the future. I beg you not to keep this question open any longer, because it creates a very weak and ambiguous situation for us both when I am negotiating finance, and am unable to present any written contract for the plays I am discussing with the groups concerned.

I really don't understand, GBS, why the contracts should not be made in my name. When you gave me the contract for 'Pygmalion' I had two-

and-a-half shillings from a borrowed pound in my pocket. I managed not only the artistic but the business side of the picture very well. Your only complaint was that you received too much money, which ruined you with the taxes; and if the war had not come to upset every kind of free planning and to imprison me, during the making of 'Major Barbara,' in all kind of wartime regulations, I should have made by now at least half-a-dozen of your pictures, and would today be a sterling millionaire, able to command the respect of all the parasites. If I had wanted to enrich myself on your contracts, which apparently is what you fear, I had plenty of opportunities to do so before the war, when I had the most exciting fairy-tale propositions from Metro and other Companies, offering me millions; but I refused them and kept my artistic integrity, and my devotion and faithfulness to your interests alone. Since 'Pygmalion,' I have practically been working in martyrdom. If the reward for all this is that I am not worthwhile enough to have the film contracts put in my name, then I should not be worthwhile enough to make the pictures – which perhaps I am not.

So let's clear this situation once and for all, because I find it undignified for both of us. I shall be satisfied with any decision you may come to. All I am asking is to know clearly what my position is ...

Our sweet English friends are trying to belittle the big box-office success of 'Caesar and Cleopatra' in America, but I received yesterday the enclosed letter and accompanying article from 'Box Office,' the official paper of all the exhibitors of America. This paper makes, four weeks after the premier, an Award of the Month to the greatest box-office hit throughout America. Our picture started on August 15th and was shown in about 120 cinemas up to the end of September; so this Blue Ribbon Award is the answer to all the doubters ...

[Gabriel Pascal]

Former commander of the Free French Air Force, General Edouard **Corniglion-Molinier** (1899–1963), a film producer, was president of the Gaumont film company. Canadian-born Mary **Pickford** (née Gladys Smith, 1893–1979), internationally popular American film star, founded her own company in 1916 and co-founded United Artists in 1919. Jean-Louis **Barrault** (1910–94), French stage actor and director, is famous as the mime in the film *Les enfants du paradis* (1945). The Comédie Française, founded 1680, is the French National Theatre. Salvatore and Michele **Scalera** owned Scalera Film. Patrick Farrell, not **O'Farrell**, owned a chain of cinema theatres. *Uncle Silas* (1947) is a suspense film based on the novel (1865) by Joseph Sheridan Le Fanu (1814–73). Ira **Margulies** was an attorney in MGM's legal department. Lester **Cowan** (d. 1990, age 83) was an American film producer.

196 / To G. Bernard Shaw

[Mumford's Farm
Chalfont St Peter. Bucks.]
14th November 1946

[TL(c): Delacorte: U]

Marjorie Deans and Walter Mycroft (1891–1959), former scenario editor at British International Pictures, had prepared a draft of The Doctor's Dilemma.

... I have finished the shooting script with Marjorie, all the set sketches are ready, and we both agreed on casting. Before I came back I had several talks with Sir Aubrey Smith, Sir Cedric Hardwicke, Herbert Marshall, Roland Young, and Montgomery Clift, and they would be happy as they waited so long if I can make this picture next. In particular Sir Aubrey Smith gave up a contract to be able to play Sir Patrick ...

A propos, I had a most interesting luncheon with Dulanty, the Irish High Commissioner, and the great hero Dan Breen. Dan Breen is the most amazing figure of an honest adventurer I ever met. He is exactly the opposite of your Bluntschli in ARMS AND THE MAN ...

[Gabriel Pascal]

John Whelan **Dulanty** (1883–1955) was high commissioner for Eire 1930–50. Dan **Breen** (1894–1969), Irish Republican and member of the Dáil (Parliament) 1932–65, was on the board of Irish Screen Art Ltd.

197 / To Gabriel Pascal

Ayot St Lawrence. Welwyn. Herts.
14th November 1946

[APCU(p): Delacorte: U]

Are you mad or am I?
Who is to finance The Doctor's Dilemma?
Rank?
Pickford?
Irish Pictures?

GBS

198 / To Gabriel Pascal   Ayot St Lawrence. Welwyn. Herts.

14th November 1946

[APCS (tr): Delacorte: U]

The Doc's Dil. must be a British or Eirish film, *not* made in America. If
you make it now you will have to make it in Dublin, where the capitalists of the new company will not agree to keep it in the can. It must
therefore be the next production, on which Mary may be calculating.
This chopping and changing every ten minutes makes business very
difficult.

You need a rest very badly. There are passages in your long letter
which are sheer lunacy.

Ask Dan Breen how a film called *When Eire Was John Bull's Other Island*
would appeal to him.

GBS

Mary is Mary Pickford, whom Shaw knew personally. When a new constitution, adopted by
plebiscite in 1937, declared Eire (Ireland in English) a sovereign, democratic state, the
title of the play *John Bull's Other Island* (1904) was out of date.

199 / To G. Bernard Shaw   [Mumford's Farm

Chalfont St Peter. Bucks.]

27th November 1946

[TL(c): Delacorte: U]

My dearest GBS

You are right. A grievance is the worst obstacle to creative work, and I
am so grateful that you told me so at our last meeting. Really in my heart
I have no grievance at all, only a nervous tension which is partly due, as
you say, to my bad health, which starts in October every year when I winter in England – I cannot stand the climate here. The other part is due
to my anxiety to get our production programme straightened out,
because only then can I quieten down my nervous state of mind, go
away for a month to the South of Italy where I have an invitation, and
forget telephones, telegrams, contracts, and every possible kind of business, and then come back and start the preparation of our next picture.

My understanding is that we agreed at our last meeting that it would be unwise to put the licensing contract for our two American pictures, DEVIL'S DISCIPLE and BLANCO POSNET, in Mary Pickford's name; and that it should instead be put in the name of Dr Bernard Giannini, Director of the Bank of America, who is doing the real financing. This Bank, when Bernard Giannini's father was alive, advanced about $400,000,000 to American independent producers. From this you can judge of its importance in film financing.

The two pictures which I will do in France (the second partly in Spain) are contracted with General Corniglion Molinier. They are SAINT JOAN and MAN AND SUPERMAN; and these are also to be made in French versions.

The two pictures to be made in Rome with Rank's opposite numbers, Scalera and Mosco, are ANDROCLES AND THE LION and ARMS AND THE MAN. Like Rank over here, Scalera owns all the studios in Rome; while Mosco has the biggest distributing organisation in Italy, on a par with GFD here.

The two pictures to be made and financed in India by the Maharajah of Baroda are THE SIMPLETON OF THE UNEXPECTED ISLES and CAPTAIN BRASSBOUND'S CONVERSION.

DOCTOR'S DILEMMA, since you are against its being made in Hollywood, should be made in England or Ireland, in between the above-mentioned pictures, when the opportunity arises. The same applies to CANDIDA and THE MILLIONAIRESS. Maybe I shall get studio space here one of these days, although for the moment it looks hopeless for at least two years to come.

Ireland: Cox writes me that the Government finally agreed that I should go ahead with the small scheme with Patrick Farrell, owner of the Capitol and other cinemas; and this will be incorporated later in the big scheme, which will be discusssed in the Cabinet next spring. So it would be wise, as this smaller Company which I will form with Farrell will be the basis of the Irish Studios and Productions Limited, to put the contracts either in Farrell's name or in that of Irish Studios Limited ...

[Gabriel Pascal]

The duties of Dr Bernard **Giannini** (d. 1954, age 43), nephew of the founder of the Bank of America, were mainly motion-picture-industry loans and accounts.

200 / To Gabriel Pascal   Ayot St Lawrence. Welwyn. Herts.

29th November 1946

[ANU(tr): Delacorte: U]

Paul Czinner tried to persuade Shaw to reconsider his refusal to allow him to direct a film version of Saint Joan. Anderson's *Joan of Lorraine* had opened on Broadway.

I have cabled No decisively. But note that all the assurances that the Anderson Joan would not come off have proved false.

[GBS]

201 / To G. Bernard Shaw   [Mumford's Farm

Chalfont St Peter. Bucks.]

2nd December 1946

[TL(c): Delacorte: U]

My dearest GBS

Thanks for your note, telling me that you had given a definite 'No' to Czinner. I think your instinct is right, and that Anderson's play is not such a big failure, in spite of the fact that it is supposed to be very bad; but Ingrid Bergman saved it. Here is a write-up from the Herald-Tribune, and my secretary in New York, Miss Buonocore, is airmailing me a very important article from the New York Times, practically to the effect that it was a childish attempt to make another Saint Joan, when your play has recreated Joan for all eternity ... Don't worry, I will find our Joan very soon.

What I *did* find over the week-end, to my great joy, after searching for hours through every possible file and index, was your original George III scene for DEVIL'S DISCIPLE, and I am sending you a copy. To my astonishment, I see that you yourself put it in picture sequence! Some idiotic technician of mine (Marjorie was not yet with me at that time) tried to follow up your scene with the execution of Peter. Here is your remark to that scene:

This scene completely ruins the play. The climax of the play is the threatened execution of Richard and the reprieve. This scene anticipates and utterly destroys it by making it an unbearable repetition. It also spoils Richard's first entrance.

The author of the sequence has mistaken his profession and thinks I have mistaken mine.

GBS

So now be an angel, and as you have finished your play – which you call 'hopeless,' though I am sure it will be delightful – give yourself two hours' time and write me the Boston Tea Party, and send it to Marjorie, and she will send it to me in Rome. I can work on the shooting-script on my holiday, and send my suggestions to Marjorie, who will finish it in four weeks until I am back. I would like that you read and approve it before I go over to start preparations ...

Cox promised me on the phone that as soon as I am back from my holiday he will come over, when I will bring him out to you, and he will report to us on the whole Irish situation, which seems now to be definitely under control ...

[Gabriel Pascal]

Michelina **Buonocore**, an American-born author in both English and Italian, wrote poetry and journalism. Shaw's **George III scene** is published in *The Collected Screenplays of Bernard Shaw*. The **execution** of Peter Dudgeon is in the 1959 film of *The Devil's Disciple*.

202 / To Gabriel Pascal   Ayot St Lawrence. Welwyn. Herts.
3rd December 1946

[ALS(tr): Delacorte: U(e)]

What Shaw, with unwarranted optimism, considered good luck for Pascal and him was an announcement that Maxwell Anderson would adapt Joan of Lorraine to the screen; its title changed to Joan of Arc.

My dear Gabriel

What a stupendous stroke of good luck!!! Anderson, without stepping on my grass, has given us a film advertisement that will make all America rush to see Ingrid as the real and only possible St Joan. She now cannot do without us nor we without her; so let her know at once that we must have her; and put the Swiss girl and all the other postulants out of your head: Anderson has settled the cast for us.

As to the general program we must not license more than one play at a time, and not until you are ready to produce it within, say, 6 months or so. St Joan ought to be produced in France; but as we are bound to Ireland you must give up the idea of combining a French version with the English one, and let C-M do it independently.

As to Androcles in Rome I do not believe that the Colosseum will be of the smallest use to you; you must have to build it or spoil the play. Even the forum must not be what is left of the real forum. There is no hurry about Androcles: you need only chat about it to the financiers as a possibility.

The only pressing contracts are St Joan and the 2 American productions. I am not *quite* convinced about the Doctor's Dilemma: but I think the Maharajah must be attended to soon.

GBS

C-M is the French film producer Corniglion-Molinier.

203 / To G. Bernard Shaw   [Hollywood Athletic Club
6525 Sunset Blvd. Hollywood]
31st January 1947

[TD TEL(c): Delacorte: U]

DEAR GBS: I AGREED DEAL WITH MARY PICKFORD'S COMPANY, ARTISTS ALLIANCE, FOR DEVIL'S DISCIPLE STOP THE BANK OF AMERICA WILL GIVE 75% OF THE FINANCIAL BACKING AND THE REST WILL BE GIVEN BY MARY'S COMPANY, ARTISTS ALLIANCE STOP MARY IS PUTTING HER OWN STUDIOS CALLED THE GOLDWYN STUDIOS AND HER PREFERENTIAL DISTRIBUTION CONTRACT WITH UNITED ARTISTS AT MY DISPOSAL STOP THE ENTIRE ADMINISTRATION AND FINANCING OF THE PICTURE IS TAKEN CARE OF BY MARY'S COMPANY AND I HAVE THE SOLE AND FULL ARTISTIC CONTROL OF THE PRODUCTION OF OUR PICTURE STOP I AM GETTING $50,000 SALARY AS PRODUCER/DIRECTOR DURING PRODUCTION AND $50,000 AFTER NEGATIVE COSTS RECOUPED AND 45% OF PROFITS STOP BANK OF AMERICA

AGREED TAKE OVER YOUR CONTRACT IN TRUSTEESHIP AND PAY 10% ROYALTIES ON THE DISTRIBUTOR'S GROSS DIRECTLY TO YOU ACCORDING YOUR CONTRACT STOP WILL YOU PLEASE CABLE ME AT THE HOLLYWOOD ATHLETIC CLUB 6525 SUNSET BOULEVARD HOLLY-WOOD CALIFORNIA THAT YOU AGREE SEND A NEW CONTRACT TO THE BANK OF AMERICA AS WE AGREED BEFORE I LEFT YOU WHICH CONTRACT WILL GIVE FIVE YEARS NEW LICENSING DATED FROM FIRST RELEASE OF THE PICTURE IN THE UNITED STATES OR ENGLAND STOP THE PRODUCTION WILL START THIS SPRING AND MUST BE FINISHED BEFORE THE END OF THIS YEAR AND MUST BE RELEASED NOT LATER THAN NEXT YEAR STOP HOWEVER I ADVISE YOU TO INCLUDE IN YOUR CABLE ALSO THE LICENSING OF OUR SEC-OND AMERICAN PICTURE BLANCO POSNET BECAUSE I HAVE THE FINANCING AND THE SAME DEAL FOR IT STOP HOWEVER IN YOUR LETTER THIRD DECEMBER 1946 SENT TO ME IN ROME YOU WROTE AS FOLLOWS QUOTE AS TO THE GENERAL PROGRAM WE MUST NOT LICENSE MORE THAN ONE PLAY AT A TIME AND NOT UNTIL YOU ARE READY TO PRODUCE IT WITHIN SIX MONTHS OR SO UNQUOTE STOP FOR THIS REASON I ARRANGED WITH MARY'S COMPANY ONLY TO PUT INTO PRODUCTION DEVIL'S DISCIPLE AND I WILL ARRIVE IN LONDON FIRST WEEK OF MARCH TO DISCUSS THE CAST WITH YOU AND THEN WILL RETURN AND START PRODUCTION STOP BEGINNING NEXT MONDAY MY HEADQUARTERS WILL BE AT THE GOLDWYN STUDIOS WHICH ARE OWNED BY MARY PICKFORD AND I WILL START PREPARA-TIONS SO THAT SETS CAN BE PREPARED WHILE I AM EN ROUTE TO LONDON TO SEE YOU STOP IN YOUR SAME LETTER THIRD DECEMBER IN THE LAST PARAGRAPH YOU WROTE QUOTE THE ONLY PRESSING CONTRACTS ARE SAINT JOAN AND THE TWO AMERICAN PRODUC-TIONS UNQUOTE STOP AS I CABLED YOU FROM NEW YORK I SAW INGRID BERGMAN AND SAW HER HUSBAND HERE BUT I AM AFRAID WE MUST ABANDON HER BECAUSE SHE IS INVOLVED WITH MAXWELL ANDERSON AND CANNOT DISENTANGLE HERSELF FROM THIS MORAL OBLIGATION AND HER MANAGER IS ASKING THREE HUNDRED THOU-SAND DOLLARS AND FIFTY PERCENT OF THE PROFITS WHICH WOULD OVER-BURDEN THE PICTURE FROM THE BEGINNING WITH A TERRIFIC BUDGET AND IN COMPARISON WITH YOUR TEN PERCENT ROYALTIES AS AUTHOR IS AN ARROGANT REQUEST BUT THERE ARE SOME FOOLS

WHO ARE READY TO GRANT HER THESE CONCESSIONS STOP GREER
GARSON IS VERY ANXIOUS TO PLAY THE PART AND I AM READY IF YOU
WISH TO MAKE A TEST WITH HER AND BRING IT TO YOU STOP I WILL
BE GRATEFUL IF YOU AUTHORIZE ME IN A SEPARATE CABLE TO
ANNOUNCE THAT WE WILL GO INTO PRODUCTION IMMEDIATELY
AFTER DEVIL'S DISCIPLE AND WILL START PREPARATIONS AT ONCE AS
OUR SCRIPT IS ALREADY WRITTEN BY YOU AND IF INGRID BERGMAN IS
NOT CLEVER ENOUGH TO PREFER YOUR PLAY TO ANDERSON'S AND
GREER GARSON'S TESTS SHOULD NOT BE SATISFACTORY, YOU
AUTHORIZE ME TO TAKE AN UNKNOWN YOUNG ACTRESS SUBJECT TO
YOUR APPROVAL STOP ... GABRIEL

In 1937, Ingrid **Bergman** married Dr Petter Aron Lindstrom (b. 1907), a dentist. In 1949,
she created a scandal when she left him for Roberto Rossellini (1906–77), an Italian neore-
alist film director, whom she married in 1950.

204 / To Gabriel Pascal   [Ayot St Lawrence. Welwyn. Herts.
                                            received 2nd February 1947]

[TEL(p): Delacorte: U]

AGREED FOR DISCIPLE ON MY PART BUT YOU MUST HAVE SEPARATE
AGREEMENT REMEMBERING THAT UNDEFINED NEGATIVE COST WILL
INCLUDE YOUR HUNDRED THOUSAND DOLLARS YOUR FORTYFIVE
SEEMS TOO MUCH TO BE GOOD FOR BOTH SIDES AS ALL GOOD BAR-
GAINS SHOULD BE BLANCO MUST WAIT SO MUST JOAN AS INGRID
MAY DISENTANGLE   [GBS]

205 / To Gabriel Pascal   Ayot St Lawrence. Welwyn. Herts.
                                            3rd February 1947

[TLS(tr): Delacorte: U(e)]

My dear Gabriel

I enclose the draft agreement for the Disciple. I have sent a copy of the
two last clauses to Mary Pickford. She will make her own agreement with

the Bank. You will make your own agreement. She will take care of herself: you must do the same.

In my cable to you I omitted to warn you that if you persist in making a profit sharing agreement instead of a percentage (say Ten) of the receipts the expenses will include not only my royalty and your $100,000 but any rent Mary may fix for the Goldwyn Studios.

Any attempt to define the expenses will probably end in a dispute and a lawsuit, and end in your losing money even if you win your case.

If the Bank will sign my contract on the dotted line cable the word Agreed. If not, let the Bank cable or air-letter its amendments. When we are agreed I will immediately have the document engrossed and despatched with my signature for execution by the Bank.

Now as to Ingrid. The difficulty in assuming about her is mere foolishness. She is assuming, or rather Anderson's company is assuming that if she films my Joan she cannot film Anderson's as well. On the contrary she must film both. Her success in Anderson's makes her not only the only possible Joan for him but for me also. The two will advertize each other enormously, to A's benefit as well as ours. Ingrid will get two big salaries instead of only one, and be pleased into the bargain. And there will be no interference of her company with ours; both will be entirely independent and will profit equally. No question of entanglement or bad faith can arise.

Renew the negotiations on these terms.

The weather is so bad here that it has been impossible for me to see Marjorie: but this was not in the least necesary; she is on the telephone. Nor is it necessary for you to see me: take care of your health and stop rushing about needlessly.

It will be easy to authorise Blanco if and when our relations prove satisfactory. I positively will not license more than one film at a time. Nor should you.

G. Bernard Shaw

206 / To Gabriel Pascal   [Ayot St Lawrence. Welwyn. Herts.
                                        received 8 February 1947]

[TEL(p): Delacorte: U]

At Pascal's instruction, Marjorie Deans gave Shaw his cable quoting a press statement that The Devil's Disciple *would be produced in America. The 'flat falsehoods' are that the British film industry has a monopoly on Shaw's works, that Pascal would produce two Shaw plays for United Artists, and that Shaw gave his unqualified approval to Pascal's contract with Pickford.*

PLEASE REPUDIATE MONSTROUS LIE THAT HOLLYWOOD HAS CAP-TURED US IT WILL HARM US HERE AND MAY MAKE DUBLIN IMPOSSI-BLE THREE OTHER STATEMENTS ARE FLAT FALSEHOODS AND SHOULD BE CONTRADICTED TELL THE PRESS NOTHING KEEP THEM ASKING AND GUESSING   UNSIGNED

207 / To G. Bernard Shaw   [Scripps Metabolic Clinic
                                                     La Jolla. California]
                                                     8th February 1947

[TDS TEL(c): Delacorte: U]

Pascal had entered the Scripps Metabolic Clinic for a general check-up.

DEAREST GBS: I ALREADY REPUDIATED ALL THE STUPID LIES AND REFUSED TO GIVE ANY MORE INTERVIEWS STOP IN THE LAST INTER-VIEW THE NEW YORK TIMES ASKED ME IF WE HAVE A CONTRACT FOR MORE THAN THE ONE PICTURE DEVIL'S DISCIPLE AND I SAID NO AND EVEN SHOWED THEM YOUR CABLE TO PROVE THAT ALL OTHER RUMORS ARE WISHFUL THINKING ON THE PART OF CERTAIN HOLLY-WOOD GROUPS STOP DON'T WORRY ABOUT DUBLIN STOP I AM IN STEADY CONTACT WITH THEM AND EVERYTHING IS ALL RIGHT WITH THEM STOP THEY ARE INFORMED THAT I AM DOING DEVIL'S DISCIPLE HERE AND WILL SEE THEM WHEN I AM PASSING THROUGH DUBLIN ON MY WAY TO YOU THE FIRST WEEK OF MARCH STOP I FOUND FOR DUBLIN A NEW STUDIO SCHEME WHICH I AIRMAILED THEM ALREADY AND WHICH WILL REVOLUTIONIZE PICTURE MAKING BOTH ECONOM-ICALLY AND TECHNICALLY AND WILL MAKE DENHAM AND HOLLY-WOOD OLD FASHIONED BUT IT WILL TAKE AT LEAST A YEAR BEFORE THE IRISH STUDIOS CAN OPERATE STOP DON'T WORRY MY DEAR MAS-TER AS WE HAVE A WONDERFUL POSITION AND WE ARE HOLDING THE WHIP OVER THE HEADS OF ALL THE COMMERCIAL SPECULATORS STOP IT IS IMPORTANT HOWEVER THAT I AM CONVINCED I WILL

MAKE WITH MY ASSOCIATION HERE A GREAT PICTURE IN RECORD TIME AND A THIRD AS ECONOMICAL THAN I COULD DO IT IN ENGLAND STOP I WILL STAY A WEEK LONGER AT SCRIPPS METABOLIC CLINIC LA JOLLA CALIFORNIA STOP MY DOCTOR'S NAME IS FRANCIS SMITH WHO IS TAKING CARE OF ME AND I WILL COME BACK HEALTHY WITH MY STOMACH CLEAN FROM POISONS AS MY MIND IS ALREADY SEMPRE GABRIEL

208 / To Gabriel Pascal   [Ayot St Lawrence. Welwyn. Herts.
                                              received 12 February 1947]
[TEL(c): Delacorte: U]

INGRID MAY DO FIFTY JOAN PLAYS AND FILMS FOR WANGER BEFORE OURS DO NOTHING TO STOP HIM THEY WILL ADVERTISE OURS WE WILL WIPE THEM OUT UNTIL THIS IS SETTLED DO NOT MENTION DEB[ORAH KERR] ANNOUNCE ONLY THAT MY TWO AMERICAN PLAYS WILL BE FILMED IN AMERICA AND THE REST IN THE BRITISH COM-MONWEALTH.   [GBS]

Walter **Wanger** (né Feuchtwanger, 1894–1968), American, produced *Joan of Arc*.

209 / To Gabriel Pascal   [Ayot St Lawrence. Welwyn. Herts.]
                                              17th February 1947
[ALS(tr): Delacorte: U(e)]

Pascal was still at the Scripps Metabolic Clinic.

Dear Gabriel

As far as possible impress on the newspapers that my two American plays will be filmed in America *before* St Joan, which will be a British film. We must choke the canard about our being annexed by Hollywood. Let your slogan be 'Shaw is British; Pascal's address is The World.'

Of course Ingrid will regard St Joan as Porte St Martin melodrama, in which she would have nothing to do but look pretty and come on the stage half burnt already; but if she has any real power the play will knock that out of her unless she is a born fool. Even if she is, she can make a Pitoëff-Bergner success. But that would be a horror artistically. She looks intelligent; and the Anderson-Wanger affair is all to the good; but you must use your judgment and keep Deborah up your sleeve.

The weather here is damnable: stay chez Scripps as long as you can.

GBS

In the nineteenth century the *Théâtre de la **Porte-Saint-Martin**,* built in Paris in 1781, was the home of melodrama.

210 / To G. Bernard Shaw [*no address*]
21st February 1947

[TDS TEL: Delacorte: U(e)]

Whether the doctors diagnosed cancer is unclear. Since they mentioned the Mayo Clinic to him, as he revealed on 16 July 1949, it is unlikely that, whatever their diagnosis, they said he had recovered.

DEAREST GBS: HAVE SEEN WITH YOUR DRAFT CONTRACT BERNARD GIANNINI FROM THE BANK OF AMERICA AND THE BANK'S LAWYER IS WORKING OUT THEIR SUGGESTIONS FOR CERTAIN LEGAL CHANGES WHICH I WILL BRING WITH ME FOR YOUR APPROVAL AND A LETTER TO THE MANAGING DIRECTOR OF THE BANK OF AMERICA OF LONDON WITH THE AUTHORIZATION FOR HIM TO SIGN THE CONTRACT ON BEHALF OF THE BANK IN YOUR PRESENCE STOP SAILING DEFINITELY ON QUEEN ELIZABETH MARCH 7 STOP I AM COMPLETELY RECOVERED FROM MY ILLNESS AND COUNTING THE DAYS UNTIL I SEE YOU AGAIN   EVER GABRIEL

211 / To Gabriel Pascal Ayot St Lawrence. Welwyn. Herts.
17th March 1947

[ALS(p): Delacorte: U(e)]

My dear Gabriel

I read through your agreement and marked 30 places where it needed alterations.

When I came to the end I found that you had signed it. It is too late now to do anything but leave you to your fate.

All I can say is that being now cognisant of the agreement I disapprove of it and must not be assumed to be bound by it nor to admit any of its propositions as to my copyrights.

You are incorrigible; and there will be no profits unless they are afraid of losing you.

I have just been talking to Kieran Tunney, a clever young Catholic playwright, related to Gene. He says that both Ingrid and Deborah are wrong for Joan, and suggest[s] Mary Morris as just right for her physically.

Do you know her? I never heard of her.

He wants to get in with the Irish company. As he is a Catholic of Irish descent it may be worth while to make a note of this.

Ayot has jumped from the depth of winter to the middle of spring on this St Patrick's day. The snow has vanished.

GBS

Born in Ireland, Kieran **Tunney** (b. 1922) – journalist, biographer, and dramatist – emigrated to England, then America. **Gene** Tunney (1898–1978), American heavyweight boxing champion, won the world title in 1926 and retired in 1928; he and Shaw, a longtime boxing enthusiast, were friends. Mary **Morris** (1895–1970), American actress, played Abbie in *Desire Under the Elms* (1924) by Eugene (Gladstone) O'Neill (1888–1953).

212 / To G. Bernard Shaw Mumford's Farm
Chalfont St Peter. Bucks.
19th March 1947

[TLS(c): Delacorte: U(e)]

My dearest G.B.S.

I received this moment your letter of March 17 and I think you wrong me again. I am not incorrigible – on the contrary, since my fourth year when I started an independent life as an orphan I corrected myself every day and every hour, and the result is not so horrifying as you try to make me believe.

Before I received your cable of approval 'Agreed for Disciple on my part but you must have separate agreement,' I cabled you all the conditions of my contract; and even in that cable you told me that my forty-five per cent 'seems too much to be good for both sides as all good bargains should be.' This cable was unfortunately read by Mary's Company, and created a good deal of controversy, making them think that you believed they had made a bad bargain with me; but to protect ourselves I provided in the contract (page 4, paragraph 3) that 'if, for any reason, said George Bernard Shaw does not approve the said screen adaptation, then this agreement shall terminate forthwith and each of us shall be released from any obligation to the other except that you agree to repay to us, on demand, all monies which we have advanced to you.'

Then came your second cable telling me that you had omitted to advise that instead of profit-sharing I should take a 10% royalty like yourself, because I should never make a cent of profit otherwise. By this time, on the basis of your previous cable, the agreement had already been signed by Mary and myself; so I immediately corrected the situation, and agreed with Mary's business manager that if you did not approve the contract as such it would be declared null and void, and I would return all salaries which I had by then received. So I was and am doubly covered – even trebly, because there is a further provision in the contract that if you do not approve the choice of the leading actor the contract may then too be cancelled.

So nothing is wrong. All it needs is a little bit of patience and a little bit of goodwill to put it right; and I would be grateful if you would therefore write me a letter tomorrow morning telling me the thirty places where, according to you, alterations are needed. It is also in your own hands to write a separate letter to Mary Pickford that you don't believe in any profit-sharing business, and that you would prefer they pay me ten per cent of the producer's gross income, without any deductions of negative costs or overheads; and I am convinced that they will accept whatever you suggest.

I will send my chauffeur to you after lunch for the letter. I would also be grateful if you would give me back the letter from the Metabolic Clinic and the letter from Barry Fitzgerald enclosed in my yesterday's letter.

I note your remark about the young Irish playwright Kieran Tunney. He certainly is right about Ingrid, but I don't think he is able to judge Deborah Kerr, because he has not seen her latest work. His Mary Morris suggestion is wrong. I know her very well. I tested her years ago and she is a notorious Lesbian, so pathological that she ruins every part she plays through this publicly-known abnormality of hers, and now also she is too old for the part. I considered her very seriously before 'Major Barbara,' when we doubted that Wendy Hiller would be the right choice for 'Joan,' and I dropped her then, as she had a rather masculine, harsh and unpleasant voice; but although your young playwright may not be very useful as a casting adviser, he could certainly be a worthwhile addition to the Irish Company, so please tell him to contact me here at the Duke's Hotel, or at the Shelbourne Hotel, Dublin, where I will be for a week from the day after tomorrow (Friday).

I was delighted that St Petrus is smiling down to you, and that the Spring has set in at Ayot St Lawrence.

> Ever your Devil's Disciple,
> Gabriel

P.S. I am sending back the contract, maybe you need it for the suggested thirty alterations.

In 1936 Barry **Fitzgerald** (né William Joseph Shields, 1888–1961), Irish actor and veteran of the Abbey Theatre, had moved to Hollywood, where he became a popular character actor in movies. Pascal wanted him to play Androcles.

213 / To G. Bernard Shaw [Shelbourne Hotel. Dublin]

23rd March 1947

[TDS TEL(c): Delacorte: U]

DEAREST GBS HAVE RECEIVED MYSELF COPY OF DRAFT AGREEMENT AND EXPLANATORY LETTER ABOUT IT FROM LOUIS SWARTS AND AGREE WITH YOU THAT DRAFT AGREEMENT AS IT STANDS IS NON-SENSE STOP MICHELINA IS BRINGING YOU TOMORROW LETTER TOGETHER WITH LETTER FROM MYSELF ANSWERING YOUR QUESTION WHO IS MORE SOLID UNITED ARTISTS OR MP AND PLEASE DO NOT WRITE TO ANYBODY UNTIL YOU RECEIVE THESE LETTERS STOP OUR IRISH PROJECT IS PROGRESSING BEYOND ALL EXPECTATIONS WE SELECTED THE STUDIO GROUNDS SATURDAY AND ARE DISCUSSING FINANCE ARRANGEMENTS WITH BANKS TODAY AND TOMORROW RETURNING WITH COX ON FRIDAY AND LIKE TO VISIT YOU WITH HIM

SATURDAY AFTERNOON FOUR OCLOCK WHEN HE WILL REPORT TO
YOU ABOUT THE PAST PRESENT AND FUTURE OF OUR IRISH PICTURE
COMPANY   SEMPRE GABRIEL

Louis E. **Swarts**, Pascal's Hollywood lawyer, was with the firm Swarts, Ziffren & Steinberg.
MP is Mary Pickford.

214 / To Gabriel Pascal   [Ayot St Lawrence. Welwyn. Herts.]
                                                        25th March 1947
[HPCS(tr): Delacorte: U]

*The next day Shaw wrote to Swarts, Ziffren & Steinberg in Los Angeles. U.A.A.
is United Artists Alliance.*

I am in correspondence, not with Mary but with Swarts.

   The draft agreement with the Bank which he sent through you is so
absurdly incompetent that I am telling him high handedly that as neither he nor the Bank understands the case they must sign my draft
(which they have ignored) on the dotted line, or cry off the transaction.

   No further letters from them can alter this. They simply do not know
what they are about; and I do. I must therefore dictate the terms: take
them or leave them.

                                              GBS
Michelina has just given me your letter. It makes no difference. I note
the point about the U.A.A. but I have made no contract with them. The
%age does not concern me.

215 / To G. Bernard Shaw   [Mumford's Farm
                                               Chalfont St Peter. Bucks.]
                                                        25th March 1947
[TL(c): Delacorte: U(e)]

My dearest G.B.S.

I received your postcard, and am sending herewith the explanatory letter of Mr Louis Swarts, which is no longer of much service, because I
agree with you that the Bank agreement as they worked it out is useless,

so the preliminary agreement you made with Artists' Alliance also falls down.

I don't like to argue with you my dear G.B.S. about my incorrigibility, but if you would realize how clever I am in these matters, you would give me your Rodin bust as a present. I have not committed myself to anything, but the opposite party are committed if you agree on the deal, so practically nothing is signed from our side. I told them when your cable arrived the story about Arthur Rank; how you made a deal with him for me for ten percent of the gross income; and how Arthur Rank persuaded me in the car coming from your place to change the Agreement, otherwise he would not finance the picture; and how you rubbed it under my nose on each occasion that I betrayed you and myself; and I predicted to them that if they don't change it before I arrived there would be no contract. So as my nose is long enough, I do not want any rubbing on it any more.

I decided over the weekend, when I reflected about our future plans, that I am not willing to go on with the deal. I am old enough now to work in harmony, and I will not do anything in life any more which upsets my nerves and my health. 'Caesar & Cleopatra' was a bad picture because I was surrounded by saboteurs and I made it without joy and without inspiration. I hate the memory of it, so I don't like to go into a business which starts with a disharmony between you and myself.

The only man who can arrange the whole thing is Louis Swarts who cannot be bribed either by Mary Pickford, Lester Cowan or United Artists. The more powerful partner for your personal contract is United Artists and not Mary Pickford, because United Artists has Charlie Chaplin, who is more solid and straighter in his business dealings than the vain and cunning Mary. But I beg you to wait with the letter to Louis Swarts and Mary Pickford until my return, because I must explain to you also a very important thing about the Preferential distributing deal which according to my contract with Mary Pickford's Company she must deliver to us as a major inducement to enter into the deal at all. According to this Preferential distribution deal, we are charged only 10–17½ percent distribution charges, instead of the usual 25 percent which every shoeshiner can obtain from United Artists; and only in this case has she the right to present the picture herself. Unfortunately, you did not know this in drawing up your Draft Contract in which you provided that she presents the picture in any case; and already they are jubilant that they need not give us the ten percent Preferential distributing deal which was a part of the agreement, and without knowing the conditions of the Goldwyn Studio situation that they can overcharge us for the studios as much as they please.

Let us discuss all this when I see you. Either we can have a contract which makes both of us happy, or we should forget it altogether.

I hope to see you on Saturday afternoon with Arthur Cox.

[Gabriel Pascal]

(François) August (René) **Rodin** (1840–1917), French sculptor, did a bust of Shaw that Shaw contributed in 1908 to Dublin's Municipal Gallery, which was founded in 1906 to house modern art.

216 / To Gabriel Pascal   Ayot St Lawrence. Welwyn. Herts.

15th May 1947

[ALS(p): Delacorte: U(e)]

The article Shaw enclosed does not appear in the Sunday Express *of 4 May or 11 May.*

The enclosed may make frightful mischief. Our business is to start an enterprise which is above all Irish, Irish, Irish.

And here comes a Hungarian from Arthur Rank's camp, who is to buy up the whole affair without a single Irishman or a penny of Irish capital in it.

You must write to the Sunday Express contradicting the whole article and declaring that you will own nothing in Ireland but your artistic talent; that the capital will be Irish capital, the shareholders Irish, the actors Irish, the chief author Irish, the financial and political control Irish, and no foreigner concerned in the project (an Irish project) except your humble self, chosen for your peculiar job by a famous Irishman. Nothing short of this will undo the mischief and turn it into an advertisement.

Mrs Laden says you are coming again on Saturday. Dont. Within these ten days I have had seven engagements, and I can make no more until after the 23d: I *must* have some days of uninterrupted work and a quiet hour or two. We have nothing to discuss until I hear from Cox.

GBS

Alice **Laden** (1901–79), a Scotswoman, was Shaw's cook and housekeeper.

217 / To G. Bernard Shaw
[Mumford's Farm
Chalfont St Peter. Bucks.]
17th May 1947

[TL(c): Delacorte: U]

Pascal's letter does not appear in the 18 May, 25 May, or 1 June issues. Shaw wrote to Pickford, who received his letter by the 26th, that The Devil's Disciple *must be postponed for two years, which from her viewpoint meant that the project was cancelled and her contract with Pascal violated. She sued Pascal to recover his salary advances.*

My dearest G.B.S.

I am in receipt of your note of the fifteenth instant and you can see from the stupid article that it was printed without my knowledge and it is very difficult to prevent some gossip from sneaking out in Ireland ...

I understand my dear G.B.S. our motto 'Irish Ueber Alles!' and according to your wishes, I wrote the enclosed contradictory letter to the editor of the Sunday Dispatch. I will telephone you as soon as I am back from Berlin, and in the meantime, I trust we will have definite news from Mr Cox.

As I told you in my letter of yesterday, Marjorie communicated with me that Mary Pickford insists that 'Devil's Disciple' should be done in America. She does not mind if it is postponed until the end of next year and she is ready accept all your suggestions and modifications, but, she insists that the preliminary contract should be honoured. I don't know what the legal position is as according to my knowledge, the contract is only valid if you approved it. For this reason, to avoid misunderstandings, I asked you originally to write a letter to her with me because I had plenty of reasons to cancel the preliminary contract without getting legally in trouble with this over-clever business lady whose vanity is now injured; so I like to talk it over with you as soon as I am back and certainly, if a legal action can be prevented, it would be wiser.

Mary Pickford is ready to come over herself or send some one to make a new deal with us for Disciple, and I am afraid that we must receive her or her envoy to avoid complications, but please do not write to her again until you have spoken with me, because in my opinion, we are one hundred percent covered, if we act diplomatically. We need the American market for the distribution of our pictures and it is no use to create an unpleasant situation when with a clever move, Mary Pickford can be calmed down and satisfied with 'Devil's Disciple' made at a future time when most convenient to us.

For the moment, we have plenty to do with 'St Joan' in Italy and we can always use the 'Devil's Disciple' deal with Mary if the building of the Irish Studios should be delayed, but a complete rupture with Mary Pickford and United Artists would be very harmful as it was years ago the rupture with R.K.O., but one thing is certain, we have finally the upper hand in the situation in every country and we must use our entire tact not to lose the power again.

[Gabriel Pascal]

218 / To Gabriel Pascal   Ayot St Lawrence. Welwyn. Herts.
4th June 1947

[APCS(p): Delacorte: U(e)]

The letter to de Valéra has not been located. Shaw wired the message to Cox the day before. Ultimatum notwithstanding, Shaw, Cox, Dan Breen, and others continued to negotiate. Shaw recognized that Breen had been overly optimistic in expecting to raise the money quickly. To Irish investors, he knew, film making was unfamiliar territory in which they trod warily or did not tread at all, particularly since Patrick Farrell, whose cinema chain linked him to Hollywood and Hollywood's viewpoint, believed the venture to be ruinous.

I have written to Dev. by Air Mail.

I have also wired Cox that unless at least quarter million Irish money is on the table on Friday I withdraw.

Do not engage yourself to the Italians until the Irish question is settled. If the Irish money is forthcoming Rome is only a location job.

If not, there must be a new contract for Androcles, not for Joan.

I am assuming that £250,000 will cover the cost of St Joan and leave you enough to begin building at Shanganah.

GBS

The plan was to build studios at **Shanganah** (or Shanganagh) Estate, in the townland of Shanganah, South County Dublin, two miles north of Bray and one mile inland from Killiney Bay; the estate was later bought for Ardmore Film Studio.

---

219 / To G. Bernard Shaw   Hassler Hotel. [Via Sistina.] Rome
19th July 1947

[TD TEL(c): Delacorte: U]

DEAREST GBS HAVE DELAYED WRITING TO YOU BECAUSE ITALIAN COMPANY INSISTED AND INSISTS TO GIVE THEM OPTION FOR FINANCING ST JOAN BESIDES ANDROCLES WHICH AM NOT ABLE TO AGREE BECAUSE YOU GAVE OPTION TO DAN BREEN STOP HAVE FIXED MEETING FOR TWENTY SEVENTH IN LONDON WITH DAN BREEN AND COX BUT PREFER TO SEE YOU AND REPORT ABOUT ITALIAN SITUATION BEFORE SEEING THEM ... GABRIEL

---

220 / To G. Bernard Shaw   [Mumford's Farm
Chalfont St Peter. Bucks.]
22nd August 1947

[TL(c): Delacorte: U]

Because Pascal could not leave Rome until the 31st, he postponed the meeting until 2 August, but this did not come about. He flew to Dublin the first week of August to discuss possible arrangements. Cox and Breen were confident that if they began with a capital of £50,000, they could raise £100,000 within three months and another £100,000 within the next three. They could then proceed, with Pascal producing Androcles and the Lion *for them in Italy.*

Dearest G.B.S.

... When the engrossed agreement arrived, I sent Mr Cox a telegram asking him to send me the old draft agreement which I brought to you before I went to Italy with his two or three corrections in red ink, which at the time you approved and told me to write to him to engross the agreement. Unfortunately, this draft and his letter arrived only yesterday after I have seen you, so I am sending it to you now that you are redrafting the original agreement as maybe, you like to see it ...

As I told you Wednesday, the 'St Francis' script that I left with you is not the right one and finally, I received yesterday from Rome the correct one where the story is straight and not told by three different persons, so disregard the other script and kindly give it back to my chauffeur and keep this one and let me know if you need a translation of it ...

[Gabriel Pascal]

A film on **St Francis** of Assisi (né Giovanni Francesco Bernardone, 1182–1226), founder of the Franciscan Order, who devoted his life to poverty, would be directed by Roberto Rossellini: *Francesco – Giullare di Dio* (1950, English title *Flowers of St Francis*).

221 / To Gabriel Pascal   [Ayot St Lawrence. Welwyn. Herts.]
                                                                8th September 1947

[ALS: Letters]

The same day Shaw sent the agreement to Cox, he sent Cox a press statement that hailed Ireland's appropriateness as a film centre. 'I am ready to give Ireland the first call on my valuable film rights,' it said. 'I have in fact actually executed an agreement which will have that effect if the project meets with the necessary public approval and financial support.'

My dear Gabriel

I have executed the agreement and sent it back to Cox, who should have sent it directly to me.

You have now to make your own agreement with the company. My agreement makes you indispensable: that is all I can do for you. So take care of yourself. A share of the profits (strictly defined) would give you an interest in keeping down the expenses; but it should not take the place of royalty and production fee (or salary) and expenses.

I do not want to see you. I do not want to see
ANYBODY.

I find that when I have a visitor my work falls into arrear for half the day. I have a book to see through the press – two books in fact – no, three!!! I have a production to arrange for Evans in America, and a revival of You Never Can Tell for London at Wyndham's. There is the Irish business to draft and redraft. Pressing private correspondence for which I have to keep my afternoons turns up by every post. I want to go on with my literary work, even to write another one now that my new one has not finished quite so badly as I feared. Mrs Laden is going away to Aberdeen for a holiday.

Keep away, Gabriel. Keep away EVERYBODY. Come only when there is the most pressing necessity unless you want to kill me.

GBS

The Maurice **Evans** production was *Man and Superman* (1902), which opened on Broadway on 8 October to great critical and popular acclaim. *You Never Can Tell* (1896) opened on 3 October. The **new** work was the play *Buoyant Billions*, completed 13 July.

222 / To G. Bernard Shaw   [Mumford's Farm
Chalfont St Peter. Bucks.]
11th September 1947

[TL(c): Delacorte: U]

My dear G.B.S.

Thanks for your letter of 8th September and your kind advice as to how I should make my agreement with our Irish Company and will try my best to follow your precious advice.

I wanted to see you this week not only for business reasons but for private reasons. You remember before I went to Italy you told me I should marry a woman who is not a spoilt star to whose bedroom I must bring tea in the morning, but one who makes the coffee and brings it to me in the morning and devotes her life to me that I can do my job.

I found such a miraculous woman when I was on the Continent and she arrived here two weeks ago. I wanted to bring her out before I bound myself to the slavery of marriage, to show her to you and to get your fatherly blessing.

After your last letter I gave up hope to bring her out so I married her to-day in the Amersham Registry Office and before Christmas in Italy in a little Irish Franciscan chapel in Rome we will have the blessing of the Church.

She is gay, healthy and simple and will make me happy. She is on her mother's side Hungarian and on her father's side Dutch and has rather a Scotch tendency, like the Dutch all have, for economy, order and cleanliness, exactly what I needed after all these years of vagabondage.

So, when your great work gives you half an hour's freedom, after Mrs Laden is back from her holiday, write me a note and I will be happy to bring her out and you can judge for yourself if I made the right choice.

I will go next Wednesday to Dublin where we have a kind of Board Meeting and will ring you as soon as I am back from Dublin.

P.S. I think that Mr Loewenstein misunderstood me on the 'phone. I don't care if my name is never mentioned either on the screen or in any press announcement, my whole desire is to translate your works to the best of my artistic ability and conscience to the screen and the public's acceptance shall be my only reward. This is sincere and please don't write to me about this press statement as I have nothing to do with it.

[Gabriel Pascal]

The **woman** was Valerie (Valeria) Erzsebet Henrietta Jakabffy (née Hoecker, age 28), a stage and screen actress born in Budapest. After much discord, she and Pascal divorced in June 1954; she later married the American publisher and philanthropist George Delacorte (1894–1991). Dr F(ritz) E(rwin) **Loewenstein** (1901–69) was a refugee from Nazi Germany whom Shaw befriended and helped financially by designating him as official bibliographer and giving him access to the papers at Shaw's home in Ayot St Lawrence.

223 / To Gabriel Pascal   Ayot St Lawrence. Welwyn. Herts.
                                12th September 1947

[APCS(p): Delacorte: U(e)]

Too late now, Gabriel.
Youve done it.

Mrs Laden will be back on the 22nd.

Sybil Thorndike is coming on the 26th.

GBS

224 / To G. Bernard Shaw
[Mumford's Farm
Chalfont St Peter. Bucks.]
22nd September 1947

[TL(c): Delacorte: U]

Dear G.B.S.

... I would like to know if you are writing something for Saint Francis or not as I must confess to you that I am not very keen to go on with this picture if you do not write the dialogue or even your own story of it ... If you change your mind and do not like to write the script please let me know. I should be grateful if you can see me next Saturday or Sunday afternoon.

Dan Breen asked me to give you the message that the money questions of the production are all settled and the first two pictures are fully financed.

Also, I received a letter from Mr Cox that the Department of Industry and Commerce has accepted the change of the name of the Company to 'Irish Screen Arts Ltd.'...

[Gabriel Pascal]

225 / To Gabriel Pascal
[Ayot St Lawrence. Welwyn. Herts.]
24th September 1947

[APCS: Letters]

I think we had both [better] leave Saint Francis alone. You do not care a rap about him; and my view of him and of Savonarola and of Jesus is that their propaganda of Holy Poverty and amateur Communism was mischievous and ignorant. This would not suit the Italians.

As to Saturday or Sunday or any other day come if you must: I cannot shut my door to you.

GBS

226 / To G. Bernard Shaw
[TL(c): Delacorte: U(e)]

[Mumford's Farm
Chalfont St Peter. Bucks.]
1st October 1947

My dearest G.B.S.

... I confess to you that all these weeks my mind was overshadowed by the doubt which should be the first picture for our Irish Company, and as you said the General of the Franciscans saved us from this problem because we all feel that the Italian story is old-fashioned and has not the right basis for ST FRANCIS.

I told my Irish partners that maybe you are willing to write your own story of ST FRANCIS but at a later date, and we should do it after ANDROCLES and not before.

After long reflection we decided that the small picture about THE THIEF OF THE BICYCLE is not the right vehicle to do it in English because it is a typical Italian story. So I would like to select for the first picture, as always 'Mohammed comes to the mountain,' one of your earlier plays like CANDIDA, YOU NEVER CAN TELL – I shall see a revival of this comedy tomorrow evening – or CAPTAIN BRASSBOUND, because I feel, and my partners agree with me, that our Company is founded on your name and we should start definitely with one of your plays.

I have good news from Pisa that the Americans will leave the Italian studios in six weeks. So we could start shooting at the end of the year. I am going to Dublin with my Roman lawyer, Signor Graziadei, on Saturday to establish the co-operation with our Irish Company and the Italian Studio, and I shall decide which of these three plays is easiest to cast to get a dignified and easy start for the first picture and not over-burden the Company with great expense for the first venture.

I will come back from Dublin and submit to you our proposition, and then you can advise us if you like our decision. I could not do ARMS AND THE MAN for the first picture because Cary Grant is only free at the end of next year, and I know that you are not very keen on DOCTOR'S DILEMMA, so I discarded this play for the first picture ...

[Gabriel Pascal]

The Bicycle Thief (*Ladri di Biciclette*), directed by Vittorio De Sica (1902–74), would become a major Italian film (1948). Pascal alludes to the proverb 'If the mountain will not go to Mahomet [or **Mohammed**], Mahomet will go to the mountain,' derived from *Essays* (1597–1625) of Sir Francis Bacon (1561–1626), who wrote, 'If the hill ...' A revival of *You Never Can Tell* opened at Wyndham's Theatre on 3 October – the day after 'tomorrow.' Count Ercole **Graziadei** (b. 1900) was also head of Nuovo Rinascimento (New Renaissance) Films.

227 / To Gabriel Pascal   [Ayot St Lawrence. Welwyn. Herts.]
2nd October 1947

[TLS: Letters]

My dear Gabriel

I do not see how I can collaborate with the Italian authors of the St Francis scenario. I have strong views as to the character of St Francis, who was an apostle of Holy Poverty, whereas my doctrine is that poverty is a social crime and the root of all evil for individuals. In any version made by me the saint would appear, not altogether as a hero but as a wellintentioned but dangerously mistaken enemy of the Vatican, who, had he lived longer[,] would have shared the fate of Savanorola, Hus, and Jesus. My heroine would be St Clare.

The result would be a film which the Church might find it hard to sponsor; so I think I had better let it alone. The necessary revision of the existing scenario had better be made by some practised Italian playwright who accepts the popular view of St Francis as an example to all the world of holy living.

I should like to have a look at the comedy you mention as a substitute.

G. Bernard Shaw

Jan **Hus** (1369–1415), a Bohemian whose preachings urged reforms of the Church, was convicted of heresy, excommunicated, and burnt. In *Saint Joan*, Shaw echoed his exclamation, 'sancta simplicitas,' when a peasant threw wood on the pyre on which Hus was burning. **St Clare** of Assisi (1194–1253) was a follower of Saint Francis; but Shaw may pun on the name of his neighbour, Clare Winsten (b. 1898?), a painter and sculptor who drew Shaw and from whom he commissioned a bronze statue of St Joan, which she completed in 1947. In April 1968, the statue was stolen from Shaw's garden at Ayot. By the time it was found, it had been irreparably damaged.

228 / To Gabriel Pascal   Ayot St Lawrence. Welwyn. Herts.

8th October 1947

[ALS(tr): Delacorte: U(e)]

The longer St Joan is held up the greater will be the expectation and success. I will not let it be made anywhere except in Eire.

I will not touch St Francis. All I have to say about saints is in St Joan. Of course they would like me to go on repeating myself like Jannings and the Green Goddess man whose familiar name I forget (I forget everything) or like Priestley and Coward; but I WONT.

We must go straight on with Androcles. Then Arms and the Man Cary or no Cary. He is not indispensable; nor is he growing younger.

But Brassbound is a possible alternative if Phyllis Neilson Terry plays Lady Cicely. I got a glowing account of her lately.

Consider this.

I shall be glad to see your lady when you return.

GBS

George Arliss acted in the stage (1920) and silent (1923) and sound (1930) screen versions of *The Green Goddess* by Shaw's friend, fellow-critic, and Ibsen translator William Archer (1856–1924). J(ohn) B(oynton) **Priestley** (1894–1984) was an English dramatist, novelist, and essayist. Phyllis **Neilson-Terry** (1892–1977), British actress, was a member of the Terry dynasty, older cousin of Sir John Gielgud (b. 1904) and niece of Dame Ellen (Alice) Terry (1847–1928), who was Sir Henry Irving's leading lady and who conducted an epistolary romance with Shaw. Their correspondence was published in 1931. Pascal brought his 'lady' to Ayot on 18 October.

229 / To G. Bernard Shaw   Hotel Hassler. [Via Sistina.] Rome

[received 10 November 1947]

[TELS(c): Delacorte: U]

MY STUDIOS WILL BE FREED IN DECEMBER STOP UNIVERSALIA ASSIGNED TO ME ALL COSTUMES SETS EVERYTHING NECESSARY FOR ANDROCLES STOP ROBINSON LEFT ROME SUNDAY WITH PROMISE TO WIRE AT ONCE WHEN IRISH BOARD AGREED PUT PRODUCTION MONEY AT MY DISPOSAL STOP HE WIRED YESTERDAY THAT BOARD CANNOT GIVE ME DECISION THIS WEEK STOP REMEMBER THEY STATED TO YOU AND ME THAT THEY WILL DISPOSE 250 THOUSAND

POUNDS BEFORE YOU SIGNED CONTRACT STOP IF THEY FOOLED ME
AGAIN I MUST GO ON WITH ANDROCLES WITHOUT THEM STOP
ARRIVING NEXT WEEK STOP LOVE BUOYANT BILLIONS HAVE EXCEL-
LENT CASTING SUGGESTIONS   SEMPRE GABRIEL

John J. **Robinson**, former president of the Irish Institute of Architects, was perhaps Dublin's leading architect.

230 / To Gabriel Pascal

[Ayot St Lawrence. Welwyn. Herts.]

10th November 1947

[HD TEL(c): Delacorte: U]

Written on verso of Pascal's overseas telegram.

My contract signed last September covers all my unfilmed plays including Androcles. Incur no liability until money is banked. You cannot go
on without them.

GBS

231 / To G. Bernard Shaw

[*no address*]

19th November 1947

[TL(c): Delacorte: U]

Under the terms of their contract, in which Pickford gave Pascal a salary in
advance of earnings on the Shaw movie he would direct, he was obliged either to
carry out his contract or to cancel it by returning the sums her company
advanced. Pickford sued him and won her case.

My dearest G.B.S.

You mentioned to me in our last conversation that Mary Pickford has
written to you that she will be obliged to sue us, and you doubted that
she would do so.

Apparently without waiting for your answer they have already
attached my future income from Metro, which is supposed to come to
me from the selling of my Deborah Kerr contract to them next Spring,
in the amount of $50,000 which was my only capital if the whole Irish
deal should fall through to start with Universalia and Nuovo Rinascimento Films on my own.

I would be grateful if you would glance through these documents and advise me what I should answer to Metro. My lawyers in New York called me up that they are ready to stop the attachment if you cable to Mary Pickford that within two years DEVIL'S DISCIPLE can be made. But I leave it to your judgment to advise me what to do ...

... I hope to let you know if they have sufficient money for ANDROCLES or not next Monday.

[Gabriel Pascal]

232 / To Gabriel Pascal Ayot St Lawrence. Welwyn. Herts.
[undated, stamped received 21 November 1947]
[APCS(p): Delacorte: U]

The writ tells me nothing except that you are being sued, not for a debt but for damages, which they must have proved, as this cannot be done *ex parte* [from testimony of one side only].

Did you sign a contract? If so, what did you undertake to do, and did it fix a date for the doing? I am utterly in the dark and cannot advise until I am enlightened ...

GBS

233 / To G. Bernard Shaw [*no address*]
29th November 1947
[TL(c): Delacorte: U]

My dear G.B.S.

I received yesterday a copy of the letter Cox sent to you, and I replied to him acccording to the enclosed copy, pointing out to him that it is not as he states in his letter to you that 'if the Irish Company should ever find itself brought to a standstill and quite powerless to proceed,' but as it was decided that if they are not able to do what they were supposed to do months ago before they even signed the contract with you – that they give bank proofs for the £250,000, and all the necessary permissions which they promised to procure before Christmas – they must send back the contract to you.

I am enclosing the original report of the Board Meeting, and have underlined the most important points for your attention.

[Gabriel Pascal]

234 / To Gabriel Pascal Ayot St Lawrence. Welwyn. Herts.
30th November 1947

[APCS(tr): Delacorte: U(e)]

Shaw wrote this postal card on Sunday morning. Apparently, Michelina Buono-core informed Pascal of what Shaw learned when he read Arthur Cox's letter and the minutes of the board meeting, which revealed that the Irish film project had failed. On this date, Shaw replied to Cox that, since only £41,000 had been raised, the venture must be wound up and his contract cancelled. The project collapsed when Joseph McGrath (1887–1966), millionaire financier and founder of the Irish Hospital sweepstakes, withdrew his support. On 2 December he wrote to Éamon De Valéra a summary of what had happened, which clarifies his statement to Pascal: he suggested that Irish Screen Art Ltd. should keep its capital and build studios in Ireland to rent to any film company on commercial terms.

Do not worry about Buonocore's news. Nothing will come of it: Robinson will jump at any suggestion that they should go in for studio building on commercial lines, and get rid of me. Public proceedings against me would expose their hopeless financial failure.

I am sending a line to Mary to say that the Irish project is off, and that the American plays must be filmed in Hollywood after all.

GBS

235 / To G. Bernard Shaw [Mumford's Farm
Chalfont St Peter. Bucks.]
10th December 1947

[TL(c): Delacorte: U]

Dearest G.B.S.

Regarding the Mary Pickford matters, ... the contract was signed only after your telegram arrived.

I would be grateful, as you promised yesterday, if you would send me a letter that you never definitely agreed, after reading my contract which I brought you back, on the contract, because you have never received from the Bank of America the guarantees for your royalties, which was the basis of my preliminary contract with Mary Pickford and my cable to you, of which I quote a contract:

> BANK OF AMERICA AGREED TO TAKE YOUR CONTRACT IN TRUSTEE-SHIP AND PAY 10% ROYALTIES ON THE DISTRIBUTOR'S GROSS DIRECTLY TO YOU ACCORDING TO YOUR CONTRACT.

[Gabriel Pascal]

236 / To Gabriel Pascal 4 Whitehall Court. London SW1
12th December 1947

[TLS(p): Delacorte: U(e)]

Dear Gabriel Pascal

I have now seen for the first time the agreement you signed last January with Artists Alliance as quoted in the summons served on you pursuant to the order of a Justice of the Supreme Court of New York dated the 21st day of November last. You cannot have understood this agreement, obviously drafted by the Plaintiff, when you signed it; or else you left its approval to me. It is incredible that I should have countenanced such a document even had I been legally able to do so.

It is assumed throughout the agreement that you possess the entire copyrights of every kind in The Devil's Disciple, defined as 'the right to broadcast said play by television, to broadcast all or parts thereof by radio, and to publish summaries and novelizations of the said play and/or photoplay for publicity purposes.'

To this I reply that you own no rights whatever in The Devil's Disciple nor in any work of mine. I never sell, assign, or alienate my copyright or any part thereof. As sole owner of all such rights my invariable practice is to issue licences for performances and publications, retaining all my rights intact. Many such licenses are still in operation; and some of them are exclusive, and for their duration make it impossible for me to authorize the clause quoted in the preceding paragraph above.

Clause 9 begins with 'We shall be entitled to, and you hereby grant, transfer, and assign to us, all rights of every kind and character whatsoever in said motion picture.' This makes it doubly clear that the plaintiffs assumed without foundation that you own 'all rights of every kind' whereas in fact you own none. This assumption may have been founded to some extent on a misinterpretation of a cabled message sent by me to you warning you to make 'a separate agreement.' This had no specific reference to any particular transaction: the fact that you have no rights makes it necessary for you to have a separate agreement in all cases, your share in all our enterprizes being secured by a clause in my licences naming you as artistic director as of the essence of the contract.

Apart from all this your agreement must have fallen through because an indispensable condition of my consent was that the Bank of America should guarantee the financing of the film. When the bank refused to do so, there was nothing more to be said: the deal was off; and you proceeded to make other arrangements. I must explain, however, that I preferred the bank's responsibility to that of Miss Pickford as President of United Artists not from any doubt of her solvency or good faith but because our friendly personal relations would have prevented me from treating any contract with her as a matter of business.

There are other points in the agreement to which I should probably have objected; but enough is enough.

As a film licence for The Devil's Disciple is now in the market, there is nothing in what has passed to prevent the play being eventually produced in Hollywood under reasonable arrangements.

G. Bernard Shaw

237 / To Gabriel Pascal Ayot St Lawrence. Welwyn. Herts.

13th December 1947

[APCS(p): Delacorte: U]

I forgot to say in my last *private* letter that you should impress on your American lawyers that the allusions to *my contract* in our cablings refer, not to any specific contract with U.A. or anyone else, but to the printed form of agreement which I always use for my film business, and which contains my customary terms and conditions for all film corporations.

GBS

Keep me informed of your address in Italy.

238 / To G. Bernard Shaw

[Mumford's Farm
Chalfont St Peter. Bucks.]
15th December 1947

[TL(c): Delacorte: U]

Dear G.B.S.

... I think you are mistaken that I assumed throughout the agreement that I possess the entire copyright of every kind in DEVIL'S DISCIPLE. I mentioned it is stated in the preliminary contract that an old contract was signed in 1939 with the right to make a motion picture of DEVIL'S DISCIPLE, and that I had a verbal agreement with you that as soon as the arrangement with the Bank of America is concluded, you will give me a new agreement as the old agreement had no more value.

That was our understanding when you let me go to America to make a contract with Mary Pickford. I never stated in this contract that I have the rights for broadcasting etc., on the contrary, that 'I will use my best efforts to obtain separate permission from George Bernard Shaw permitting the right to broadcast said photoplay by television, to broadcast all or parts thereof by radio and to publish summaries and novelizations of said play and/or photoplay for publicity purposes.'

You are right that Paragraph 9 begins 'We shall be entitled to, and you hereby grant, transfer and assign to us, for the term of this contract, all rights of every kind and character whatsoever in said motion picture,' but you forget that this paragraph is only a consequence of Paragraph 5 which starts: 'Promptly after the screen adaptation is approved by George Bernard Shaw, we will prepare a production schedule,' so I had, according to my own lawyer, I don't know how many paragraphs in that contract which needed your own approval; only after your approval the contract could operate.

For that reason it is provided in the preliminary contract, about which you are reproaching me so much, that if you disapprove the contract, then I must pay back the 1000 dollars weekly salary which I accepted for preparation work because the Treasurer refused to give me dollars, and I did not want to borrow money from anybody.

So your advice that 'I must plead that as the agreement was subject to your approval, it was clear that the copyright was yours, and therefore, I paid no attention to the rest of the mass of verbiage, knowing that I could safely leave its criticism and correction to you' is the best because it is the *true situation.*

I told my lawyer that maybe one day we will make the two pictures, DIS-CIPLE and BLANCO, in America, but I have not promised anything. I don't deny that I was careless, but may I refresh your memory: when I came back from America, I gave you a copy of the contract, and you started to correct it with red ink. Then you had your correspondence with Louis Swarts, and only when the Bank of America refused to agree on your condition to be a partner in the deal, you broke up your correspondence with Louis Swarts and wrote to Mary Pickford that the deal was off ...

[Gabriel Pascal]

239 / To G. Bernard Shaw

Villa Manzoni
Tomba di Neroni, via Cassio 91. Roma
20th January 1948

[TL(c): Delacorte: U(e)]

Neither Shaw's letter of 26 December 1947 nor Pascal's telegram has turned up. Despite Pascal's difficulties in concluding a contract for a new film, he maintained a sufficient sense of humour to poke fun at his tendency to send excessively long cables.

My dear G.B.S.

Please forgive me that I am answering your letter of the 26th December only to-day. The letter crossed my 10,000,000 words telegram and since then I received a long letter from Arthur Cox which I will bring you.

I am advised, as I wired you, by my lawyer, before making any new deal for ANDROCLES with 'Universalia,' to wire to Cox giving him a last chance so that no reproach could be made that I abandoned my obligation to them to wait until the 25th of December but, apparently, my fear was justified, they had not obtained, as Cox wrote to me, the approval of the Department of Finance, yet Cox insisted that they had all the £250,000 at their disposal already at the last Board meeting and so insisted Dan.

There is something pathological in this whole situation. I, who was already insane that I could not start to produce, what reason could I have, if they had the £250,000 to tell you they had only £40,000? I would have come back and jumped with joy, instead of making you doubtful as I became doubtful myself. Or the extract of the Board meeting, which all the members read, should have been immediately contradicted and corrected that there were not £40,000 but £250,000. Maybe your clear mind can find the definition of this contradiction.

I have not occupied myself here in Rome until now with the business side at all, waiting also that the chaotic political situation will be cleared. So I have used these weeks of the bank strike where every business was held up in Rome, to work on the shooting script and on preparation of the picture. I hope that at the end of this week the contractual questions with 'Universalia' will be cleared and then I come back at once to see you and liquidate the Irish situation before signing the definite contracts with 'Universalia.'

Regarding the Pickford contract, I am glad that you reminded me of my mistake. During the holidays I tried hard to concentrate myself in order to remember what had happened – and I see it now clear and ask you[r] forgiveness for my error.

What I have read and what I brought you to read and correct was the contract the solicitor Louis Swarts sent to me to give it to you for your approval, and that contract you started to correct with red ink. And suddenly it came clear to me that I told you, when you asked me what is with my Pickford contract, that it was no use to waste your energy to read it until your own contract is settled. How could I have mixed in my mind that you have been correcting your contract, which was the basis of the deal and which my lawyer had sent to you, believing it was my own stupid contract as producer, is unexplicable to me, but I am glad you helped me to remember and now I can see everything clear. I can do nothing else but ask your forgiveness ...

I am so sorry for you, dear G.B.S., that this happened, because after you had written to Mary Pickford that the picture cannot be done now but could be done maybe in two years' time, I left everything to my lawyer, instead of writing myself a registered letter to Mary Pickford telling that I cannot go on with the deal because your contract had not been signed and she had not lived up herself to several of its promises. Had I written such a letter, they could do nothing against me ...

[Gabriel Pascal]

240 / To Gabriel Pascal [4 Whitehall Court. London SW1]

16th February 1948

[TLS(tr): Delacorte: U]

Dear Gabriel Pascal

I never made nor contemplated any contract with Miss Mary Pickford for the production of The Devil's Disciple or any other play. It was explicit between us that as our personal and artistic relations would make it impossible for me to enforce such a contract she could give me no real business security.

Consequently the proposed contract for the production of The Devil's Disciple had to be with the Bank of America on its sole security. I drafted an agreement accordingly. The Bank demurred, and refused to be responsible.

The project then fell through, leaving Miss Pickford under no obligation to me nor I to her.

faithfully

G. Bernard Shaw

241 / To G. Bernard Shaw [Mumford's Farm

Chalfont St Peter. Bucks.]

24th May 1948

[TL(c): Delacorte: U(e)]

My dear G.B.S.

... I was away in Paris to see a great comic Mario Cantinflas who is supposed to be superior to Charlie Chaplin, for the part of Androcles. He is by birth Mexican and he has a new fame in America. I will report you my impression personally.

... As soon as the Bank of England approves Rex [Harrison]'s salary there should be no further obstacles in starting our production with 'Arms and the Man' ... I hope that all these formalities will be settled at the latest next week and I can forget all these horrifying tribulations and get on with my work for 'Arms and the Man' and without interruption continue with 'Androcles and the Lion'...

[Gabriel Pascal]

Cantinflas (né Mario Moreno y Reyes, 1911–93), Mexican, was one of the most popular comic film actors in Spanish-speaking countries. In English-speaking countries, he is best known as the servant in *Around the World in Eighty Days* (1956).

242 / To Gabriel Pascal

Ayot St Lawrence. Welwyn. Herts.

15th February 1949

[ALS(p): Delacorte: U]

During the nine-month gap that separates this letter from Pascal's last letter to Shaw, Pascal tried to reach an out-of-court settlement with Mary Pickford. Details of Pascal's project in Malta, which collapsed by the end of October, are unknown, as is the name of the Marquess mentioned in the next letter.

Remember that I cannot draft an agreement for Malta until I have the names of the firm and all the other necessary particulars.

Without the agreement nothing can be concluded.

GBS

243 / To Gabriel Pascal

Ayot St Lawrence. Welwyn. Herts.

23rd February 1949

[ALS(p): Delacorte: U(e)]

Although Pascal's fortunes had deteriorated considerably, he attempted to maintain his lavish lifestyle, partly because he liked it and partly because a film producer who seemed impecunious was less likely to attract large capital than one who seemed prosperous. Before 1948 ended, he sold Mumford's Farm and moved to the fashionable, expensive Connaught Hotel in London. In February, he and Valerie rented a flat with an exclusive address in Mayfair, 51 South Street.

Dear Gabriel

Here is the agreement with the counterpart for the Marquess's signature.

We should have sent him a draft for his approval. Apologize and say that the time was too short. If there is anything that he dislikes it can be remedied. It is the best I can do for him and for myself. It leaves open the question of what plays we shall begin: 3 before the end of 1950, and 2 per year after that.

You must make your own bargain as producer. Take care not to let yourself in as you did with Mary. You have no rights in the plays; but unless you are supreme artistic director the agreement falls through.

The Connaught and South St are needlessly expensive, and are for the idle rich and tourists and not for business. NW, SW, or Fitzroy Square would have given you more and better accommodation for less than half the money.

However, as you seem to have unlimited millions always at your command, it does not matter.

GBS

244 / To G. Bernard Shaw   Mayo Clinic. Rochester, Minnesota
16th July 1949

[TL(c): Delacorte: U(e)]

Whereas, according to Pascal, a Harley Street doctor had recently assured him that his rectal bleeding was only a hemorrhage, the bleeding recurred during a vacation in Switzerland. His wife Valerie suspected cancer, but although he refused to see a doctor while on holiday, he promised to do so in New York, which he did. The diagnosis confirmed his wife's suspicions. Refusing to undergo the surgery the doctor insisted was necessary to save his life, he threatened to leap from the office window instead. He went to Hollywood. On his way back to New York he stopped at the Mayo Clinic. Despite his assurances to Shaw, no dates were fixed, no firm commitments made, and no contracts signed.

My dearest G.B.S.

Since my last cablegram from Hollywood I tried every day to write to you and explain the whole situation, but, even though everything seemed to be settled when I cabled you, it changed every day because not only the British picture industry is bankrupt but the American industry is nearly so.

From Hollywood, on my way to New York, I stopped at Mayo Clinic, which Clinic I had already heard of two years ago when I was at Scripp's Metabolic Clinic and it was advised that I should go there for a general checkup. As I have had a strange pain for many months in my rectum, I believed it would be best to find out what it was all about before I started working. After the general checkup, they said that my heart, my lungs and all my organs are in perfect condition but there is a polypoid growth in my rectum and they said if they do not operate upon me it will become malignant and dangerous. I tried to explain to my doctor, Dr Harold Habein, who is taking care of me, and to the head of the Mayo Clinic, Dr Charles Mayo, that it would be tragic for me to stay at the Clinic at this time and that I promised to go back to England after I finished my last picture. Doctor Mayo insisted that I should give him my word of honor to come back in two weeks' time. He said he could not allow me to go on a strenuous picture production before I am cured.

Before this happened, when I arrived in New York I met Robert Clark, the executive director of the Associated British Films Limited, who offered me a distributing deal and that I should make DEVIL'S DISCIPLE in England. But he tried to dictate such horrible conditions – to change the script even after you approved it and to cut the picture on their own will even after you have seen it – that I told them to 'go to hell.' I remembered then our last conversation before I left England and it was ringing in my ears what you said – that you felt we should go on with ANDROCLES AND THE LION with my Roman friends and ARMS AND THE MAN as you felt that they are your two most timely comedies which I should make now. You had the impression that I was not listening and not considering your suggestions, but I made up my mind as soon as I left your place to postpone DOCTOR'S DILEMMA, to refuse DEVIL'S DISCIPLE, and to work out the deal with my New York friends for these two pictures. I can tell you with good conscience that I succeeded.

I went to Hollywood only to check with the Metro Company the dates for Deborah Kerr for the part of LAVINIA, and as I saw in New York a wonderful actor called Jose Ferrer (who is since Coquelin the best Cyrano in the whole world) I wanted to fix the contract with his manager for ANDROCLES. Everything went well in Hollywood. After I cabled you I cabled my Italian partners to not give the costumes away to anybody that I would be down in a few weeks to start the picture. Then this incident happened here at the Mayo Clinic. I think we should be very grateful to Doctor Habein and to Doctor Buie, who will operate upon me, and to Dr Charles Mayo that they insisted that I come back here to make me healthy. Meanwhile I have lost about 25 pounds and I feel very well and

I am confident that the operation, with God's help, will succeed and in a few weeks I shall see you – healthy and full of vigor to start production. I had all kind of difficulties to postpone production until the beginning of September, but I succeeded and all of the dates are fixed for early spring with Rex Harrison and his wife Lilli Palmer to play BLUNTSCHLI and LOUKA in our ARMS AND THE MAN. I will have for RAINA Jean Simmons and for the father, Noel Willman, who had very great successes in Stratford in similar parts last year – in the last instance when he played KING DARIUS. The important thing now is that I get healthy, come back to England with the contracts for your approval and go to Italy and start production. I feel very confident that everything was for the best and that I have not made the picture all this time because the whole old school of picture making, as are all the camera tricks, outdated. I knew that our hour would come when everybody failed and my American friends recognized this and came immediately to my assistance and I feel that I will make these two plays of yours even bigger successes than with PYGMALION because I know what you want and I know what I want now and know what I must do and I will do it! I feel that I will overcome all obstacles and I am completely free from Hollywood and Rank's monopoly and our pictures will make history.

According to the doctors I must stay here at least for three weeks. I am so sorry that I cannot be back for your birthday but I hope I will be able to be at Malvern for the opening of BUYON'S MILLIONS. I have sent you today the following cable: 'Forgive long silence. Tried to avoid to let you know that I am at Mayo Clinic, Rochester Minnesota. An operation next Monday indispensable but not dangerous. Stop. Our next two pictures ANDROCLES AND THE LION and ARMS AND THE MAN all financed and American distribution fixed and can start work in a few weeks, as soon as released from Clinic. Stop. My explanatory and also doctors' letters forwarding today.' I am enclosing the letters of Dr Charles Mayo and Dr Harold Habein, which are self-explanatory. After the operation I will cable you if everything succeeded so don't be nervous about me. I think this illness was necessary to start living a new life in a simple, modest way, consecrating all my work for you and disregarding all the rest. If your last play is already printed I would be grateful if you would give instruction to Loewenstein to airmail me at the Clinic one copy.

Valerie arrived here a few days ago because Doctor Buie, the doctor who will operate upon me, believed it was best to have her stay with me when I am operated. I am so sorry that these things happened exactly when I established our new program, but blame the Food Minister of England who ruined my whole metabolic system with starchy food. I have good news for you also in that I gave up smoking since I discovered this illness and I feel I never will be weak again to fall back on this horrible vice.

Thanks for your patience with my troubles. God bless you and keep you in good health and good mood.

[Gabriel Pascal]

Head of the Mayo Clinic, Dr Charles William **Mayo** (1898–1968) was the son and nephew of the brothers who founded it in 1915. Dr Harold **Habein** practised there. Robert **Clark** (1905–85) was director of the Associated British Film Corporation until 1969. José **Ferrer** (né José Vincente Ferrer de Otero y Cintron, 1909–92), born in Puerto Rico, came to the United States at age six. The high points of his career were his performances in *Cyrano de Bergerac* (1897) by Edmond Rostand (1868–1918) in New York (1946) and on film (1950), for which he received an Academy Award for acting. French actor Benoît Constant **Coquelin** (1849–1949) first played Cyrano. Doctor Louis **Buie** was a surgeon at the Mayo Clinic. German actress and international film star Lilli **Palmer** (née Lillie Marie Peiser, 1914–86) was then married to Rex Harrison. Jean **Simmons** (b. 1929), British, who had a bit part in *Caesar and Cleopatra*, acted Lavinia in Pascal's *Androcles and the Lion.* Noel **Willman** (1918–88), born in Ireland, later became a director. **King Darius** is a character in *Adventure Story* (1946) by British dramatist Terence (later Sir Terence) Rattigan (1911–77). *Buyon's Millions* is an error for *Buoyant Billions.*

245 / To Gabriel Pascal

[Ayot St Lawrence. Welwyn. Herts.]
27th July 1949
(I was 93 yesterday)

[ALS(p): Delacorte]

The day before, Shaw wrote to Sydney Box (1907–83), British screenwriter, director, and producer, refusing him screen rights to The Devil's Disciple *and* The Doctor's Dilemma. *'Gabriel has the whole boodle as long as he is alive and efficient.'*

My dear Gabriel

Whenever I see the word Operation, especially Trifling Operation, I at once write off the patient as dead, and begin to consider how to replace him. In your case this will be so difficult that I am deferring it on the off chance of your achieving the Miracle of Resurrection and popping in here some afternoon alive and hearty.

Meanwhile, what else can I say?

Absolutely nothing.

GBS

246 / To Gabriel Pascal

[*no address*]

27th October 1949

[ALS(p): Delacorte]

Pascal was staying at the Plaza Hotel in New York City.

Dear Gabriel

I have just seen Valerie, looking so well with her perfectly dressed classical head, that though it is against all my principles I told her that she is Lavinia to the life and ought to play her.

Spanish and Hungarian accents do not matter. American accents *do*. English accents are a drawback in Androcles.

Cantinfla[s] is justified in refusing an engagement on approval, and standing on his reputation. I do the same myself as an author. But of course he will stand a dozen tests if you do not impose them on him.

The captain must not make his speeches to the Christians colloquially. He should rehearse them to a side drum beating a march rhythm.

After the collapses of Malta and Boston I have no confidence in the solvency of the Atlas Investment Corporation. But we can do no better: all the financial concerns are as likely to be bankrupt next year as I am myself. So Odlum can have the contract.

The accounts of your health are highly satisfactory. I look forward to seeing you in November on your way to Rome. Valerie must go with you, even if she has to set up a ripieno [supplementary] husband when you persist in working longer than from 10.30 to 16.30, which is quite long enough.

GBS

Mrs Laden is enchanted with her new nylons.

247 / To G. Bernard Shaw   Mayo Clinic. Rochester, Minnesota
                                                7th November 1949

[TL(c): Delacorte: U]

Dear G.B.S.

I received your letter of October 27th only a few days ago but since then I am walking full of happiness and strength again. Last Saturday I finally agreed to the terms of Cantinflas with his business manager and he is very happy and proud that he can play the part. Metro heard about the negotiations and offered him four times the salary I agreed with him but Cantinflas said he preferred to play the part for the small salary because he believes that he is Androcles – and he is. I will send you some photos of him when I am back in New York.

I am dictating this note from Rochester, where I am at Dr Charles Mayo's farmhouse. Today I had my examination. My surgeon, Doctor Buie, said that he is completely satisfied with everything and I can go on and make my picture. After I finish the picture I should come back for another checkup, which is just a routine thing with the Mayo Clinic ...

You are right regarding Valerie. She must come with me to Rome and help me on the picture. I am not sure but that she can give more help to me by being on the set and seeing that everything is under discipline than by playing Lavinia. I have learned in these months that Valerie is a very shrewd business woman and a wonderful, practical girl. She gave me excellent advice in my negotiations. But I leave this question open to discuss with you when I am back.

Regarding Atlas. You don't know my dear G.B.S. what a great truth you have spoken when you say that maybe all these financial concerns are bankrupt next year. They are already on the edge of bankruptcy now, but I have faith in Odlum and when I see him the second half of this week when I am back in New York I will tell him that you agreed on the contract ...

... I was invited to a luncheon when Nehru was speaking. It was the luncheon given to him by the Overseas Press [Club]. I think the Americans have been rather puzzled because they have not been able to find out to which part of the world India gives her sympathies. Nehru said, 'The struggle will be won by that part of the world who has more spiritual integrity in the future.' I also met Vincent Sheean, who wrote the book about his experience with Gandhi called 'Lead, Kindly Light.' He offered me the picture rights. I told his publisher that for the next two or three years I will not be able to do a picture about Gandhi and I will do it only if Nehru invites me to do so ... So if you happen to see Nehru again ask him if in two or three years such a Gandhi picture would be at his pleasing because I have a group in Calcutta who would give me all the money for the Gandhi picture and your SIMPLETON OF THE UNEXPECTED ISLES. But that is too far away to worry about now. I am concentrating all my strength on ANDROCLES ...

[Gabriel Pascal]

Pandit Jawaharlal **Nehru** (1889–1964), India's first prime minister, admired Shaw since, as a Cambridge undergraduate, he heard Shaw lecture. In 1949 (James) Vincent **Sheean** (1899–1975), American author and journalist, published his **book** on Mohandas K(aramc-hand) **Gandhi** (called Mahatma, 1869–1948) who, through his policies of civil disobedience, non-violence, and non-cooperation with Great Britain, led India to independence.

248 / To G. Bernard Shaw

[Mexico]
1st December 1949

[TLS(c): Delacorte: U(e)]

My dear G.B.S.

Cantinflas, his real name Mario Moreno, insisted that before I go back to London I should come to Mexico and see the studio possibilities and all the rest to judge the possibilities of proposition of my future Bernard Shaw picture in Mexico.

What I found here that is not from this world are that the studios are better equipped than any studio in England or Hollywood. Everything is wonderfully organized, the unions are strong but just and work very hard from nine to five in the studios, but with a great gay spirit and I think I could make our picture in the most economic and most faithful way in this country. But I will report to you all the facts personally when I am back in London over next week. The Cantinflas contract is signed. I signed up Diego Rivera as art director and he has started to work on the sketches because he convinced me that my Italian sketches are too old fashion. Strangely enough Laurence Langner from Theatre Guild, told me in New York when they produced 'ANDROCLES AND THE LION' that their director was a young Mexican painter and now we have the greatest Mexican painter ever lived. The plan is that we make our exteriors in Rome and all the studio scenes here in Mexico because everything is much cheaper here and the sound equipment is the latest Hollywood produced and that was as I told you always the big work, in Rome the sound equipment is antiquated ...

[Gabriel Pascal]

Diego **Rivera** (1886–1957) was a Mexican painter and muralist. Lawrence **Langner** (1890–1962), Welsh-born American, co-founded the Theatre Guild. On 23 November 1925, its production of *Androcles and the Lion* opened on Broadway. The **director**, Philip Moeller (1880–1958), was American, but the scenery and costume designer, Miguel Covarrubias (1904–57), was Mexican.

249 / To Gabriel Pascal   Ayot St Lawrence. Welwyn. Herts.
[*c.* 2nd January 1950]
[ALS(p): Delacorte: U(e)]

Although Pascal reported that he consummated all financial arrangements, nothing had been completed.

My dear Gabriel

Do not come on Thursday.

Your letter convinces me that I must take the Androcles affair into my own hands; and I have written to Rinascimento and will not see you or utter a word on the subject until I have their reply.

Four of your arrangements have collapsed and you have had to pay damages to Mary P.

It is my turn now.

GBS

250 / To G. Bernard Shaw   [Hotel Hassler. Via Sistina. Rome]
4th January 1950
[TL(c): Delacorte: U]

My dear G.B.S.

I received your letter yesterday and thank you for your kind offer to take my problems in your own hand.

I do not think there will be any problem with Rinascimento. I postponed my going to Rome for one week, because Mr Graziadei, who is the head of Rinascimento Films and my great adviser in all Italian affairs (and the most outstanding lawyer in Rome) would not be back in Rome until the end of this week. It is to Graziadei's merit that at the time of the Irish venture, he saved me from making a joint Contract with Universalia and the Irish Group, and it was his advice that 'Androcles' should be made through Rinascimento.

I sent Graziadei on Monday 2nd instant, by registered post, the two Contracts, asking him to return one copy, duly signed, direct to you. I enclose herewith a copy of my letter to him.

I am sorry that I am not able to see you before I leave and that my short note of the 30th December made a bad impression on you, because I received an important letter from Mr Gaxiola, partner of one of the richest men in Mexico, General Rodriguez, ex-President of Mexico, and I wanted to submit this letter to you personally. However, I enclose it herewith and it is self-explanatory. You can get all the information about Gaxiola and General Rodriguez from the Mexican Ambassador, Mr Jimenez O'Farril, Mexican Embassy, 8, Halkin Street, Belgrave Square, S.W.1.

In this matter, I would be grateful for your kind help, as I consider this proposition of life importance, because everything we missed with the Irish Company we can realize with the Mexicans. There in Mexico is good will, the best studios in the world and limitless capital at our disposal. All they need is your stories and me as producer.

So I would be grateful if you would, after you receive satisfactory reply from Graziadei for Rinascimento, advise me at the Hotel Hassler in Rome what I should reply to Gaxiola. There is no urgency in the Mexican matter, because I shall be occupied the whole Spring with the making of 'Androcles.' But certainly, I would not like us to neglect this unique opportunity offering us both security for the future.

I am delighted that it is your turn now, and I am confident that the change of the wind will again save 'Orleans.'

> Sempre tuo fedele
> [Gabriel]

Francisco Javier **Gaxiola**, Jr (1898–1986?) was on the board of directors of several banks, insurance companies, and financial institutions. Businessman and banker General

Abelardo Luis **Rodriguez** (1889–1967), who had fought against revolutionary general and national hero Francisco 'Pancho' Villa (1878–1923), was elected interim president of the Republic of Mexico for two years in 1932 by the Mexican Congress. Ambassador Federico Jiménez **O'Farril** (d. 1977) owned hotels in Mexico.

251 / To G. Bernard Shaw [51 South Street. Mayfair. London]
7th January 1950

[TL(c): Delacorte: U]

... I am worried about your income from CAESAR AND CLEOPATRA. There is at least £100,000 due to you, according to my information of what the picture has done until now, and I am afraid if you do not take the money, the General Finance Corporation will never be able to pay it, because they are on the verge of bankruptcy.

What a prophetic sense you had when you wrote to me in New York regarding Odlum, that next year all the big financial concerns would be bankrupt. Things are cracking there also, so for heaven's sake take the General Rodriguez and Gaxiola offer seriously, because Mexico is the only country in which real money exists. One can go from the streets to any bank and buy as much gold as one wants without being arrested by some British civil servant or a spy of the Tax Inspector.

Mario Moreno telephoned me yesterday, saying that he saw Diego Rivera, and Diego is sending the first sketches to me to be shown to you. Valerie will not be joining me in Rome until the end of next week, so I have asked her to take the sketches out to you as soon as they arrive and to bring them to me in Rome with your eventual corrections or suggestions.

I will write to you from Rome as soon as I arrive. In the meantime, I hope you have received your copy of the Contract, duly signed. In the Contract there is one mistake. The old Contract was for the English and Italian languages because, if a picture is produced in Italy, the Government rules that it must be produced in the Italian language as well as in English, so be so kind as to write a letter to Ercole Graziadei, c/o Rinascimento Film S.A., Via Vittorio Veneto 96, Rome, that you agree that he should add to the Rinascimento copy of the Contract 'the Italian language,' and you add it to your copy ...

[Gabriel Pascal]

252 / To Gabriel Pascal   Ayot St Lawrence. Welwyn. Herts.
                                      1st February 1950

[APCS (p): Delacorte: U]

Shaw resolved the legal issue by proposing a separate agreement for an Italian-language film if his terms were accepted for the English-language film. Rinascimento agreed.

I have settled everything with Graziadei.

Rinascimento has my licences for 5 years ending 31/12/1956 to film Androcles subject to the condition that you are to be artistic director exclusively.

It is up to you to make your own bargain with Rinasci.

The agreement goes to Graziadei by this post, but may be delayed by the censorship by a day or two.

The films must be released on or before 31/12/1952.

                                      GBS

253 / To G. Bernard Shaw   Hotel Hassler. [Via Sistina.] Rome
                                      8th February 1950

[TL(c): Delacorte: U]

... Graziadei received the contracts with great delay, apparently the censorship is holding back everything for days. But as soon as Graziadei remitted the contracts to Rinascimento its directors signed them and sent them to you.

I will be back in London before the end of this month to present the shooting script to you. I will ask you for some help and advice on it. I am bringing with me the first Rivera sketches, which Rivera sent to London and the post office here forwarded on to me in Rome. They will certainly arrive here with great delay.

I am glad you have taken the negotiations with Graziadei into your own hands and brought them to conclusion, and thank you, dear GBS, for giving me personally all the protection in the contract for my artistic work. As you advised me I will make my own bargain with Rinascimento.

I am including you herewith three photos (one without make-up, in a serious part and one in a comical part) of the actress AVE NINCHI who is the first stage comedienne of Italy and very popular in South America where she acts also in Spanish.

I am considering her for the part of Megaera. She speaks English with the same accent as Cantinflas. I think therefore, that they will match each other very well. Please let me have the photos back and tell me your reaction about her ...

[Gabriel Pascal]

Ave **Ninchi** (b. 1914), Italian supporting actress, appeared in French as well as Italian and Spanish films into the 1970s.

254 / To Gabriel Pascal

Ayot St Lawrence. Welwyn. Herts.
13th February 1950

[ALS(p): Delacorte: U]

Why send me these photographs? A N Y B O D Y can play Megaera. But a low comedian would be better. This lady looks like a second rate prima donna assoluta [absolute prima donna].

I think we must not get rid of the plan we devised for the Irish affair, and deal with all comers in the ordinary course as we are dealing with Androcles ...

GBS

255 / To Gabriel Pascal

Ayot St Lawrence. Welwyn. Herts.
5th March 1950

[ALS(p): Delacorte: U]

The Devil's Disciple is not available for filming until the end of Maurice Evans's revival of it in New York and its possible extension to London.

These day-to-day changes make business impossible.

The nearest available play is Blanco Posnet.

I am submitting a draft agreement to Gaxiola with the title of play left blank; but I greatly doubt whether this Mexican adventure will come off at all. I will not include England.

GBS

The Devil's Disciple opened at the New York City Center on 25 January 1950 for a two-week run. Reviews were so enthusiastic that it transferred to Broadway, where it ran from 25 February through 27 May. It did not move to London.

256 / To Gabriel Pascal Ayot St Lawrence. Welwyn. Herts.
6th March 1950

[APCS: Letters]

On thinking it over I conclude that the Mexican experiment had better be with Blanco Posnet acted by popular Mexican actors in Spanish, and, if you find when you arrive there that they have a good enough leading man and lady, The Man of Destiny. No English rights nor players. All my other plays would be too foreign in Mexico.

GBS

257 / To Gabriel Pascal Ayot St Lawrence. Welwyn. Herts.
10th March 1950

[TLS: Letters]

There is not time to consult with Belgrave Square. The ambassador can do nothing. I enclose the agreements. With them in your pocket you can arrange everything. The name you have given me for the Company is not sufficient: an agreement cannot be made with a studio; only with a person or body of persons ...

If Usigli makes the translation he must be billed as the translator and not as Editor nor Adaptor nor script writer: only as Translator.

We must take our chance as to security, and be content with the President's letter, of which I have a copy. But the President lasts only until the next election or until he is assassinated; and his successor may be against the film business.

However, we can do no better. Any breach of the contract leaves us free to make a new one as best we can.

If Ipeca complains that we did not submit a draft asking them to sign on the dotted line, say I *did* submit one, and it was returned without comment or objection.

Bon voyage!

GBS

Rodolfo **Usigli** (1905–79), one of Mexico's most prolific and influential playwrights – as well as a poet, actor, drama critic, and director – was an acquaintance of Shaw.

258 / To G. Bernard Shaw

Mayo Clinic. Rochester, Minnesota
3rd April 1950

[TD TEL(c): Delacorte: U(e)]

Pascal's cheerful statement was untrue. He told neither Shaw nor his wife that the doctors had found new malignant tissues and had prescribed radiation therapy. Against their advice, he went to New York and Mexico. Later he suffered a relapse.

I am sorry not to be able to give you the joy of outliving me. My doctor declared today that I am completely cured, younger and healthier than ever and will release me from the Clinic Wednesday. I will go to New York to meet Gaxiola and return with Gaxiola to Mexico City to start work. Mexico trip successful. Have sent informative letter to Valerie to give to you with comments. Sempre. Gabriel

259 / To G. Bernard Shaw

Mayo Clinic. Rochester, Minnesota
8th April 1950

[TL(c): Delacorte: U]

Pascal did not post this letter, dictated after he regained his strength, until 18 April, after he had left the Mayo Clinic, when he did so as an enclosure to a letter of that date, below. Since Hollywood film companies and their financiers would not accept all of Shaw's terms, and since Shaw did not let Pascal negotiate for the playwright, there is some truth to Pascal's complaints. Still, Pascal's desire to exonerate himself, which after years of frustrated efforts to finance Shaw films is understandable, leads him to distort the record by blaming Shaw, whose refusal to give him carte blanche was rational, since Pascal's agreement to inadequate financial and artistic terms for himself in order to get a film contract strongly suggested to Shaw that Pascal would act similarly for Shaw, and indeed, as their correspondence has revealed, tried to do so more than once. As it has also revealed, the Pickford affair was not entirely as Pascal describes it, and Benjamin Stern gave legal advice but did not beg Shaw to approve any contract. As the headnote to letter no. 137 indicates, on at least one contract involving R.K.O., Stern did not counsel approval. Shaw's response to Pascal's charges, if he responded, has not been discovered.

My dear G.B.S.

Valerie told me about her visit with you and her long talk with you regarding the English versions, that there is no use to make Spanish versions alone because there is no justification for it economically. I give you an extract from a letter I received from my Hollywood lawyer, Louis Swarts, who is the greatest copyright lawyer in the world, which is as follows:

'... In connection with your suggestion that you do BLANCO POSNET in Spanish, I want to call your attention to the following general information. South American money is to a considerable point tied up; from Argentina no money comes out; Peru paid up to the first of the year but is inclined to withhold; Brazil is supposed to pay but is a whole year behind; Chile allows partial remittances; Colombia the same; from Spain no dollars can be remitted but on outright sale of film. The Spanish money is made useful by different forms of trade, such as the purchase of olive oil and the like. Of course you know the English situation and the various European countries. France is frozen; Italy is frozen; and Egypt, Denmark, Holland and others withhold part of the money.

'You should find out immediately what gross may be expected in Mexico and the free remitting countries of South America, including among the free moneys the income from the border states of the United States. This is a fairly considerable sum for the number of theatres involved, amounting perhaps to $30,000. I have not checked this recently.

'I should think it would be difficult to make a picture in Spanish costing anything over $100,000 and expecting to recoup. However, I simply warn you to be sure to investigate this point.'

Valerie cabled me that she believes that you are not opposed to giving the General the English language rights also and that you told her that she should not worry about these problems and you will write to me directly.

I shall try as sincerely and simply as I can to explain to you what I feel is the real problem between us. It is very difficult to give you a real explanation but it is my duty to you and to our friendship to try to do so.

While I was ill, which was almost for two years, I did not have the courage to push things and to come to conclusions because I felt that perhaps I would not be able to even go through with the picture, but now – like through a miracle – I am cured from a grave illness and cured completely and feel younger, healthier, better, and cleaner in spirit and in body than I have felt for twenty years – the time when I start a new career more mature, more relaxed, not hunting after Spanish castles but knowing what I want, what my duties are, and what my responsibilities are towards you, towards my finance backers, and towards the world's public – now on this important crossroad it is imperative that the relationship between you and me, which seemed to be over-shadowed through many happenings, created not only through intrigues through others or gossips but through my physical and spiritual impotence, should be cleared and harmonized because without your co-operation and your complete approval and blessing I cannot be successful ...

After CLEOPATRA, as you know, I wasted two years for the promotion of the Irish Company. That Irish venture cost me about 20,000 pounds and I went into it only to please you and give you the security of having continuous film production of your plays. I remember even as though it happened yesterday, I called Blanche up one Sunday telling her that you shouldn't write the letter to Cox which you intended to do for I felt that that letter would destroy two years of hard promotion. But, you sent the letter and everything fell to pieces.

When I had the deal with Mary Pickford, the deal did not fall through because no money was there or the Bank of America was unwilling to put up the guarantees to you, and she has not made the lawsuit against me because it was no business understanding between her company and me, but, you wrote two letters to her which she misconstrued and misunderstood and she had no other revenge than to attack me.

But before that, I had a deal with R.K.O. to make four pictures. It was a wonderful deal. Your lawyer in New York, Benjamin Stern, begged you to approve the deal and you refused it ...

The Odlum proposition, which you approved, I didn't want to follow up because Odlum didn't want to give you a percentage. His idea was to buy you out and I felt it would be a betrayal to even bring you a draft contract.

Every major company which tried to get your film rights, when the formal contracts came to their legal departments, they tore them to pieces. No major company and no bank is willing with such restrictions risking any money.

So, it was not my inability all these years to start production; it was one of these strange circumstances where the Master did not have the courage to give full faith to his pupil. Through some strange influence you lost this faith which you had years ago, and maybe you are justified also in losing this faith, but practically you buried me last year, as I heard from Cedric Hardwicke and others, and as you wrote it to myself you looked for a successor of mine.

Therefore, when I showed your letter of approval to Odlum to Gaxiola, I had no doubt that Gaxiola and General Rodriguez – who are much wealthier than Odlum and have their own film studios and their own organizations – would be granted by you at least what you granted to Odlum. Why should these people be less good to you or to me than Odlum was? You say you don't want the Irish formula anymore. All right, then let's co-operate on another formula without dictatorship and without knocking on my head when I try to raise it and justify to you, to God and to the world my talents, my courage and my artistic integrity. You cannot treat me like the Inquisitors treated your Saint Joan, signing a letter and take my freedom away. My spiritual freedom is my life goal, creating a series of your plays in films. I refused I don't know how many pictures, honors, money – to stick to you. Therefore, let's create a free, harmonious co-operation now that I was so lucky to finally find the backers who, as they repeated to me two weeks ago in Mexico, are ready to accept your harsh financial conditions. But what they want is a real artistic program because BLANCO POSNET (even in Mexico) is a very doubtful proposition for the censorship as the church is very strong again there. They want at least four of your plays in the contract, as I cabled to Valerie (you have the cable in your possession).

... I am not compromising any more – not even with you, G.B.S. God gave me, like to your shepherd girl, the inspiration that I will do miraculous artistic work now. If you like that I am doing it for you, which was the desire of both of us on the basis of our friendship, I am only happy to do so. If you feel that I am not the right man for you any more then really it is better that you tell me so and I will take the consequences ...

Regarding Mario Moreno (Cantinflas) I agreed what you said to Valerie, that if he has the Charlie Chaplin mania to change everything then the hell with him. Everything is prepared and ready in Rome to start the first of September and I have a very great comedian in New York waiting only for my cue to leave his play on Broadway and come to play ANDROCLES for the picture. But as soon as I arrive in Mexico I will have another heart to heart talk with Cantinflas. Then if he is scared from the long speeches then he is not the right man for us because we can't cut one iota from ANDROCLES' lines. In my opinion, it is not as Moreno says that he is talking too much, on the contrary, he is too silent in the second act ...

[Gabriel Pascal]

260 / To G. Bernard Shaw   The Plaza. Fifth Avenue. New York City
18th April 1950
[TL(tr): Delacorte: U]

... I wanted to meet Gaxiola in New York before writing to you. My meeting with him was very satisfactory. At the meeting he expressed the hope for the General and for himself that they can count in their contract with you on the English language, besides the Spanish one, and they would like to incorporate in the contract an option on DEVIL'S DISCIPLE and another play to be chosen in mutual agreement between you, themselves and myself. I think it is only reasonable, because the General has already put important money in production and it is much better that he reserves the money for our picture and does not waste it for all kinds of Hollywood rubbish.

I will return to Mexico City the end of this week because I waited for my Labor Permit as you cannot work in Mexico with a tourist visa, which is the ordinary visa to go to Mexico, but Gaxiola arranged it already that when I got today to the Mexican Consul I will find my Labor Permit there. The General also invited Valerie as his personal guest, to come over with me to Mexico and see if she likes it there because he wants her opinion if she can live there before we sign my personal contract as the producer of your pictures. He is a very wise man, and he knows if a producer's wife is not happy, the producer cannot do good work.

You are a wise man also, because you tried to put Valerie in ANDRO-

CLES to make her happy, but we must be happy also that she can play the part, so I will make a test with her in Mexico before I decide upon it. As soon as you suggested to me originally that she should play the part of Lavinia, I cancelled my deal with Deborah Kerr and promised her Jennifer in DOCTOR'S DILEMMA, which I will do the latter part of next year ...

[Gabriel Pascal]

261 / To G. Bernard Shaw   [Hotel Hassler. Via Sistina. Rome]
                                                            10th June 1950

[TL(c): Delacorte: U]

I received your registered letter with the English contract for 'Arms and the Man' four weeks after you dispatched it from Welwyn.

Waiting all these weeks wasted my time because nothing could be concluded with the General's company offering the Spanish version alone. Before your English contract arrived, the General had meanwhile left for the North of Mexico to his estate for personal business, and on the way he had a car accident in which his wife was gravely wounded, and Gaxiola was helpless to decide anything without the General.

I waited two weeks for his return, then I lost the confidence that I could do a picture in Mexico before starting 'Androcles' in Rome. The last decision that caused me to abandon the whole scheme was that that Cantinflas fellow behaved very stubbornly, insisting on all kinds of changes in the scenario, which I naturally refused. In the end I lost my patience and told him to go to hell. So I left the country, and this is the end of the Mexican experiment. It is too far away from civilization.

I don't understand what you mean in your last letter when you say I suggested Cantinflas for the 'Emperor.' I never did so, and this part is reserved for Rex Harrison.

I arrived here in Rome a few days ago and will hurry up 'Androcles' and stick to the Italian company ...

I have spoken with the President of Nuovo Rinascimento and the company would be very happy to take over your contract 'Arms and the Man' in English and Italian, to be produced immediately after 'Androcles.' The President of the Company will write to you regarding this directly.

[Gabriel Pascal]

262 / To Gabriel Pascal   [Ayot St Lawrence. Welwyn. Herts.]
                                                      18th June 1950

[TLS: Letters]

My dear Gabriel

Another fiasco! Have you brought back the agreements? If not, the case
is very serious; for if they have been executed Mexico has a hold on us
under the clause which provides that if you are unable *or unwilling* to
direct, a substitute shall be agreed on. I gather from your letter ... that
you have the agreements and can put them in the fire, leaving us quite
free; but I should like to be sure of this; so let me know positively.

Meanwhile there is nothing on hand but Androcles. I will make no
more agreements until we see how you get on with the Milan people. I
dread another fiasco.

I have been uneasy about you lately. You are laying out your life as if I
were sure to live another fifty years, and putting all your eggs in that
quite illusory basket accordingly. It is extremely unlikely that I shall live
another three days; and when I die your connexion with me will have
been a mere episode in your career. You will have half your life before
you which you must fill up with new friendships and new interests and
activities. Otherwise you will starve. Never forget that dealings with very
old people can be only transient. Make young friends and young clients.
Look for a young Shaw; for though Shaws do not grow on the goose-
berry bushes there are as good fish in the sea as ever came out of it. Anyhow you must live in your own generation, not in mine.

Devotion to an old crock like me is sentimental folly.

                                                                     GBS

263 / To Gabriel Pascal   Ayot St Lawrence. Welwyn. Herts.
                                                      22nd June 1950

[APCS(p): Delacorte: U]

This is to remind you that as American copyright lasts only 26 years and
can be renewed only once, my first seven plays (P. & Unp) will fall into
the public domain in 1954 in the U.S.A. They were published in 1898.

To secure another 52 years for them they must be screened in the next 3 years.

GBS

264 / To G. Bernard Shaw　　　　　　[Hotel Hassler. Via Sistina. Rome]

3rd July 1950

[TL(c): Delacorte: U]

My dear G.B.S.

As I wired to you, I brought back your contracts with General Rodriguez and will bring them back with me to London; I don't like to send them by mail. So we are quite free from the Mexicans. You will laugh to know that two of his friends flew to Rome to convince me to sign the contract with them and they will bring back the General in the deal. I said to them: 'It is too late now. I decided to make my pictures in Italy and in England.'

Don't you dread any other fiasco. The period of fiascos is over: I will have only successes now. Regarding the future I don't look for another young Shaw; you are young enough for me and my inner voice, answering to your 'sentimental folly,' tells me that devotion to an 'old crock' like you is the most clever thing I have done in my life, because the devotion originates from my heart.

Regarding your postcard of 22/6/50 ... The solution, in my opinion, is the following. From the seven plays four are first-class picture material and they are as follows: 'Arms and the Man,' 'Mrs Warren's Profession,' 'Candida,' and 'You Never Can Tell.'

I like to do 'Arms and the Man' immediately after 'Androcles.' Gertie Lawrence told me in New York that she is very keen to play Mrs Warren whenever I call her for it. For 'Candida' three outstanding actresses are waiting for the grace of you whenever we like it, and that is Ingrid Bergman, Greer Garson and Deborah Kerr. Both of the latter are with the Metro Company and they could get permission to get freedom for this part. And for 'You Never Can Tell' I have the whole cast ready from English players whenever we like to do it. I hear you saying: 'To hell with the cast. Where does he get the money?' And I answer to you that I think I am on the way to solving now these money problems for ever. Also when I am back in London I will give you the proof for it.

You are right that these four plays to secure other 52 years must be screened before 1954; also I will prove to you how I can achieve that. I am not a legal expert, but in my modest opinion the most important thing would be to deposit in Washington the printed shooting scripts, but to make it sure that this is the right procedure I will write with your permission to my Hollywood lawyer, Louis Swarts, who is the greatest author-rights expert, if that is the right procedure to protect you.

I am back at the latest in two weeks with definite good news. A propos, I have made peace with Rank for the services of Jean Simmons; our whole fight was created by his business man, John Davis, who made up his mind to steal this most talented young actress from me, and Arthur was very decent and honest and gave me back the actress for three pictures, so she is at our disposal for Raina. The whole English public and press is shouting for a good part for her and I think she is now mature to play Raina. As I told you when I discussed this little girl with you, she has the greatest natural talent ever discovered in the English screen, and while I was indulging my years of passive resistance they nearly ruined her, but Raina would put her right. What is more important she is today the best Raina I could imagine, because when I talked to you that she is maybe not mature enough for the part I had not seen her for two years, but I saw her a week before I went to Mexico and saw her last two pictures and she would be exactly the right cast.

I had a long talk with the President of Rinascimento, Ambassador Sola, and he promised to write to you. He has gone to Belgium and he likes to go over to England in the middle of July. I think you should see him if you can afford the time; he is a very interesting and serious man.

[Gabriel Pascal]

Gertrude **Lawrence** (1898–1952) was a British acting and singing star. John (later Sir John) **Davis** (b. 1906), a business executive, later became chairman of the Rank Organisation.

265 / To Gabriel Pascal   [Ayot St Lawrence. Welwyn. Herts.]

3rd July 1950

[TLS(p): Delacorte: U(e)]

My dear Gabriel

Some tons of green figs have just arrived from you. You must be perfectly mad. I do not eat a green fig oftener than six times a year; and there is nothing I need that Mrs Laden cannot buy for me. I object strongly to people sending me food as if I were a pet child in their care. Drop it.

In your letter to Mrs Laden you say you are coming to England TO SEE ME. I will not see you until you have given serious consideration to what I wrote to you about your future. Unless you have business of your own in London you must not come back until you have finished Androcles. I will have no more of your damned sentiment on any terms. If you will not take care of your interests and think of your prospects when I am dead I must do it for you.

So stop sending me victuals and stay where you are. Dont force me to break with you for your own sake. Much as I value your art work I dont want to ruin you. Above all dont come back with a sackful of vegetables and oblige me to go over all this again.

GBS

266 / To Gabriel Pascal   Ayot St Lawrence. Welwyn. Herts.

5th July 1950

[APCS(p): Delacorte: U]

This is the last known postal card or letter that Shaw wrote to Pascal.

A fiaschetto [failure]! Ugo Sola writes that you cannot have the studios until October.

Meanwhile you will have nothing to do but come back and slobber sentimentally over me, wasting your time and mine.

It is exasperating.

As to the scenarios I am consulting my own American lawyers, Stern & Reubens.

GBS

267 / To G. Bernard Shaw   [Hotel Hassler. Via Sistina. Rome]

12th July 1950

[TL(c): Delacorte: U]

MGM was filming the third movie version of Quo Vadis *(1951), a Christians-to-the-lions epic based on the novel (1895) by Polish writer Henryk Sienkiewicz (1846–1916). The 'great advantage' Pascal mentions may be his ability to arrange a deal to use sets already built.*

Thanks for your postcard. Definitely no more sentimentality, figs or vegetables; that period is over.

I have only one aim in life now that I am cured and healthy – to work and keep my promise to you, who have been so patient with me.

'Androcles' I will shoot in October and November and finish it in record time and for less than 10% of the cost of 'Quo Vadis.' It is a great advantage that we waited so long, because I will be able to do a very fast job. I will explain the details to you when you are anxious to know about it. I shall arrive in England next Friday. Ambassador Sola will also be in London next week and he will contact you directly. You will listen to him and judge yourself what he has to say. I have nothing more to say either to you or anybody – the finished pictures will speak for me.

[Gabriel Pascal]

268 / To G. Bernard Shaw   [Mayo Clinic. Rochester, Minnesota]

14th October 1950

[TL(tr): Delacorte: U]

On 14 September, Alice Laden cabled Pascal in Bombay that Shaw's operation at the Luton and Dunstable Hospital had been successful. This letter, whose second page is partly torn in the upper right-hand side, is the last that Pascal wrote to Shaw.

My dear G.B.S.

I have not written to you because Blanche notified me that I should not write to you until further advice. Finally I received word from Mrs Laden that you are back at home and you can receive letters.

It is very hard to find the right expression for my joy that you are safe and well.

I also had a strange experience. When I arrived in Rome back from India, my surgeon wrote to me that for my own protection, before I start shooting ANDROCLES I should come over for a last check-up to see if there is any recurrence from last year's operation. When he examined me, he exclaimed – 'The miracle that G.B.S. wished for and predicted before the operation has happened! I cannot see even the scar of the operation!' I think he has written to you from the Clinic.

My brain was darkened when I read in the American papers what you said leaving the hospital. And now I understand what you meant.

Strangely enough, I met in Bombay, on the way back from New Delhi, the perfect Master – a saintly man who initiated me, 20 years ago when I was in India. His name is Shri Meher Baba. Gandhi loved him dearly, and Nehru also believes that he is a saintly man with great spiritual powers.

Meher Baba and I spoke about you and he told me there is no danger for G.B.S. He will live for many years to come because he has something more to say in the world. But what use if the staying here longer is not a joy for you any more? When your desire is to go back to Nirvana and use your soul power in service of the whole universe instead of in the service of this ordinary little globe.

It must be exciting to go away for the greatest adventure and leave back the suffering and the small illusions, but I wish that you could find the desire again to stay a while longer, because I believe you will witness great happenings and inspire their development. Nehru believes in your judgement very much. I am convinced he holds the last 'a tout card' [trump card] of the world's destiny in his hands.

My meeting with the Maharajah was very sucessful. [All] the finance for the future is at my disposal. [The studios] in Rome will be freed the end of next month, and I [will] begin shooting in December.

I leave for Rome at the end of next week, and I will stop for a few days in London only to see you. I will telephone Mrs Laden to ask for an appointment and I hope to find you completely recovered and in gay spirits.

[Gabriel Pascal]

On 4 October, after twenty-four days in hospital, Shaw left, without answering questions of the one reporter who was present, which makes it unclear what Pascal read that discouraged him. On the 12th, in his wheelchair in the garden of his home in Ayot, Shaw gave an interview to F.G. Prince-White, a journalist friend who was a correspondent for the Hearst newspapers. 'I don't think I shall ever write anything more,' said Shaw. Possibly, this was the statement that darkened Pascal's mind.

An Indian mystic and philospher who wrote books on spirituality and mysticism, Shri (Mr) **Meher** Baba established a Universal Spiritual Centre in Byramangala, Mysore, India. When 'Baba,' which connotes a saintly or holy man, is appended to his surname, his first name is dropped, for it is considered disrespectful.

Afterword

Two years after Shaw's death, Pascal produced *Androcles and the Lion* for RKO, the Hollywood studio that had almost persuaded Shaw to permit it to film *The Devil's Disciple* with John Barrymore. The movie was directed by Chester Erskine, a writer and producer whose motion-picture directing credits were few and undistinguished but who had experience as an actor, director, writer, and producer in New York. Erskine collaborated on the screenplay with Ken Englund, whose screenwriting credits were routine. Nevertheless, Pascal obtained a top-drawer cast, including Jean Simmons (who had become a star since playing the harpist in *Caesar and Cleopatra*) as Lavinia, Robert Newton as Ferrovius, Maurice Evans as Caesar, Elsa Lanchester as Megaera, Alan Young (a prominent radio and TV comedian on whose popularity the studio gambled) as Androcles, and Victor Mature as the Captain.

When RKO released *Androcles and the Lion* in 1953 in both the United States (14 January) and England (16 October), it was a critical and box-office disaster in both countries. In Hollywood, Pascal had no artistic control and, as he later admitted, made too many concessions. Shaw was not present to guide him and to stop him from compromising, or to intercede with those who radically changed his play, anticipating that they were improving it by removing almost all of the comedy from it, not to mention many of its major themes. Apart from Pascal's compromises and lack of control, Howard Hughes, who at that time ran RKO, held Pascal in contempt. When Pascal was away from the studio, Hughes had additional scenes shot, the romantic aspect boosted, and the film recut. On seeing the movie today, the critics who savaged it and the public who assessed it by not attending seem entirely justified. Only Jean Simmons and, perhaps surprisingly, Victor Mature come off creditably. *Androcles and the Lion* finished Pascal in motion pictures. It was his last film.

His life too was almost finished. Despite his use of the word 'cure' to Shaw, doctors still do not use the term in relationship to cancer. The disease, whose existence let alone its gravity he tried not to acknowledge to his business associates, did not go away. Once again, he was hospitalized. On 6 July 1954, at Roosevelt Hospital in New York City, Pascal died of cancer of the liver.

Although he did not die on a note of artistic or financial triumph, he had posthumous success in both. *Androcles and the Lion* was not his final venture. In the summer of 1951, he conceived the idea of turning *Pygmalion* into a stage musical, based partly on new scenes in his film version. Although Shaw had on at least two occasions strenuously rejected proposals to musicalize *Pygmalion*, even with Noël Coward as a possible composer (*Letters*, 813, 817), Pascal persuaded the Shaw Estate to agree to the idea. He sought a number of first-rate American composers – including Cole Porter, Leonard Bernstein, and Rodgers and Hammerstein – but came to terms with none of them. Finally, in October 1952, Alan Jay Lerner and Frederick Loewe contracted to write it. They did not complete the work until after Pascal died. On 15 March 1956, their musical version of *Pygmalion*, titled *My Fair Lady*, opened on Broadway, starring Rex Harrison as Higgins, Julie Andrews as Eliza, and Stanley Holloway, the police constable in the opening scenes of Pascal's *Major Barbara*, as Doolittle. While the result was financially successful beyond even Pascal's wildest expectations, it was not he but his Estate, and Shaw's, that profited. The worldwide stage success of *My Fair Lady* was surpassed by the 1964 movie version, with Audrey Hepburn replacing Julie Andrews in the title role. The film won eight Oscars, including Best Picture and Best Actor.

Table of Correspondents

Index

(Since the names of Shaw and Pascal appear on most pages of the volume, they are not included in the index except where specific works by Shaw are mentioned.)